The Art *of* Negotiation

How to Improvise Agreement in a Chaotic World

Michael Wheeler

HARVARD BUSINESS SCHOOL

SIMON & SCHUSTER

NEW YORK   LONDON   TORONTO   SYDNEY   NEW DELHI

Simon & Schuster
An imprint of Simon & Schuster, Inc.
1230 Avenue of the Americas
New York, NY 10020

First Simon & Schuster hardcover edition October 2013

SIMON & SCHUSTER and colophon are trademarks of Simon & Schuster, Inc.

For information about special discounts for bulk purchases, please contact
Simon & Schuster Special Sales at 1-866-506-1949 or business@simonandschuster.com.

The Simon & Schuster Speakers Bureau can bring authors to your live event. For more
information or to book an event, contact the Simon & Schuster Speakers Bureau at
1-866-248-3049 or visit our website at www.simonspeakers.com.

Designed by Akasha Archer

Manufactured in the United States of America

10   9   8   7   6   5   4   3   2   1

Library of Congress Cataloging-in-Publication Data

Wheeler, Michael.
    The art of negotiation : how to improvise agreement in a chaotic world / by Michael
Wheeler, Harvard Business School.
        p.   cm
    1. Negotiation in business. 2. Negotiation. I. Title.
    HD58.6.W49 2013
    658.4'052—dc23

                                2013005793

ISBN 978-1-4516-9042-2
ISBN 978-1-4516-9044-6 (ebook)

For Cally, Edie, and Kate
With love and gratitude

Contents

The Art *of* Negotiation

For every complex problem,
there is a solution that is simple, neat, and wrong.
—JOURNALIST AND ESSAYIST H. L. MENCKEN

[1] Embracing Chaos

As manager of a private investment firm, Jay Sheldon bought a small cable television company in the Midwest some years ago. He didn't know much about the industry, but the $8 million price seemed right, and the purchase would let him test the water. Jay and his partners quickly got the business into the black. A year later, they wanted to expand by acquiring nearby systems. After running the numbers, they figured that they could pay $11 million, maybe $12 million tops, to buy a second cable company in a neighboring city.

Jay began an extended series of talks with its owner, but after two months of back-and-forth, it became obvious that the parties were far apart on price. "Listen," the other owner said. "I didn't post a For Sale sign. You came to me. You'd have to dump fifteen million in cash right on my desk to tempt me. And I'd probably kick myself if I took it."

Sheldon understood that this wasn't a bluff, but he also felt the demand was unrealistic. By conventional logic, the parties were deadlocked. If a seller's bottom line is three million *higher* than the buyer's absolute top dollar, you can't have a deal.

Or can you?

"Let me ask one last question," Sheldon said before getting up to leave. "If you think your system is worth fifteen million, how about ours?"

"Oh, yours is a bit smaller," was the answer. "I'd say fourteen or so."

Sheldon turned the deal upside down. He adroitly became the *seller* instead of a *buyer*. In a little more than a year, he flipped his own system for almost twice what his firm had paid for it (and much of that had been leveraged). He was still bullish on cable, but when he encountered this particular owner, who was rabid about the industry, Sheldon had the agility to transform an apparent impasse into a lucrative sale.

His solution was clever. More important, though, was his nimble mind-set. In the impediment to his hoped-for acquisition, Sheldon spotted the seed of another deal that would serve him even better. When he let go of his initial plan, the insight arrived in a flash.

Sheldon's agility is the mark of a master negotiator. Yes, preparation is important, but negotiation is a two-way street. **We can't script the process. Whoever sits across the table from us may be just as smart, determined, and fallible as we are.** We can't dictate their agendas, attitudes, or actions any more than we'd let them dominate us. Adaptability is imperative in negotiation from start to finish. Opportunities will pop up. So will obstacles. Power ebbs and flows. Talks that crawl along can race forward or veer off in another direction. Even our own objectives may evolve. We have to make the best of whatever unfolds.

Negotiators like Sheldon are great improvisers. When things aren't going well, they'll float a clever proposal, crack a joke, or even challenge the other side. If need be, they'll also make major changes in strategy. What's odd, though, is that there isn't much about improvising in standard negotiation books. That's true both for the hardball manuals on dominating the other side and for the "win-win" texts that preach joint problem solving. In spite of their obvious differences, both approaches start with the same static premise that you have your given interests and I have mine. The win-win message is that by laying your cards on the table, you can expand the pie by making mutually beneficial trades. The hardball line tells you to chest your cards (and maybe slip a couple up your sleeve).

But there's much more to negotiation than bluffing and trading. The challenge lies in the fact that preferences, options, and relationships are typically in flux. Theorists may have sidestepped this reality, but top negotiators understand this very well.

I've seen this in my own research and also thanks to the work of colleagues at the Program on Negotiation (a cross-disciplinary consortium of negotiation experts at Harvard, Massachusetts Institute of Technology, and Tufts University). In a ten-year project led by Jim Sebenius, we've analyzed the work of great negotiators in a wide range of fields. They've included diplomats such as George Mitchell, who mediated peace in Northern Ireland; investment banker Bruce Wasserstein; and the visionary artists Christo and Jeanne-Claude.

The contexts in which these virtuosos negotiated differed. Their personalities ran the gamut as well. Some had a certain gravitas, while others were warm and entertaining—even funny. Yet in our workshops with them, they all emphasized the dynamic nature of negotiation and the importance of agility. The late ambassador Richard Holbrooke, who forged the accord ending the bloodshed in the Balkans, described negotiation as being more like jazz than science. "It's an improvisation on a theme," he said. "You know where you want to go, but you don't know how to get there. It's not linear."

UN special envoy Lakhdar Brahimi, having mediated in some of the world's most violent and unpredictable trouble spots, used a nautical metaphor to express the same idea. Negotiators must always "navigate by sight," he cautioned. No matter how diligently we prepare, we're bound to encounter surprises, pleasant and otherwise, that warrant course corrections.

Donald Dell, the sports agent-marketer, made his mark by hammering out huge contracts for basketball players Patrick Ewing and Moses Malone and earning millions in endorsement deals for tennis stars Arthur Ashe and Jimmy Connors. He's orchestrated bidding wars between rival television networks for broadcasting rights to events like the French Open.

Dell has also done very well negotiating on his own behalf. In 1998 he sold his sports management firm ProServ to an entertainment company for what he describes as "the proverbial offer I couldn't refuse." A few years later, after buying much of it back for twenty cents on the dollar, he then resold his interest to Lagadère Unlimited, where he is group president in charge of TV deals, events, and tennis.

For all his success, though, Dell is quick to say that things often don't go according to plan. "I can't tell you how many times I arrived prepared for a negotiation, only to have someone or something come up that upset or changed the deal I thought I was doing. *The only way to protect yourself one hundred percent against this situation is to assume there is something you don't know.* This advice will not only keep your mind up to speed with the deal and force you to consider other parties' motivations, but it will also keep your ego in check."

LEARNING, ADAPTING, AND INFLUENCING

Lesser known but highly talented deal makers make the same point. Tom Green is a remarkable negotiator who has worked in both the private and public sectors. Tom was a key figure in the sale of a storied baseball franchise and helped restructure a failing health maintenance organization (HMO) that many thought was headed for bankruptcy.

Tom also served on the public interest team that resolved massive litigation against the tobacco industry. Until that time, Big Tobacco had never lost a case or paid a dime to settle health claims out of court. When Mississippi, Massachusetts, and a few other states filed suit to recover Medicaid costs for smoking-related illnesses, their effort seemed quixotic. Yet one by one, Green and his colleagues enlisted forty other states to join the effort. That momentum brought the tobacco companies to the bargaining table. In 1998 the industry bowed to more stringent regulation and agreed to pay $350 billion in damages.

I wrote a case study about this meganegotiation for my MBA course. Tom visited the class the first time I taught it and listened as students analyzed the deft coalition building and old-fashioned horse trading that led to the unexpected outcome. Near the end of the discussion, I asked Tom for his own conclusions. After complimenting students on their observations, he added something that surprised them. The secret of his success, he said, has been "making chaos my friend in negotiation."

When Tom speaks about embracing chaos, he's not talking merely about cases involving scores of parties, thorny issues, and messy politics. Rather, he knows that all negotiations, large and small, are chaotic, since they take place in fluid and often unpredictable environments. But that's not to say that negotiation is random. The process is propelled by how the parties interact. Understanding how seemingly small moves or gestures can change the course of negotiation can mean the difference between agreement and deadlock.

Saying that negotiators like Tom are agile improvisers doesn't mean that they make everything up as they go along. Far from it. They're well prepared, but they don't hobble themselves with rigid plans. **They understand that effective negotiation demands rapid cycles of *learning*, *adapting*, and *influencing*.**

Each of those italicized words is critical. Learning, adapting, and influencing take place in most negotiations, of course, but all too often only by happenstance. Instead, I'm talking about *deliberate* learning. It entails updating your expectations on three levels: (1) the scope of the issues under discussion, (2) the best means for resolving them, and (3) the nature of your relationship with counterparts. "Another way of saying it," Ambassador Brahimi asserts, "is keep an open mind and be ready to change and adapt to the situation. Don't ask reality to conform to your blueprint, but transform your blueprint to adapt to reality."

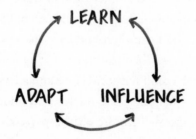

The learning can't be passive. It's not like browsing in a store, checking stock prices, or reading a text. Latent information in those contexts is unchanging. A book has the same number of pages whether you skim it or read it word for word. But the fact is that much of what you must learn in negotiation can only come by interacting with the other party.

Let's say that you reveal your priorities to your counterparts, hoping to foster a cooperative exchange. If you're right, you may proceed down a collaborative path. But if, instead, they interpret your disclosure as a sign of weakness, the negotiation could take a turn you wouldn't have chosen.

Or you make a proposal. It doesn't work for them. They counter with something that's not so hot from your point of view. But the two ideas together prompt both of you to come up with a third option that neither party would have conjured on its own. When the issue under discussion changes, you must adapt accordingly. It may be a slight adjustment, or, as it was with Jay Sheldon, it may be a major shift.

Likewise, you seek to influence those on the other side, to convince them of the value of what you're offering. What they say in response—and how they say it—speaks to that particular point, but it is also feedback on how effectively you're engaging your counterpart. Maybe your style suits them. If not, you'll need to change your approach. Beyond the dollars and cents of a potential deal, you are negotiating how to negotiate.

SUCCESS AND FAILURE

Decades ago, in a low-rise section of Manhattan, the governing board of a church on a corner lot asked the Julien Studley real estate firm to conduct an appraisal. Board members hoped that they could fetch a price that would allow them to build elsewhere and have enough money left over to fund their social programs. The firm's figure was far less than they needed, however, so the church paid the appraisal fee and abandoned its plan.

The young broker handling the matter had another idea, though. What if he could somehow acquire all the parcels on the block? The whole assembly would be worth far more than its component parts. But there were lots of challenges. For starters, his firm didn't have the resources to buy all the properties, nor did it have a deep-pocketed buyer lined up. And there was the risk that its acquisitions would invite competitors and potential holdouts.

It took time, but the broker and his firm pulled it off. Parcel by parcel, they met the different needs of various owners. They paid the moving expenses of some elderly tenants in one case. In another, they kept a restaurant open so that its employees would have work until construction began. They even worked out a condo arrangement in which the church could rebuild on its current land. But the firm also got tough with potential competitors. If you ever happen to be in Midtown, just look up, and you can see the result: the gleaming Citibank tower with its sharply angled top. The story of how it came to be offers powerful lessons about adaptive, improvisational negotiation.

Other cases don't end as well. The board of a co-op apartment building enacted a rule requiring everyone to install and pay for child safety bars in the windows. One particular owner refused to pay, insisting that the board pick up the cost: in that case, $902. The board, made up of his neighbors in the building, felt compelled to uphold its legal authority and filed suit, hoping the owner would relent. Instead, he retained his own attorney, and the parties were off to the litigation races.

The co-op board won before the trial judge, lost on appeal, and then got the original judgment reinstated by a still higher court. This battle dragged out almost five years. By that time, their combined legal bills had ballooned to more than $80,000—almost one hundred times the amount originally at stake.

They weren't finished, either. The objecting owner gave up trying to overturn the judgment, but the parties turned to fighting over whether he had to reimburse the board for its legal costs. When they were finally done, they had broken through the $100,000 barrier.

From the start, each side assumed that the other would come to its senses and abandon the fight. Instead, they both dug themselves ever deeper and kept on shoveling. Nobody planned on investing so much time, money, and emotion in a lose-lose proposition, yet that's the outcome they got.

The apartment owner himself finally learned his lesson. "I'm a man converted," he said afterward. "Anything you can possibly do to avoid a lawsuit, do it." The lawyer for the co-op's board wasn't chastened, though. "I think the expenditures here were appropriate and were pretty much kept to a minimum," he said. He claimed that his clients "had an idea of what was going on" throughout the case. "There were no surprises." His attitude betrays a fatalistic commitment to a strategy even when there's mounting evidence that it's not working.

Maybe the owner could have "donated" $902 for some other common use without having to back down on the legal principle. Or another resident, caught in the cross fire, might have made the case go away by anonymously sending the board $902 in cash to cover the cost of the window bars—a bargain compared with being assessed for the mushrooming legal costs. The fiasco also might have been averted if just one board member had asked the right question when they filed suit: namely, What's the worst thing that could happen here? An obvious answer would be that the owner would be just as obstinate as they were.

Cookie-cutter strategies crumble in the turbulence of real-world negotiation. Persistence is often a virtue, but clinging to an obsolete plan is not. Jay Sheldon was intent on buying the nearby cable system. When it became clear that its owner wouldn't budge on price, however, he didn't try to beat him down further or cave on his own valuation of that business. Nor did he walk away. Instead, he adapted by crafting a superior plan B. But remember that it was Sheldon's agility that made it all happen. His counterpart, sitting at the same table, looking at exactly the same facts, didn't imagine being a buyer until Jay proposed it.

WHAT'S MISSING IN THE CONVENTIONAL WISDOM

The groundbreaking negotiation text *Getting to Yes: Negotiating Agreement Without Giving In,* by my colleagues Roger Fisher, Bill Ury, and Bruce Patton, was first published thirty years ago. Its timing couldn't have been better. The book offered a constructive alternative to the then prevailing view that negotiation is inevitably a win-lose proposition, a game won by muscle and deception. Many people were weary with conflict, however, whether in protracted litigation, work stoppages, or in troubled areas of the world like the Middle East.

The authors presented a five-point method, one relevant to any context, from renting an apartment to international diplomacy:

1. Focus on interests, not positions.
2. Separate the people from the problem.
3. Invent options for mutual gain.
4. Insist on objective criteria.
5. Develop your best alternative to a negotiated agreement, or BATNA (your walkaway if there is no deal).

This interest-based approach was widely embraced as win-win negotiation (although that term never appears in *Getting to Yes*). At the core, it was an appeal to enlightened self-interest.

The book remains a strong rebuttal to old-fashioned hardball tactics. Rather than locking into fixed positions, negotiators should dig deeper and work from underlying interests. If you're seeking a new job, don't haggle over salary and risk getting the relationship off to a bad start. Instead, look for other benefits that might be more valuable than a few more dollars of straight pay. With a little inventiveness, you can transform many zero-sum problems into opportunities for mutual gain. And even tough bargainers with no concern about fairness should be tempted by the prospect of expanding the pie.

Readers were also reminded of the importance of relationships and reputation. Aggressive tactics may work in one-time, price-only transactions between strangers, but there are costs. Most people who've been strong-armed once don't come back for another drubbing. Books such as Jim Camp's *Start with No: America's Number One Negotiating Coach Explains Why Win-Win Is a Disastrous Strategy, and How You Can Beat It* ignore the fact that in today's highly networked world, what goes around often comes around. Nor do they explain what's achieved if both parties stonewall and just wait for somebody to blink.

Sometimes the bargaining table is tilted, of course. When that's the case, *Getting to Yes* emphasizes the importance of improving one's BATNA. It's a matter of weighing offers on the table against the best you realistically can do if there's no deal. Having a good fallback naturally strengthens your bargaining hand. If you're holding lousy cards, then you may have to accept terms that you're not wild about.

So two cheers for win-win negotiation. Books based on that model freed negotiators from the notion that "more for you means less for me." They opened people's minds to the problem-solving potential latent in many negotiations. A lot of good work on negotiation has been done since the publication of *Getting to Yes*. But the basic framework rests implicitly on static assumptions about interests, options, circumstances, and relationships, when these factors tend to be fluid and ambiguous. Just as military strategists acknowledge the fog of war, negotiators must confront the haze that obscures the territory that they explore.

The standard model doesn't capture the complexity of real-world negotiation any more than stuffed birds in a museum reveal the marvel of flight, or show us how those creatures dart and soar in the breeze. Instead of a snapshot, we need a moving picture that illuminates how the negotiation process evolves over time. That's the aim of this book.

I'm not out on a limb saying that basic win-win theory whistles past thorny negotiation problems. Roger Fisher himself often began presentations by ripping his bestseller in two to demonstrate the need for fresh thinking. To see why, take a second look at two celebrated axioms on which the conventional model rests. One is "Focus on interests, not positions." The other is "Develop your BATNA" (your walkaway option).

First, regarding interests, **the hard truth is that we often can't know what our interests are until we're really negotiating.** The suggestion that we don't know our own minds may seem strange, even insulting. But seasoned negotiators know this well. Bear with me.

Negotiation often leads us somewhere unexpected, sometimes happily so. Say that you're trying to buy a particular house. After analyzing the market (and your bank account), you swear that the absolute maximum you'll pay is $350,000, preferably much less. Yet several days later, you shell out $375,000 to close the deal. Does that mean you negotiated badly? Possibly, if you got fast-talked into overpaying. Then again, maybe not. Violating your initial limit could make sense if the property proved to be in better shape than you expected or you learned that similar homes in the area recently sold for much more. You paid more than you planned to, but maybe you still got a bargain.

Interests are fluid, so we need to be flexible ourselves. But that complicates negotiation strategy and decision making. Stable goals give us discipline. They help us know when to say yes and when to walk away. If we dispense with objectives, we can rationalize any outcome. Surely that can't be right. When Tom Green told my students about the importance of embracing the chaos of negotiation, he tacked on a critical corollary. It's imperative, he said, "to stay on beam."

Likewise, the BATNA concept is crisp in theory but messy in practice. It presumes that negotiations come down to a simple decision: deal or no deal. Were that true, whenever someone offers you something slightly better than your walkaway, you should take it. That could mean settling cheap when, with some creativity, you might grow the pie (or by persisting, get a larger slice of it). Then again, you don't want to push so hard that you risk losing what you already have in hand. Knowing when to say yes can be tricky.

The standard BATNA model also isn't helpful when you're negotiating with no clear fallback. Just ask a business school graduate interviewing for jobs with no other offer in hand. When she's negotiating with one company, her BATNA is the uncertain prospect of landing a position elsewhere. How should she figure her walkaway when she has no immediate options? Few books address this common problem. This one does.

The elusiveness of interests and messiness of BATNAs collide when you have to juggle multiple negotiations. That's what happens when you comparison shop for a car at several dealerships. You may know generally what kind of vehicle you'd like, but you still want a great price. When you're negotiating with one salesperson, your fallback is often the uncertain prospect of how well you might do with another.

My colleague (call her Carol Griffin) and her husband, Don, faced this problem when they were looking for their first house. Carol is a brilliant decision theorist, so her preparation was off the charts. She researched the local market and compared school systems. She even test drove different commuting routes. Then she plugged all the data into a spreadsheet and weighted the factors so that they could rank different properties.

Looking back now, however, Carol admits that she and Don didn't know what they wanted until they toured various properties and began to negotiate. One house was priced right but needed a lot of work. Another had smaller rooms but also a gorgeous yard. Still others that had looked good online somehow had less appeal in person.

Some factors that they cared about—heating costs and the proximity to schools—were easy to compute, but how they actually felt about different places was not. With their apartment lease about to expire, they faced hard BATNA choices. For the house they *loved*, should they keep bargaining to knock down the price to an affordable number? Or should they settle for a less expensive place that they liked all right before some other buyer snapped up that one? (We won't even think about how much harder this would have been if Carol and Don didn't see eye to eye themselves.)

How we resolve such dilemmas isn't put to the test until we have to decide between a given bird near at hand versus the chance of snaring a more enticing one deeper in the bush. It's not simply how much better the latter might be objectively. We also have to reckon the odds of winning it—and taste how we'll feel if we end up losing out on both deals.

Savvy real estate brokers understand that, like the Griffins, many clients don't really know what they want. University of Virginia psychologist Tim Wilson describes how his own agent listens politely when prospective buyers list their priorities, but then blithely ignores them and shows them many different properties. "On the initial visits, the agent pays close attention to her clients' emotional reactions as they walk through the houses, trying to *deduce* what they are really looking for." According to Wilson, brokers have a saying: "Buyers lie." It's not deliberate. People just don't know their own minds. "One reason my real estate agent is so successful is that she is quite skilled at inferring what her clients want and often knows their preferences better than the clients themselves do."

Carol and Don played it safe by working out a deal for the less expensive place. Sometimes, though, they get wistful driving past their dream house, four blocks away. They wonder if they could have haggled a lower price by being more assertive. But because of the inherent uncertainty of negotiation, they can never know for sure.

That kind of second-guessing does little good. Instead, you're better off critiquing *how* you negotiated. On this score, the Griffins did well. Carol's meticulous preparation could only reflect attributes that were easy to quantify. It couldn't capture how they felt about particular houses until they took their tours. Still, it served as a valuable template against which they could check their judgments. Before scratching a house that they had rated high, it forced them to ask what it was that they didn't like and how much that mattered. They shifted their priorities but in a disciplined manner.

The Griffins learned and adapted along the way. Some owners they negotiated with seemed to be testing the market on the chance that somebody would make an offer they couldn't refuse. Others were in more of a hurry to sell, which gave the Griffins more leverage than they anticipated. In the end, the people who sold their home to the Griffins understood they were careful shoppers and gave them a price that was too good to pass up.

DYNAMIC NEGOTIATION

This book explains how to become a more agile and effective negotiator. It's not a matter of being somewhat prepared and a little flexible. If you try that, you'll fall between the cracks. **Instead, managing uncertainty should be the cornerstone of your negotiation strategy**. Part 1 lays out a dynamic model for analyzing and conducting negotiations. Part 2 is about mind-set and the techniques for learning, adapting, and influencing on the fly. Part 3 situates these concepts in each phase of negotiation, from openings, through critical moments, to closing. Part 4, "Mastery," knits together creativity, ongoing learning, and ethics.

Specifically, the first part—"A Sense of Direction"—deals with the role of ambiguity, change, and luck inherent in any negotiation. Understanding the nature of the environment is step one in developing adaptive strategy for traversing it. But simply acknowledging uncertainty is not enough. Master negotiators bake it into their strategy and turn it to their advantage.

The upcoming chapter, "A Map of the Pyrenees," digs deeper into the underlying challenges of unpredictability introduced here. It poses three key questions you should address before negotiating. The chapter after that, "Prospecting," offers preparation tools for setting goals, weighing trade-offs, assessing the upside, and determining when to walk away. While chapters 2 and 3 focus on *what* you are seeking (your substantive goals), chapter 4, "Plan B," is about strategy and process—the *how*—of searching for agreement. It spells out nine strategic principles for venturing forward.

The second part of the book—"Improvising"—zeroes in on micro-interactions on a tactical level. Being nimble is about both mind-set and technique. This section begins with a chapter entitled "Presence of Mind." To perform at your best, you must be prepared to negotiate both mentally *and* emotionally. That requires a paradoxical ability to be both calm and alert, patient and proactive, creative yet fully grounded.

Other chapters in this second section dig into improvisational principles and techniques. In the chapter "The Swing of Things," you'll see how jazz musicians, even complete strangers, create new music on the spot. They know when to solo and when to harmonize. They even dare to make mistakes. Then, as counterpoint, in "Situational Awareness," you'll see how concepts from the battlefield, chess, and competitive sports apply not only to hardball settlement of lawsuits and labor disputes but also to collaborative transactions.

The third part of the book—"Managing the Process"—applies these practices to the flow of negotiation. The "Openings" chapter compares transcripts of two pairs of veteran negotiators dealing with the same problem. One pair slips into taking potshots at each other. The other, instinctively following the rules of jazz and improv, just as quickly gets into sync.

Then the "Critical Moments" chapter examines tipping points in negotiations: junctures where you have to make decisions that are hard to unwind. Making an offer that you can't take back is one example. Dealing with threats or outbursts is another. A chapter on "Closing" wraps up this section. If someone makes you an attractive proposal, when should you take it and when should you press for more?

The last portion of the book—"Mastery"—illuminates the attributes that separate capable negotiators from the stars. One is creativity, as you'll see in the chapter "Silk Purses." People such as Jay Sheldon (the investor who salvaged his cable deal) have the knack for finding agreement where others might see only deadlock. Mastery also entails an intriguing mix of confidence and humility. In the chapter "Wicked Learning," you'll discover that the best negotiators learn the right lessons from their experience. They aren't intoxicated by prior success.

The book's concluding chapter, "Fair Enough," examines ethical issues inherent in all negotiations. The most difficult choices aren't about right and wrong; rather, they require reconciling competing values and obligations. Then the appendix presents twenty-five reasons to embrace chaos in negotiation, a thematic listing of the key principles and methods of the learn-adapt-and-influence approach. This list is a quick refresher for crafting strategy.

I'm confident that a thoughtful reading of this book will make you a better negotiator, whether you're a relative novice or have lots of experience under your belt. The advice here is built on the best practices of top negotiators. It offers a fresh and practical slant on negotiation, one that may push you to rethink your own habits and assumptions. I hope that's liberating.

KEY POINTS

- Anticipate that goals, interests, and walkaway alternatives might evolve in ways that are to your advantage or detriment.
- Understand that negotiation is an interactive process. Your actions and statements may influence your counterparts in ways that you did not expect or intend.
- Maximize your negotiation effectiveness by crafting a robust strategy.
- Be prepared to improvise.

PART ONE

A Sense of Direction

You'd be surprised how many people don't actually know what they want with the kind of precision that a negotiation demands. Then you have to think of the two thousand ways to get where you want to go: what the trades might be, what the arguments might be, what the moves might be on the other side. And you watch carefully, and listen carefully, talk less, and remain persistent.

—AMBASSADOR CHARLENE BARSHEFSKY

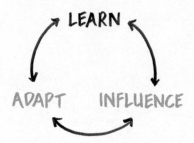

[2] A Map of the Pyrenees

Many years ago, a military patrol was caught by a fierce blizzard in the Swiss Alps. The soldiers were lost and frightened, but one of them found a map tucked in his pocket. After consulting it, the men built a shelter, planned their route, and then waited out the storm. When the weather cleared three days later, they made their way back to the base camp.

Their commanding officer, relieved that his men had survived the ordeal, asked how they made their way out. A young soldier produced the life-saving map, and the officer studied it carefully. He was shocked to see that it was a map of the Pyrenees Mountains that border Spain and France, not the Alps.

This story, attributed to Hungarian biochemist and Nobel laureate Albert Szent-Gyorgi, dates back to the 1930s. It is often cited in serious research on organizational learning and is widely regarded as true.

Whether or not the tale is apocryphal, how could the wrong map save climbers lost in the Alps? There are three explanations, and they are as relevant for negotiators as for anyone caught in the wilderness.

First, the map rekindled the soldiers' confidence. It released them from the paralysis of indecision and impelled them to take action. The men didn't bicker or wander aimlessly. Instead, they shielded themselves against the storm and waited for the best time to make a move.

Second, the map provided impetus. Heading exactly the right way proved less important than simply getting moving. That isn't always prudent, of course. If we're lost and sit tight, others may come to our rescue.

In negotiation, by contrast, we have to rely on our own wits and initiative to get where we want to go. A bias for action almost always beats being passive.

Most important, the map sharpened the soldiers' awareness. It gave them a template from which they could work. Once they were under way, portions of the map may have conformed to specific areas the soldiers encountered. Mountains have common characteristics, after all: steep headwalls, brooks, and more gentle inclines. But peaks are also distinctive in other respects. When the drawing no longer fit the scene, the men had to reconsider their position and find some other part of the map that seemed more plausible.

That constant vigilance enabled them to improve their mental model of the actual world they were traversing. This ongoing reorientation required keen attention to their surroundings. Their survival depended on a willingness to abandon earlier assumptions and accept new realities.

Confidence, impetus, and vigilance: summon that trio, and you have hardy companions when stakes are high and outcomes in doubt, whether traversing mountains or negotiating agreements.

The soldiers' map was wrong, but not *that* wrong. A map of the Sahara or of Lake Erie would have done the soldiers no good. To be useful, the map had to correspond roughly to reality. If it weren't plausible, the men wouldn't have had confidence in themselves. And it had to be appropriate to the context, or it wouldn't have provided initial direction. But it also had to be the right scale. A fine-grained map probably would have left them worse off. Overwhelmed with topographical details, they could have argued in circles about where to start rather than focus on where they needed to go.

You can't pull a printed map from your pocket, of course, when you're formulating a negotiating strategy. You have to draft one yourself. Even when you're on familiar ground and prior experience suggests a particular path, guard yourself against a been-there, done-that mind-set. The terrain may have changed since your last time around. Traditional cartographers used sextants, surveyors' transits, and altimeters to mark out territory. As Ambassador Brahimi says, negotiators must constantly use their eyes. Specifically, you need a realistic sense of three features of the landscape.

The first is a clearheaded view of where you think you are at present—that is, a reckoning of your needs, priorities, and trade-offs—as well as your fallback options if the negotiation becomes stalemated. The second is an estimate of your counterpart's circumstances so that you can gauge what might prove acceptable. (We'll get into this in depth in the next chapter.) A third element of mapping negotiation entails cataloging key factors that you *don't know* at the outset, so that you're alert for surprises as the process unfolds. Asking yourself these three questions will help you prepare strategy:

1. Should I negotiate?
2. Is now the time?
3. Do I hedge or go all in?

These questions encourage you to grapple with the uncertainty of negotiation and take it into account in mapping a robust plan.

SHOULD I NEGOTIATE?

Herb Cohen recounts stories about haggling with salesmen in his popular book *You Can Negotiate Anything*. He admits that getting a special discount on a refrigerator can take multiple trips to the store and hours of chatter, but he relishes the process. For him, the sticker price is just a starting point.

Cohen is right. Lots of things are negotiable. As he advises, you don't get if you don't ask. But asking can be risky, as Arvind Gupta learned to his regret. He was close friends with an older couple who lived in a beachfront mansion with sweeping views of the ocean. Somehow, for twenty years, they had never been billed for property taxes, nor had they ever paid them.

When a notice from the city arrived, it was for a staggering amount.

The couple had already been thinking about downsizing, and the bill pushed them to make that decision. They were childless, so they approached Arvind, whom they loved, and offered to sell him the property for $2.5 million.

Arvind realized that this was a bargain price, but it was beyond his means. So he approached another friend whom he calls "Wealthy Bill," a nickname that is also a shorthand measure of the latter's fortune. Bill recognized the investment opportunity and was glad to be a silent partner in the purchase. But Bill said they should counter with an offer of $2.25 million. If the sellers insisted on full price, he noted, they could always pay it if necessary. Arvind was hesitant, however. The asking price was already well below market.

"Nonsense," said Bill. "There's always room to bargain." Arvind reluctantly made the counteroffer, since it was mostly Bill's money that was at stake.

You probably know where this story is going. Arvind's friends expressed their hurt and anger when he tried to haggle: "We treated you like a son, and this is how you thank us?" The owners withdrew their offer, found a real estate broker, and, less than a year later, sold their property for $11 million.

Whoops!

Arvind is philosophical about the experience. He's not rich, but he's professionally successful and comfortable financially. He is also exhibit A for the principle that the only way to know just how close to the edge of the cliff you can go safely is to take one more step beyond that.

Compare Arvind's blunder with Liz and Tony Weiler's story. For twenty years, they rented a summer cottage in Salt Harbor, a charming coastal community in Massachusetts. From their back porch, they could watch their children playing on the private beach below. They befriended the elderly owner who lived next door. She encouraged them to plant raspberry and blueberry bushes. In return, Liz made fruit pies for her landlady.

From time to time, they inquired discreetly whether she might be willing to sell the property, but the owner herself had three grown children, one of whom had expressed interest in the house. The Weilers knew that they'd be able to return to the cottage every summer so long as their neighbor was still alive, but they despaired of what would happen when she died. And she was now ninety-four.

Then one August morning, the owner's eldest son appeared at their door. Without coming in, he announced that he had talked to his mother and his siblings. The family was ready to sell. "Three hundred and thirty thousand dollars," he said. "Take it or leave it. Let us know before Labor Day." Then he left.

The Weilers were in a swirl. At long last, the cottage could be theirs. But what about the price? Given the market, $330,000 wasn't outlandish, and they could afford it, but it was no bargain, either. Then again, there was nothing else in that range that they could love nearly as much. Nevertheless, Liz bristled at the take-it-or-leave-it remark. Why not make a counteroffer?

Whenever somebody makes you a proposal, either at the outset or deep into a negotiation, you must reckon the plusses and minuses of bargaining further. In the Weilers' case, the upside of countering could be saving some money. Knocking 10 percent or more off the price could be a long shot, but even saving half that amount might seem worthwhile.

What about the downside, though? Would there be any harm in asking? The owner might lower the demand a bit or insist that the price is the price. But it had taken the family years to agree to sell. Their consensus might be fragile. If the Weilers countered, any one of the siblings might regard that as an excuse to retract the offer.

Sitting on the porch of their rented cottage, the Weilers weighed the pros and cons of negotiating. Nothing ventured, they thought, nothing gained. *But they also imagined a corollary: nothing ventured, nothing lost.*

The fog of negotiation—its inherent uncertainty—makes it hard to know how much room there is to negotiate or if there's any room at all. Odds are that the Weilers could have counteroffered without exploding the deal, but for them, the pivotal question was whether the upside of saving $15,000 or $20,000 would be worth taking even a small chance of losing a house they'd come to cherish.

The conventional negotiation theory that we covered in the prior chapter doesn't address the problem of when to say yes. It just tells you to weigh whatever you're offered against your no-deal alternative—that is, your best course of action if you can't reach agreement. Viewed this way, for Arvind or for the Weilers, it's a matter of comparing two paths on a simple decision tree.

The implication is that a buyer should say yes whenever offered a better deal than he or she can get elsewhere. Real-world negotiation is more interesting, however. A more accurate strategic map would include the separate paths for saying yes to an acceptable deal or walking away, plus a third alternative, pushing for even more attractive terms.

The size and likelihood of what you might gain from continuing to negotiate have to be weighed against the downside of losing the deal. Holding on to a bird in the hand requires a sensitive touch firm enough to prevent it from flying away but not so forceful as to squeeze the life out of it. Context matters. How much risk you're willing to run depends on your temperament, as well as your resources and alternatives. **The time to stop negotiating is when the risk of pressing further outweighs possible gains.**

IS NOW THE TIME?

Many years ago, just as my uncle Al's family was starting out on a summer vacation, their car broke down. Black smoke poured out from under the hood. The engine had thrown a rod.

The timing was bad, and the location was worse. The breakdown occurred right in front of a car dealership. According to family lore, a salesman who witnessed the whole episode strode out of the showroom toward them, rubbing his hands, his face beaming.

The story had a happy ending, sort of. My late uncle bought a new station wagon on the spot. He got the suitcases from the smoldering heap and loaded them into the new car, and the family had a fine vacation. Of course, Uncle Al paid dearly. And, as it happened, the car was a Ford Edsel, a short-lived model that automotive buffs remember as one of the great lemons in Detroit's history.

Uncle Al went on to have a remarkable career in business, buying small companies and helping them grow and prosper. He was always a superb negotiator. But on that distant July day, he was in the wrong place at the wrong time. He had to have another car, and the salesman knew it.

You're better off, of course, when you can schedule negotiations to your advantage. The time to buy a car is when you don't urgently need one. It's even better if the dealer is under pressure to get cars off the lot, near the end of a promotional period. If selling one more vehicle puts the dealer over his or her quota, you'll get a great price. The only downside of coming in late is that other shoppers may have picked over the inventory, but you can always come back at the end of the next month.

Whether time is on your side depends on the stability of your BATNA: your walkaway alternative. Will your nonagreement options get better or worse in the future? Sometimes that's an easy call. If you're trying to sell a ski condo in May, it may be worth waiting till the first frost gets people thinking again about winter sports. But waiting, of course, means swallowing operating costs and condo fees in the interim and risking that the market for vacation properties will soften. Timing also depends on whether the other parties expect their own alternatives will wax or wane.

If both sides feel that time is on their side, everyone may be in for a long haul.

When Harvard economist Richard Zeckhauser was still a student, he designed a simple game that demonstrated the potential impact of time pressure in negotiation. Pairs of subjects had to divide some money, but were given different rules. If two people couldn't agree on the split, no one would get anything. With one group, most came to agreement, many splitting the money fifty-fifty, though often only after extended haggling.

Richard then gave another set of paired subjects—call them group B—the same amount to divide, but he told them that the prize would shrink with every tick of the clock. Because time literally was money, these people reached agreement quickly, almost always splitting the prize equally.

With group C, Richard added a devilish twist. Again there was a tax that grew bigger with time, but here he specified that only one side—not the other—would pay most of the entire penalty. As you might guess, the people who were more heavily taxed usually got a smaller share. The surprise was that *un*taxed parties often did poorly too.

These subjects typically overplayed their hand. Believing that time was on their side, they expected their counterparts to buckle because of the ever-mounting tax. Instead, many people in that weaker position held out, biting their own nose to spite those who were pressuring them. By the time they reached agreement, the pie had shrunk significantly, resulting in less for both sides.

People fall into the same kind of trap in real-world negotiations. In business transactions, each side may be hesitant to make a concession to close a deal, fearful that they will look weak. Likewise, litigants pour money into lawsuits, never expecting to try their case, on the assumption that they can wait out the other side. It takes only one stubborn party to create a stalemate. If both sides are committed to outlasting the other, the costs can be colossal.

The National Hockey League and the NHL Players Association ended a protracted dispute early in 2013, but only after each side suffered enormous losses due to cancellation of half the regular season. During the lockout, league commissioner Gary Bettman stated that the teams were losing between $18 and $20 million daily; in turn, the players lost between $8 and $10 million in salary every day. Even as the deadline for reaching agreement loomed larger and larger, each side assumed that the other was bound to "come to its senses" and compromise.

From the players' point of view, it seemed unreasonable for the owners to sacrifice ticket sales and television income while carrying huge debt on their facilities. The owners, in turn, couldn't see how players would risk losing a full year of income in their short careers. Each group thought that time favored it.

In many ways, this was a lose-lose negotiation. Both sides would have been substantially better off if at the outset they had somehow managed to reach the same terms that they finally agreed upon. The lost ticket, concession, and media revenue is gone for good; so are the paychecks that the players would have received if there had been no stoppage. The outcome seems all the more irrational given that both sides had been down this road before: Half a season was squandered in 1994–95, while a lockout in 2004–05 caused the cancellation of the entire NHL season.

Prolonging a negotiation makes sense only if there's solid reason to believe that you will be in a better position tomorrow than you are today. That can be the case if the added time enables you to gain leverage by improving your fallback position or winning key allies. Having more time also may allow you to be better prepared (though that's true for your counterparts, too). But conditions can also worsen. Stringing along customers may prompt them to look for better terms from your competitors. For instance, if you hold out for a better price on a new home, mortgage rates may rise.

Getting ready for an important negotiation can take time as well, but you won't be omniscient. Certain things about your counterparts—their priorities, temperament, and trustworthiness—may be learned best by negotiating in earnest. **It's time to negotiate when you can learn more by being at the table than being absorbed in private preparation.**

DO I GO ALL IN?

A few years ago, Iberia Airlines approached Boeing and asked it to propose a new midrange plane. The aircraft industry had been in a deep slump since 2001, and Iberia was one of the few carriers making money at that time. The prospect of new business for Boeing seemed a godsend to the company. Nevertheless, it was hesitant to make a proposal.

In the past, Iberia had always favored Airbus, a European consortium. It was likely that the Spanish airline just wanted to use Boeing as a stalking horse to wrangle better terms from its longtime supplier. For Boeing, the cost of bidding for the Iberia contract—and losing—would be substantial. Beyond managerial time and millions of dollars in design work and financial expenses, there were important reputational factors. Being runner-up in a two-horse race would confirm the gloomy assessments of market analysts and further weaken Boeing's hand in negotiating with other potential customers. It would also cause morale problems within the company. But any real chance of securing the Iberia contract would require Boeing to court the airline aggressively and make a bold bid. Halfway measures would not work.

Initially, Boeing decided not to bid. The odds of winning were just too small, and the costs of losing were correspondingly high. Iberia, however, didn't want to have to deal with Airbus as its sole source, so it went to great lengths to convince Boeing that the American company had a real shot at the contract. Boeing ultimately relented and invested heavily in a proposal, but Iberia chose Airbus—after the latter was compelled to make significant price concessions to match Boeing's terms.

Coming up empty-handed in this negotiation was worse for Boeing than never trying at all. Having to go all in with its proposal—and doing so publicly—compounded its problems. In hindsight, there was remorse that the company didn't stick with its original decision and stay out of the competition.

Sometimes, though, you've got to dump all your chips on the table in order to be seen as a serious player. Those chips may be your time, money, or status—or all three. When you can hedge your bets or play one possible deal off another, that's fine, but sometimes you've got to put your negotiation eggs in one basket and then manage that basket very carefully.

Nobel laureate Tom Schelling's classic *The Strategy of Conflict* analyzed situations where locking oneself in amplifies leverage. For an illustration, he described the hot-rodders' game of chicken, in which two souped-up cars speed toward each other head-on. The first driver to swerve loses face. Schelling speculated about what would happen if one of the drivers yanked his steering wheel off the steering column and conspicuously tossed it out the window. Then he'd really be all in, committed to tearing straight ahead heedless of the consequences. The other driver would have to veer away to avoid disaster.

Schelling wrote his essay at the height of the Cold War, so many of his examples have a hard edge, but his insights also apply to business today. Fox Television's prominence is due to an all-in move it made in the 1990s, when it bid aggressively for National Football League broadcasting rights. Even though audience ratings were sagging, the upstart network offered almost twice what CBS had been paying for the prime Sunday-afternoon time slot.

The preemptive strategy worked. CBS didn't even try to match the bid. With one aggressive move Fox not only won NFL rights but also elbowed a place for itself at the table with the three established networks. It might have been able to acquire the football contract more cheaply, but by making a blow-out offer, Fox ended the competition then and there.

Many negotiations don't require all-in moves. Putting a toe in the water can be all that's required. That's how Sandy Ritchie bought a beautiful property off the Maine coast. Sandy already owned a two-acre island nearby, a low-lying pile of granite with sparse vegetation. But it had a camp, and when the tide was right and the wind was calm, he could row over and enjoy being master of his little kingdom. On the way to his place, Sandy would pass Bold Island, just east of the fishing town of Stonington. It's a picture-postcard scene with a spruce forest running up above the shoreline. There's even a dock for boats and a comfortable house up among the trees.

Sandy discovered that a widow in upstate New York owned the property. He wrote her a letter, introduced himself, and asked her to let him know if she were ever interested in selling. He heard nothing back in return, but the inquiry had cost him only a few minutes of his time.

He wrote again the following year. This time he described his family's love for the ocean and what his young children had been doing in school. Again, no answer. For the next six years, he composed his annual letter, reiterating his interest in the island and updating the owner on family news. Never did he get a reply.

Finally, he sent a note saying that he hoped he hadn't been a nuisance. He would call, he said, and if she wished him to stop, he would respect her wishes. When he called a few days later, a nurse answered and told him that the woman couldn't come to the phone but that she would like him to keep writing.

Several months later, Sandy received a letter from the owner saying that she was now ready to sell. She wanted him to make an offer. Sandy calculated the most he could afford and sent a proposal, explaining his circumstances. This time the woman phoned him to say that she would accept his figure. Sandy was ecstatic. But then the next day, he got a second call, this time from the woman's lawyer, saying that the deal was off because his bid was far less than the appraised value.

Sandy wrote back to the owner that he understood the circumstances, but his offer was the best he could do given his family obligations. Two days later, the woman overruled her lawyer. Sandy now owns Bold Island. All it took to negotiate purchasing one of the jewels of the Maine coast was ten postage stamps—and a decade's worth of patience.

BEST-CASE AND WORST-CASE ANALYSIS

Answering the three core questions (Should you negotiate? Is now the time? Do you go all in?) requires projecting yourself into the future. Doing a "*pre*mortem" is powerful protection against wishful thinking. It's a strategic planning technique advocated by decision scientist Gary

Klein in his book *Intuition at Work: Why Developing Your Gut Instincts Will Make You Better at What You Do* (it has since been retitled *The Power of Intuition*).

Klein's research shows that in critiquing any plan, it's not enough to ask, "Can we foresee any problems with this approach?" Such a question will surface some concerns, but often it's a skimpy list. It's easy to be smitten with your own logic. Having mapped backward from point Z—your goal—to your starting point, A, you may persuade yourself that there is but one true way that things can go. Klein has found that slightly rephrasing the question conjures up a richer picture of what could unfold. Specifically, test your strategy by asking this:

- **Premortem Part 1:** Flash forward. Imagine that the negotiation is under way. Now imagine there's been a major setback. What is it?

  That subtle shift in framing will animate your vision. Your focus will shift from whether something bad *might happen* to assuming that trouble *will occur*. You needn't be paranoid. Put aside being hit by a meteor just as you're about to sign the deal. But consider things that are unlikely yet still could happen.

  Perhaps, for example, there's a small chance that the market will shift in the other party's favor or that after making an agreement, you learn belatedly that you could have gotten better terms elsewhere. If you think about such scenarios, you may realize that they're more probable than you'd like to admit. A seemingly simple transaction with a supplier could drag out longer than expected, for instance. If that happens, meeting commitments to your own customers could be difficult. You'd be in a weak position unless you lined up a fallback in advance.

  The point of the premortem exercise isn't to identify each and every way a deal might go wrong. That's neither possible nor necessary. Rather, it's meant to foster an attitude of watchfulness, so you'll be quicker to see that the process is going awry. If you're alert, you may be able to get back on track. If not, you'll have a plan B.

  In planning ahead, it's just as important to be open to good news, of course. Thus, you should couple Klein's premortem with an optimistic test:

- **Premortem Part 2:** Flash forward again. This time imagine that there's been some sort of pleasant surprise. *What is it?*

  You needn't fantasize that you're going to win the MacArthur "Genius Grant" for negotiation. Rather, limit your analysis to the outer bounds of reality. Think of something positive that has a 10 percent chance of occurring. If you're buying new equipment or supplies, maybe your vendor has an unexpected overstock, for example. If so, you might get a better price or faster delivery than in the past.

  Optimistic scenarios will raise your sights. Studies show that negotiators who set lofty goals get better deals. By aiming high, they don't give away as much of the bargaining range when there's ample room to negotiate. Instead of contenting themselves with outcomes they can live with, these negotiators focus instead on how much the other party might be prepared to grant. In addition, imagining upside scenarios prepare you to recognize opportunities and find creative solutions.

  Research also shows that positive and negative expectations about negotiation can be self-fulfilling. In a recent experiment on psychological priming, Adam Galinksy and his colleagues gave some subjects five minutes to write a pep talk for themselves. They were told to list the outcomes they desired and the behaviors they would use to achieve, or *promote,* them. The subjects in a second group were instructed to list mistakes that they might make and what they could do to *prevent* those errors.

  As you'd expect, the optimistic "promoters" made bolder demands than did the more cautious "preventers." While the former concentrated on what they could accomplish, the latter thought about how they could fail. But there was an added bonus: when promotion-primed negotiators were matched up against one another, they created far more value than did pairs of prevention-primed people. Those in the latter group tended to accept anything that met their minimum needs, while the promoters pushed harder for their real priorities instead of just compromising. As a result, they were more likely to spot mutually beneficial trades.

CAUTIOUS OPTIMISM

Thinking hard about both the upside and the downside simultaneously requires a healthy schizophrenia. Optimism can generate value and put you in a better position to get a goodly share of it. But being unrealistic is doubly dangerous. Dreaming that a customer will give you the sun, the moon, *and* the stars for whatever you're offering could leave you empty-handed if he or she can find a more reasonably priced provider. Ungrounded optimism can also blind you to obstacles that may pop up. The realist will be quicker to recognize that things haven't gone as hoped and to improvise accordingly.

The snowbound soldiers in the Alps drew confidence from their map. It renewed their hopes and gave them direction. Fortunately, they didn't fall into the trap of "bending the map." They didn't twist reality to fit their preconceptions. Instead, as with strategy for negotiation, they used it as a tool for ongoing learning, adaptation, and ultimate survival.

In complex cases, formal analytic tools can help formulate and test different scenarios. In a lawsuit settlement, for example, decision tree software can gauge risk at different stages of litigation. Similarly, elaborate financial models can reveal alternative ways of structuring deals in the face of turbulent markets. For most cases, though, thinking out loud and back-of-envelope assessments are sufficient.

Let's go back to Arvind Gupta's case, where he blew a bargain purchase of beachfront property. He didn't have to be clairvoyant to foresee the chance he was taking. Merely asking himself this question—"Something has gone disastrously wrong; what is it?"—would have highlighted the risk of counteroffering. Granted, Arvind was in a bind because he was playing with his silent partner's money. At the latter's suggestion, he drew up a purchase-and-sale agreement, thick with legalese, with the lowball counteroffer buried down near the bottom of the document. When the owners came to that provision, they were shocked. Arvind sheepishly tried to explain, but it was too late, and the deal was dead.

If he had thought more imaginatively about the risk of rejection, instead of just crossing his fingers, he could have managed the downside. Suppose, for example, he had begun his conversation with the owners by assuring them that he would buy the property. With that settled, he could have sought their help in solving his problem with his coinvestor. Could they come down just a bit, he might have asked, so he wouldn't jeopardize his financing? Perhaps the owners would have said no, but it's hard to believe they would have been insulted. It's even possible that they might have offered the seller financing themselves. Even if they didn't budge, it wouldn't have been hard for Arvind to go back to Wealthy Bill, who already had okayed the asking price.

And what of Liz and Tony Weiler, our other buyers, who said yes to an apparent ultimatum but still brood over whether they overpaid? They recognized the risk of countering and concluded that the upside of saving a little money wasn't worth the chance of jeopardizing a fragile agreement. There were alternatives beyond the take-it-or-leave-it options stated by the owner's son. They might have used the "principled approach" advocated in *Getting to Yes* by asking, "How did you arrive at your price?" The idea is to shift the conversation away from hard dollars and focus instead on fairness criteria (comparable sales, for example). If the parties can agree on an appropriate standard, then it may be easier for them to arrive at a workable price.

That tactic might be worth trying in other instances, though I'm skeptical about using it in a case where getting the seller to negotiate was a long and ticklish process. With little to gain and much to lose by prolonging the negotiation, it was best simply to say yes. The Weilers got the house that they wanted, after all. As with any successful deal, it came with the nagging question of whether they could have done a little better. That kind of doubt is better, though, than the regret that Arvind lives with.

You need the optimism and self-confidence that you'll be able to seize opportunity when things break your way. But you have to accept that in negotiation your fate is never solely in your hands. Some of what happens in a given case will be either unpredictable or beyond your control. Negotiation strategy must allow for that reality.

KEY POINTS

- Choose whether to negotiate further or simply say yes to an acceptable offer.
- Time negotiations to your advantage, if possible.
- Decide whether to hedge or go all in.
- Weigh best- and worst-case scenarios as you formulate strategy.
- Balance optimism and caution.

---

[3] Prospecting

Several years ago, colleagues and I organized a negotiation workshop for general managers in the National Hockey League. They earn their living by hammering out big contracts with their players—or, more specifically, with their agents. Deals for superstars add up to millions of dollars and can lock in a team for up to a decade or more. The NHL imposes an overall salary cap on teams, so signing the right players at the right prices is critical to success on the ice.

To illustrate the importance of preparation, we split the participants into two groups and put them in separate rooms. We asked people in one group to be in their familiar role of general manager. We had the others be agents. Then we gave everyone the statistics and résumé of an unsigned player, with only his name disguised. Although the participants didn't know it, everyone got the same information.

We asked everyone three questions about how he'd negotiate this contract, whichever side they happened to be on. We wanted to know their planned first offer (or demand, in the case of agent) and their absolute walkaway. Then we asked what they thought the *other party's* walkaway would be.

When we paired up people to negotiate, the most that teams were prepared to pay was almost always less than the minimum that the agent was willing to accept. In more than 90 percent of the matches, there was no room for agreement. Many participants were hundreds of thousands of dollars apart. And here's the kicker: this gap was precisely what these guys expected! Almost all of them had predicted a stalemate. They went into negotiations knowing that their best offer wouldn't be enough to satisfy the other side.

That's not to say they thought the case was nonnegotiable. Not so. They knew from experience that players and teams work things out. But for most of these GMs, negotiation is about getting the other side to cave in. Maybe it shouldn't be surprising that those in the hard-hitting world of pro hockey view negotiation as a contest of wills. But that's also how many other people picture the process, whether they're buying a car, selling a home, or even working out a salary for a new job.

This zero-sum model positions an irresistible force on one side (the player) and an immovable object (team management) on the other, with each pushing hard until somebody budges. Seeing negotiation this way makes it a win-lose proposition.

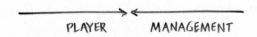

PLAYER   MANAGEMENT

The one-dimensional model fails to reflect the real-world complexity of negotiation. Because it considers only price, it fosters a "fixed pie" attitude, as my colleague Max Bazerman calls it. When people believe that there is only a given amount to be divided, the long knives come out. And even if you recognize the potential of value-generating trades, the one-dimensional framework is no help in weighing one package of proposals against another.

Take the case of my friend Jack when he was car shopping a few years ago. He likes Volvos, but only the sporty coupes and fancy sedans. On a visit to the dealer, however, he spotted a jet-black, souped-up wagon with a 300-plus horsepower engine, a six-speed gearbox, and high-tech wheels.

Although Jack usually buys brand new, he asked the salesman why this particular vehicle already had five thousand miles on it. "Oh, it was too much car for the guy who bought it." That comment was the clincher for my type-A friend, though the salesman didn't know that. Privately,

Jack loved the car, but he also loves a bargain, so he was doing his best to mask his craving.

Jack knew there would be a deal. Even then that much was certain. But he couldn't know how far he could knock down the sticker price. Nor could he know how long this little dance would take or where they'd end up.

The situation was hazier for the salesman, who was trying to assess this stranger who had ambled into the showroom. Was Jack a prospect or just a tire kicker killing time? Either way, what would be the best way to pitch him? Should he push on price or just be happy to move an offbeat vehicle off the lot? Jack dresses well. Maybe the salesman sniffed a thick wallet. Then again, Jack's self-confidence is unmistakable, so he also could look like a tough bargainer. Good salespeople have intuitions about customers, but that's not the same as hard-and-fast knowledge.

Underneath all the posturing and bantering, Jack and the smooth-talking salesman were negotiating seriously. Each was trying to scope out the bargaining range. Jack had to see this car himself, hear why it was being sold, and revise his antiwagon bias. In turn, the salesman was sizing up my friend's interest (and his budget). Walking into the showroom, Jack would have bet dollars to donuts against even looking at a station wagon. That same afternoon, after a lot of haggling, he happily drove one home—and at a good number, too.

But even in this simple transaction, price wasn't the only issue Jack had to resolve. Should he accept the dealer's offer on his trade-in or go through the hassle of a private sale? He decided on the latter. Did he want to finance the purchase? Jack had planned to pay cash, but Volvo was subsidizing a 1 percent rate. That was too good to pass up. He also got an extended warranty at cost. The terms were worked out in back-and-forth discussion. Some of the options that the salesman proposed weren't worth the money, Jack felt, but others were. In the end, price was still an important factor, but other items proved to have value too.

The familiar win-lose bargaining-range notion ignores the trading and tweaking that take place even in everyday transactions like Jack's. This chapter presents an alternative, more realistic model for conceptualizing the area of potential agreement, as well as a tool for developing appropriate strategy. Used together, these models can serve as a negotiator's map of the Pyrenees.

CONSTRUCTING A DEAL TRIANGLE

We'll start with the deal triangle shown below. It's bounded on one side by your own baseline—that is, outcomes that you prefer marginally over making no deal at all. The second side is the other party's baseline, or the corresponding set of potential deals that it finds acceptable, though just barely. The third line is made up of real-world constraints that limit the parties' ability to be creative. These might be resource shortages, deadlines, or company policies that can't be violated.

The triangle formed by these three boundaries represents the territory of workable outcomes from everyone's point of view. Any proposal beyond that is a deal breaker, since it's out of bounds for at least one of the parties.

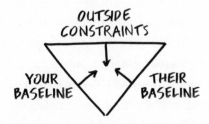

This triangle image allows parties to move into a broader area of workable deals, not just back and forth along a taut line. Where there's some room for agreement, parties will still differ about which particular outcome they prefer, of course. And when there is no deal space starting out (as with the hockey GMs), agreement may be reached by finding creative solutions rather than through concessions.

If you conclude there's little room for agreement, you should be satisfied with outcomes that are an improvement over the status quo, even if only just a bit. By contrast, if you sense that the area between the parties' respective baselines could expand, then strive to create (and claim) more value. To succeed, you need to know which one of these two situations you're in. **If you don't have a clue whether there's only a little room or a lot, you're simply tossing darts blindfolded.** It's hard to hit a bull's-eye if you can't see the target.

Explaining the deal triangle concept is easy. Getting an accurate fix on real-world possibilities is more challenging. The deal triangle isn't rigid. It can flex, grow, or vanish as conditions change in negotiation. Even so, keeping that picture in mind will help you chart your progress as you test assumptions and update your expectations.

SETTING YOUR BASELINE

The term *bottom line* rankles sophisticated negotiators, and with good reason if that's taken to mean a rigid position. Why handcuff yourself by assuming that there's only one way to satisfy your interests? What you discover as you negotiate may justify either upping your demands or softening them. On the other hand, you need a disciplined way of knowing when to say yes and when to say no. You need to draw a line somewhere, but define it broadly. Rather than putting a single stake in the ground, prepare by identifying a set of different outcomes that would be acceptable—though only barely. Together those marginal deals constitute your baseline, or the border that separates your saying yes from your saying no. Drawing the baseline involves three simple steps:

1. Establish a benchmark deal.
2. Identify equivalent packages.
3. Anticipate likely change.

The first step—establish a benchmark deal—is Negotiation 101. From the first chapter, recall the classic BATNA concept (the best alternative to a negotiated agreement). A particular offer is tempting only if it at least matches your fallback option, all other things being equal. The better your BATNA, the pickier you can be. Correspondingly, if your nonagreement alternative is poor, you may have to take less than you hope for and feel you deserve.

When going into every negotiation, identify—provisionally—a point on the scales where you'd have a hard time deciding between accepting or rejecting a firm and final proposal from the other side. It's a way of testing your resolve. It also gives you a standard for evaluating alternative deals.

Step two is to identify equivalent packages—better in some respects, worse in others—that on balance would be worth the same to you as your benchmark. Here's an analogy: let's say that you won a bag of groceries in a supermarket drawing. Everything in the bag may have some value to you, but some items you like, while others, such as fresh raspberries, you *love*. How many cans of soup would you give up to get another pint of berries? One? Two? Three? Maybe ten? I'm not talking about swaps that would improve the overall value of the mix. Rather, imagine a different assortment that would be worth exactly the same to you as the bag you won initially.

Any offer that you receive in negotiation will likewise be a mixed bag of provisions: some that you gain from the other party, and other items that you must grant in return. So identify at least two other such bundles that are of equivalent net value. Remember that the task here is to find deals that put you on the knife edge between accepting and rejecting the proposal.

Going through this preparation exercise forces you to weigh trade-offs. Thinking them through ahead of time is a whole lot better than making snap decisions in the midst of a negotiation. Mulling over your preferences also opens up your thinking the same way that warming up before a match makes a tennis player limber and focused. Research suggests that negotiators who prepare by toying with alternative solutions generate still more ideas when they negotiate with other parties.

Karen Lacey was reasonably happy in her job but was being wooed by QXData, a top-tier company that she liked a lot. She hoped that it would offer her a handsome compensation package, but she wanted to determine her baseline: the lower boundary of acceptability. Using round numbers, she figured that she might have trouble turning down a $100,000 salary and a standard benefits package. But on the other hand, she had some hesitations about the risks of changing jobs. She decided that an offer of $100,000 was her benchmark deal.

With that in mind, Karen thought next about trade-offs, using a yellow pad to note different deals that would be minimally acceptable. She asked herself, for instance, what she would require to make up for a hypothetical 10 percent lower salary. In itself, anything less than $100,000 would drop her into no-deal territory, but adding perks such as stock options, a nice company car, and a lot more vacation time might make up the difference. Getting some equity could offset living on a somewhat smaller income. Then to test her preferences further, she considered what benefits she'd be willing to surrender for a higher paycheck. Having to buy health insurance with after-tax dollars would mean that she'd need a bump of $25,000 in salary to end up with something equal to her benchmark deal.

She hoped to do better than any of these bundles, of course, but she understood the need to lay out the boundary between yes and no. That meant deliberately confronting herself with hard choices. If one of her hypothetical deals looked better than the others, she trimmed it down a bit. If another was trumped by the rest, she sweetened it. After tweaking these packages, she now had three points that constituted her baseline, the first side of the deal triangle.

PACKAGE A	PACKAGE B	PACKAGE C
$100K SALARY	$90K SALARY	$125K SALARY
STANDARD BENEFITS	STANDARD BENEFITS	NO BENEFITS
	STOCK OPTIONS	NO STOCK OPTIONS

Thinking imaginatively about your baseline is important whether the negotiation affects your career (as it would for Karen) or is a simpler transaction. If you're shopping for a car, for example, you'd take test drives, read *Consumer Reports*, and research pricing online. But having chosen what make and model vehicle you want, figure the top dollar you'd pay. (Once again you're just drawing a walkaway line, not setting any goals just yet.) But don't stop there. Next, conjure some equivalent deals. How deep a price discount would it take for you to be tempted by a demo with ten thousand miles on it? Or go in the other direction: How much more would you pay if the dealer included a premium sound system?

Such assessments should be sketched in pencil, subject to change depending on what you learn while you're negotiating. When Karen sits down to close the deal with her new employer, her enthusiasm for the job may grow. Together they may think of other items that she values (a discretionary budget, for example). As new issues and alternatives arise, her initial trade-off analysis will give her a solid foundation from which to work.

This leads to the last step in establishing a baseline: anticipating change. The analysis so far has been premised on what you know today and how you currently rank your priorities. But you'll probably learn some important things in the course of negotiation. (It would be odd if you don't, in fact.) Circumstances may change as well.

Let's use Karen's example; specifically, the three packages she identified to trace out her baseline. She imagined what might happen that would raise her minimum requirements. What if in the midst of negotiating with the new company, her current employer gave her a promotion—and the pay increase that would go with it? That would improve her BATNA significantly, in respect to both money and status. QXData would then have to offer more than the $100,000 that initially would have been tempting.

But she also considered what situational changes might justify accepting less than her original baseline. She had just bought a new home and had her old condo under agreement. But if that latter deal didn't close, she'd be stuck owning two properties in a weak real estate market. If Karen had to cover two mortgages, straight salary could look better than stock options. She might readjust her trade-offs accordingly.

When Karen took into account how her baseline could change, it looked more like a brushstroke on a watercolor painting than a clear-cut line on a blueprint. She was all right with that ambiguity. It reminded her that her success negotiating with QXData would be influenced not just by her skill but also by external factors. Moreover, she knew that her baseline was merely one boundary of the deal space, not a measure of success. If she did only a little better than her walkaway, she probably wouldn't make a great deal. Instead, she understood her baseline as simply the lowest rung on a ladder of potentially ascending value.

ESTIMATING THEIR BASELINE

The amount of room for agreement depends on how your interests dovetail with those of your counterpart, but estimating a counterpart's baseline can be difficult. One reason is strategic. People on the other side may be wary about disclosing how far they'd be willing to compromise, concerned that if you knew their limit, you'd push them right up to it. If you ask flat out, they're likely to bluff or be evasive. (Or they might turn the same question back on you.)

You must look for clues elsewhere. If you're house shopping, online services such as Zillow can give you an overall sense of the market. They can't, however, tell you whether a given owner is in a hurry to sell or is holding out for top dollar. Judgments often have to be made case by case. If Karen thinks about the negotiation from her prospective boss's perspective, she should be able to anticipate some of his concerns. Agreeing to a high salary might be hard for him if it would disrupt existing pay scales. If that turns out to be a problem, a performance bonus might be a solution.

Thinking about what other parties *should* value is always a risk, however, as they may see things differently. It's even harder if they've done a poor job reckoning their own baseline. Test your thinking with disinterested friends who may suggest other perspectives. Doing so may leave you less sure about your counterpart's priorities, but that's preferable to false confidence. Someone like Karen, negotiating a new job, can tap her network. Maybe a friend knows someone else who once worked at QXData and is familiar with its compensation policy.

After doing her homework, Karen's estimate of the other side's baseline may look less like her own brushstroke and more like a cloud of question marks. So be it. It's a signal not to treat assumptions as facts. Floating different packages will give her a feel for where her counterpart has flexibility. There may be no harm in aiming high, but if salary proves a stumbling block, she'll have already come up with an answer.

Anticipating the concerns of the other party also provides a basis for influencing its thinking—and shifting its baseline in your favor. Someone looking to buy your house might have calculated how much of a mortgage she can afford. You might persuade her to bump up her offer by explaining how special energy-saving features will reduce operating costs. Or in litigation, revealing key documents may convince the other party to reassess its chances of winning in court.

*Mis*learning is inevitable. Another car example makes the point. I was at a dealership waiting for an oil change. Alex, a genial salesman with a salt-and-pepper beard, asked, "Got a minute? I'll tell you a story on myself."

He pointed out a woman, probably in her early twenties, who was just dropping off her brand-new car for its initial service. She was wearing jeans and a tattered sweatshirt. Alex explained that she and her husband had come in two months earlier and asked about the highest-end model that the dealership sold. They wanted the sunroof, the heated leather seats, almost all fancy options, but not a turbocharged engine.

Alex didn't have such a vehicle in stock, and from what he saw, there was no way this young couple could afford it. In idle chatter, he'd learned that the husband worked on the shipping dock of a wholesale fruit distributor where the wife was a file clerk. Nevertheless, Alex ordered the car, figuring that he could sell it to someone else if this couple couldn't get financing.

Sure enough, when he phoned them after the car came in, they seemed evasive. Could you hold it for another week? they asked. Alex half expected never to see them again. But they did appear as promised—and with a cashier's check for the full amount. The couple apologized for the delay and said that they were sorry for not being straightforward with him earlier. "We just won eight million dollars in the lottery," they said, "and our lawyer told us to be careful with that information."

Alex couldn't help himself. "Why didn't you buy the turbo?" he blurted.

"We don't want to kill ourselves," the wife answered sensibly. She and her husband wanted a plush-looking ride, but with a fortune in hand, they planned to drive as cautiously as their grandparents.

It's easy to misread other people, especially at the bargaining table, where they're likely to be careful about revealing too much. Depending on our personalities and dispositions, we may hope for the best from them or fear the worst. Being observant about how a counterpart's baseline may have shifted in the course of negotiation is crucial.

IDENTIFYING EXTERNAL CONSTRAINTS

Real-world factors beyond either party's control form the third boundary of the triangle. A family may be looking to build a new home. They solicit a bid from a well-regarded contractor and are ready to sign a contract when world timber prices shoot up. What then?

The buyers will either have to stretch their budget and pay more than they expected, or shrink their plans and live in a smaller house. The builder, in turn, will have to recalculate his bid, figuring out what portion of the added cost he can pass on and how much he will have to eat. The family may end up with less house and the builder may get less profit because economic conditions narrowed the deal space. Of course, if lumber prices dropped, room for agreement would expand, leaving one or both parties better off.

Some constraints are economic. Others can be based in law. (Two competing businesses might wish to keep their prices high but be legally barred from price fixing.) The ticking clock can be a limit as well. When my friend Jack bought his souped-up Volvo, the 1 percent financing improved the deal, but it was available (supposedly) for only two more days. Company policy and procedures can be constraints as well.

Formal analysts would quibble about diagramming the deal space in this way. They'd argue that the "external constraints" line can be ignored if each party folds such factors into its respective preferences. A key element would be lost, however. Sometimes the deal space can be expanded by addressing external constraints. Let's say that Duncan owns a ten-acre parcel zoned currently for single-family homes on large lots. It's worth about $750,000. A developer would pay twice that, however, if condos were allowed. In that instance, the parties would have a shared interest in lobbying local officials for a rezoning.

Thus, all three sides of the deal triangle are fuzzy. Throughout the process, each side will be trying to fathom the other's baseline to see how hard it can push its own agenda. In time the resolve of one or both parties may wane. They may engage in less posturing or discover creative ways of breaking the impasse. When that happens, the size and nature of the deal space may change.

THE VALUE LADDER

By definition, all the outcomes within the triangle are feasible for the relevant parties, though they will rate them differently. Your own baseline is merely a floor. Outcomes above it are better for you; some may be much better. You also should set a stretch goal, something to reach for so that you don't settle too cheaply. It's not necessarily something that you'd put out as a take-it-or-leave-it offer, otherwise you could end up empty-handed.

Establishing a stretch goal calls for best-case-scenario thinking. Specifically, imagine an outstanding result, one that might have only a 10 percent chance of materializing. That's an arbitrary figure, of course. It represents a possibility that you shouldn't dismiss, but that wouldn't leave you surprised or disappointed if it doesn't come to pass.

Goal setting involves guesswork, of course. Much depends on the needs and perceptions of your particular counterpart. Start with the baseline you estimated for them. Then, because you need to stretch, go a bit beyond that by imagining what conditions or beliefs would convince the other party to be even more generous than that. From those potential deals, pick as a target whatever bundle serves you best. Call this intentional wishful thinking. Have high hopes but also ponder what conditions would have to exist to make them come true. If you're dealing with a vendor, for example, consider the possibility that the company is hungry for your business because it just lost a big order with another customer.

Updating your deal triangle, you locate that best-case scenario well above your baseline—and probably outside the deal triangle, though not much, from the other side's point of view. (point *B*, below). In turn, the people with whom you're negotiating may hope to talk you into accepting their dream deal *A*. It's high above their baseline, but a bit below yours. If the other party's aspirations are unrealistic, you will have a lot of work to do.

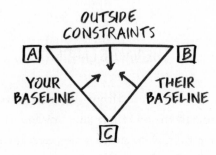

As Karen thought about her job negotiation, she felt that getting $125,000 salary plus stock options and other perks would be a long shot but not out of the question. If that's what QXData offered, she'd jump at it, but she was leery about proposing such a package herself. In addition to negotiating her compensation, Karen realized that she was also establishing her relationship with her prospective boss and colleagues. She didn't want to come on too strong.

If you're lucky, you may end up with more than you ever imagined. Jack Binion, a celebrated Las Vegas casino operator, tells of an old Mississippi family that owned some prime farmland that another developer was trying to buy. In planning their strategy, one of them said, "Let's ask five million for this property." Others in the family worried that the high number could turn off the developer, but they agreed to give it a try.

Fortunately for them, the buyer started first. "We've thought this over," he said, "and our bottom line is twenty million." After the siblings caught their breath, they said they'd have to confer privately. When they returned, they were able to bump the final figure up to $25 million.

In most cases, of course, you'll settle someplace between the pinnacle of your highest hopes and your baseline. You can think of intermediate levels of satisfaction as rungs on your value ladder, or gradients on a wilderness map that mark increasing altitude as you approach the summit. **The more you've considered different ways to tweak a deal, the more nimble and creative you'll be in the thick of negotiation.** And keeping those rungs in mind as various proposals are floated lets you judge whether you're making progress or sliding back.

From a purely strategic viewpoint, it would be ideal if you alone could see the deal space, and your counterpart could not. You'd then be able to compel an outcome that would optimize the deal's value for you and give those on the other side just enough to gain their assent. That's your target position (near point *B*) in the upper right-hand corner. Of course, if they had perfect vision and you didn't, they'd push for a result in the upper left (near point *A*) that maximizes their welfare but doesn't do much for you.

Information is power. Whichever negotiator has a clearer sense of what's feasible has the advantage. That's why people are cautious about disclosing their true needs and priorities. If nobody reveals his interests, nobody gets exploited. Then again, if there are no disclosures, no deals get made. This is the classic creating-claiming dilemma inherent in all negotiations. Out of necessity, negotiators must exchange information. Where relationships are strong and trust is high, this may come easily. In arm's-length transactions, it can be arduous.

Even if both parties were forthright and the deal triangle was transparent, there still could be jostling over where the deal should end up. Splitting it down the middle might be a practical solution in some cases, but in other situations, one or both parties may believe that they deserve the major share. One way or another, they should *not settle* near point *C*, where their respective baselines intersect. Such an outcome would work for both of them, but just barely. It would squander the potential value of deals higher up in the triangle, well above each side's baseline.

In real-world negotiation, of course, you won't be able to lay out the deal triangle with the precision of a land surveyor. But having in mind the image of what you'd like to see, were it only possible, will help you orient yourself. It reminds you what information you're looking for and organizes what you learn along the way. Seeing the deal space as an area that potentially can be expanded provides a richer and more realistic view of the process.

THE PROSPECT MATRIX

Our preparation so far has focused on the substance of deals: your interests, options, and trade-offs, as well as those of your counterparts, as best you can gauge them. Now it's time to zoom out and see how that analysis shapes negotiation strategy more broadly. The first step is determining where on a scale you'd peg the chances of reaching agreement: are they high, low, or somewhere in between?

$$\longleftrightarrow$$
0%   LOW   50/50   HIGH   100%

If you're like most people, you may waver before marking a particular spot. That's fine. Such hesitation is another reminder to be modest when making assumptions. You may prefer to sketch a broader band of probabilities instead of committing to a hard number. As for Karen, she knew that the company's recruiters wanted her on board—they had reached out to her, after all. But she wasn't certain they could put together a compensation package that would justify a move. So, not to jinx herself, she put the odds of making a deal at 75 percent.

In making an estimate for an upcoming negotiation, ask why you're optimistic (or why you're not). Does your guess reflect your personality, or is this case particularly promising (or daunting)? What specific facts or assumptions inform your estimate—and what more would you like to know to confirm or revise it? If you've dealt with this counterpart before or handled similar situations, for example, you may have confidence in your expectations. That's fine, but can you imagine a reason why your hand could be stronger (or weaker) this time than it was in the past?

Even after reflection, it may be hard to tell if there will be lots of room for agreement or only a little. You should have a good sense of your own alternatives but find it hard to gauge how badly your counterpart needs to make a deal with you. If you know only your own floor, but not their ceiling, you can't predict whether you'll be squeezed or have room to reach high. Don't wish away uncertainty. Instead, factor it into your plan. **The less certain you are about the odds of reaching agreement, the more provisional your strategy must be.**

You've now reckoned one dimension of your prospects. Call this the latitude of possibility. The next step is estimating the potential upside of a deal—the longitude, if you will. Ask yourself whether this particular deal will yield a lot or only a little, compared with your fallback plan, given the effort needed to pull it off.

To locate where you are on a scale, think back to your deal triangle, specifically the baseline you estimated for your counterpart. If you're offering something he values highly—and he has the resources to pay for it—you may have a lot to gain. We're talking best-case scenarios here, not necessarily the most likely outcome.

In Karen's case, she was of two minds. On the one hand, she didn't expect QXData to pay her significantly more than she was already getting.

Her current employer might match any offer. In dollars-and-cents terms, the upside of agreement seemed modest, at least in the short term. But emotionally, that didn't feel right at all to Karen. She liked the people at QXData and felt the company was poised for a great future. She wanted to be part of it. Going through this exercise helped her remember what mattered most to her. She drew a bold circle around *Large*.

When you're weighing your own negotiation prospects, construct a simple matrix by combining the latitude of the probability with the longitude of potential gain.

In the upper right-hand cell are the grade-*A* deals. Think of this area as standing for *abundance*, if you like. It represents negotiations where both the odds of agreement and the expected payoff are high. If your assessment of an upcoming negotiation lands you here, congratulations.

If you have competition, however, you may have to sweeten your offer to win agreement. Doing so would net you less and thus put you in the lower right-hand cell, grade *B*, which we'll call *bonus*. Again, the chance of agreement is high and the outcome is better than your fallback, but the upside is lower. You won't get rich on any one such transaction, but string together a bunch of them, and you'll do well in the long run.

The left-hand column represents relative long shots. If the potential payoff is large enough, you're in the grade *C*—*chancy*—area. Rolling the dice may be worth the gamble, so you shouldn't necessarily avoid such negotiations. But make sure you're realistic about the possible upside. You don't want to chase rainbows.

You rarely want to be down in category *D*: *dead-end* territory. Here there's little to gain and not much chance of getting even that. There are exceptions, though. Sometimes you're obliged to make a good-faith attempt at agreement even though you can already see that none is likely.

Negotiations don't magically fall into these neat little boxes, of course, but the exercise is essential when crafting a game plan. Each category calls for a different strategy. Once in a while, you may find yourself in the grade-*A* area. Good for you. But you should revisit your assessment of the upside. Maybe you're overestimating how much your counterpart needs you. Or maybe you didn't set your own baseline high enough. Rethink your BATNA. Your walkaway may be better than you expected. Others may be eager to do a deal with you.

If you're in *B* territory or on the boundaries between the four cells, think twice about how hungry you should be for this particular deal. It may well be worth pursuing, but you don't necessarily want to go all in. You also should be prepared to walk away if things don't pan out.

I once did some work for a midsized company with a CEO who said cheerfully, "In twenty-five years, we've never failed to reach agreement." Because we were in a meeting with his other senior managers, I nodded my head and smiled. Later, when we were alone, I told him that his unblemished record was an odd thing to be proud of. I quoted the old saying, "If you never miss a flight, you're spending a lot of time at the airport."

The same principle applies in negotiation. "If you always come to agreement," I said, "there are only two explanations, and neither of them is good. Either you're being overly cautious and only going after sure things, or sometimes you're saying yes when you should be walking away." There are flights you just can't afford to miss, I added, and deals that must be made, but don't agree simply for the sake of agreement.

You need to keep that in mind especially if you're in the areas *C* or *D*. If the odds of reaching agreement aren't good and the payoff is low, put serious effort into improving your fallback. If you're negotiating on behalf of a client or organization, make sure that the expectations are realistic. You don't want to be second-guessed if you come back empty-handed. And if you're operating on your own, guard yourself by setting up a trip wire. If you're exploring a joint venture, for example, and three months have passed without any apparent progress, ask yourself what reason there is to believe that conditions will be more favorable going forward. If you trudge on, you may miss other, more promising opportunities.

When Karen looked at her matrix, she had mixed emotions about finding herself in the *abundance* box. It was partly superstition, she knew. She didn't want to get her hopes up too high. But it also surfaced a conflict she was feeling. Part of her didn't want to jeopardize a great job by asking too much in the way of compensation. But Karen also didn't want to undersell herself. This inner conflict wasn't pleasant, but she realized that it was better to work through these feelings now than wrestle with them as she was negotiating.

Drawing a deal triangle and constructing a prospect matrix had bolstered her confidence. There were still question marks, many that she could resolve only in the course of negotiating, but she knew that she was in a good position. Moreover, she had thought about her baseline, her trade-offs, and different ways of structuring an agreement. Karen had even set a stretch goal. She had done her homework. Whichever way negotiation unfolded, she was well prepared to learn, adapt, and influence.

THINKING BIG

People with ambitious goals don't take their own baseline as a starting point. Instead, they focus on what they think they can persuade their counterparts to accept. They think big, make bold demands, and compromise slowly. Sometimes they succeed, but they run a greater risk of stalemate. They tend to overestimate their power and underestimate other parties' resolve.

Swarthmore College psychologist Barry Schwartz calls such people "maximizers." They press hard and worry about their decisions. By contrast, "satisficers" tend to be okay with whatever they get. In a study of recent college graduates, Barry and two colleagues found that maximizers landed jobs that paid 20 percent more than satisficers got, but (and it's a big drawback) they were *less happy* with their deals! The satisficers were content with doing a bit better than their next best offer, while the maximizers bemoaned not accomplishing their lofty goals.

It would be great if we could switch these traits on and off. During the actual negotiation, we could tap the maximizer side of our brain to expand the deal space. A maximizer wouldn't take "company policy" as a firm constraint. Unlike a satisficer, she'd try to craft a new policy or figure out a way around the old one. Yet it's hard to turn off that kind of restless thinking even when the deal is done. In its worst form, it generates self-doubt and insecurity. When we're done, we'd be better off accepting whatever we've achieved and moving on to the next deal.

Consider Hollywood producer Jerry Weintraub, who seems to embody both these traits. In his book *When I Stop Talking, You'll Know I'm Dead: Useful Stories from a Persuasive Man*, he tells how as a young promoter with no resources or reputation, he audaciously pursued Elvis Presley as a client—and eventually signed him. (We'll see how later, in the chapter on closing.) But in addition to recounting his successes, Weintraub also speaks about failures without regret. When his protégé John Denver fired him abruptly, the singer-actor asked, "Don't you want to know why?" Weintraub answered, "Why should I care?" He doesn't look back. He's always moving forward.

In 1998 he decided to produce a remake of the 1960 movie *Ocean's Eleven*, which had starred Frank Sinatra, Dean Martin, and the rest of the fabled Rat Pack. It's challenging enough to sign a single major star. Nowadays, lining up an all-star cast for relatively short money would seem next to impossible. But Weintraub succeeded, first by landing Matt Damon and director Steven Soderbergh. With them cast, it was easier to reel in George Clooney, Julia Roberts, Brad Pitt, Don Cheadle, Andy Garcia, and other big names. (When he sent the script to Roberts, he attached a $20 bill with a note saying, "We know you get twenty for a movie, but you have to work for a little less on this one.") The new version was among the top five earners worldwide in 2002.

Several years later, Weintraub wanted to do a sequel, *Ocean's Twelve*, but the chance of getting all the actors back seemed remote. (We never saw Richard Dreyfuss in *Jaws 2* or Jodie Foster in the follow-up to *The Silence of the Lambs.*) The *Ocean* actors all had commitments to other pictures, and some might not have shared Weintraub's enthusiasm for a repeat. Nevertheless, he called Clooney, Roberts, Pitt—the whole gang—and shamelessly told each one that all the others were on board. Nobody wanted to be the spoiler, so everyone signed up again. Bryan Lourd, managing partner of Creative Artists Agency, which represented many of them, knew that Weintraub was blowing smoke, but says, "Eventually we just folded."

On the surface, it may seem that this is a story about how Weintraub improved his odds of making the sequel by stretching the truth. There's more to it than that. It's a positive example of high aspirations being self-fulfilling. Weintraub's persistence and blithe denial of practicalities led him to tackle a project that no one else dared to touch. His optimism proved irresistible to the actors, all of whom had become good friends. As proof of that, they demurred again when he pulled the same stunt three years later for *Ocean's Thirteen*.

The *Ocean's* trilogy grossed over $1 billion. Back in the late nineties, when Weintraub floated the idea of the first movie, it's doubtful that even he foresaw the huge payoff. He's smart, funny, and has built a great network of relationships. But success like this can't be scripted, and Weintraub didn't try to. Instead, he took a step at a time—though they were bold steps, to be sure.

KEY POINTS

- Don't limit your vision by relying on the one-dimensional "bargaining range" model of negotiation.
- Instead, build a deal triangle that opens up the potential area of workable agreements.
- Weigh your trade-offs, and then establish a baseline of different deals that could satisfy your interests.
- Estimate your counterpart's baseline, but keep in mind that assessing his or her interests is difficult.
- Set a stretch goal, so that you don't settle too cheaply.

[4] Plan B

The Citibank Center, as it's still familiarly known, is an iconic feature of New York's skyline. It may seem as if the fifty-nine-story tower, with its sharply angled peak, has stood in Midtown Manhattan forever. Up into the 1970s, however, the block that fronts Lexington Avenue between Fifty-third and Fifty-fourth Streets was sleepy and timeworn. It was home to low-rise residential and commercial buildings, an old Gothic church, and other properties owned by various organizations, trusts, and individuals. How those separate parcels were acquired and assembled is recounted in an entertaining 1974 *New York* magazine article, "How They Assembled the Most Expensive Block in New York's History," by Peter Hellman, as well as in *Holdouts!*, a book by Andrew Alpern and Seymour Durst. The tale still serves as a master class in formulating and implementing negotiation strategy.

I'll tell the story in detail, so let me flag key themes at the outset. For starters, you'll hear echoes of concepts we explored in prior chapters, such as coping with uncertainty, creating value, and mapping the way to our objectives. You'll also see how those elements, taken together, compel a dynamic approach to negotiation, one that makes learning, adapting, and influencing paramount.

Deliberate learning was a priority for the New York Realtors who acquired the properties for Citi. It enabled them to adapt to changing circumstances and to persuade reluctant owners to sell. Sometimes the land assemblers extended an olive branch. Other times they brandished big sticks. In still other cases, they reached agreement not because of specific terms they offered but, rather, due to patient relationship building. Each acquisition was an end it itself—getting all the properties was essential—but every transaction also helped the assemblers recalibrate as they moved forward.

The project was audacious, certainly falling in the low-odds, high-payoff category in our prospects matrix. The assemblers recognized that reality. Throughout the process, they took steps to minimize their risk and improve the potential upside. Even so, the negotiations took several years to complete—and they involved scores of parties and millions of dollars. Few of us engage in deals of such magnitude or complexity, but small-scale everyday transactions require the same kind of flexible, creative, multilevel approach.

To make the moral of this story crystal clear, I'll lay out strategic precepts that apply to negotiations across the board. You may have already grasped some of these lessons from your own experience. Here are nine key principles that you will see in action:

1. **Set a Provisional Goal.** A general sense of direction is essential, but narrow objectives can make negotiation an all-or-nothing proposition.

2   **Have a Plan B.** An obstacle to agreement may harbor seeds for a different deal, perhaps even better than first expected.

3. **Envision the End Game.** Reason backward from your goal to discover plausible paths for getting there.

4. **Make Learning a Priority.** Use early tests and probes to illuminate the negotiation landscape.

5. **Adapt When You Have To.** Accept the reality that other parties won't always do what you want or anticipate.

6. **Think Like a Competitor.** Stress test your strategy by seeing how others could exploit it.

7. **Be Multilingual.** Bring along both carrots and sticks.

8. **Guard Your Exit Option.** As in poker, know when to hold 'em and know when to fold 'em; when to walk away and when to run.

9. **Always Be Closing.** From start to finish, each step should be aimed at getting closer to agreement.

This set of principles isn't a lockstep checklist. Rather, each element is a gear, lever, or spring in the machinery of dynamic strategy. In particular cases, some parts may prove more vital than others, but all must link smoothly.

1. **Set a Provisional Goal.** Don Schnabel, a young broker with the real estate firm of Julien J. Studley, had been hired by St. Peter's Lutheran Church to appraise what its fifteen-thousand-square-foot plot might fetch in what was then a hot real estate market. Famous as the "jazz church," St. Peter's had been the venue for jazz legend Louis Armstrong's funeral in 1971, but it was strapped for cash and squeezed for space. Its board hoped that a profitable sale would help expand its social services. Schnabel scrutinized all the properties on the block to generate his estimate. The figure he calculated proved disappointing, however, so the church's board decided not to sell.

2. **Have a Plan B.** That would have been the end of it, but Schnabel's research convinced him that even if there couldn't be a satisfactory sale of the church property in its own right, a deal might be fashioned by acquiring all the Lexington Avenue parcels, along with others fronting the cross streets. One unified piece of property would have much more value than the sum of its separate parts. It would be a win-win-*win*

solution: the current owners would get a premium over market value; a major corporation could erect a landmark building; and, oh yes, whoever brokered the deal would make handsome commissions.

Success, however, would depend on Schnabel reaching agreement not just once but almost twenty times with that many different owners. In figuring his baseline for each property, he'd pay a little sweetener, if necessary, over its stand-alone value, but he had to stay within a reasonable budget for the whole project. He knew the real estate market generally. To get the best price each time, however, he'd have to uncover the unique needs, attitudes, and expectations of every owner to gauge his or her particular baseline. All told, it was an all-or-nothing proposition. Getting a yes from most of them wouldn't be enough. And if things didn't work out, the downside would be unloading properties for which he had overpaid. Shutting down the project midway could be expensive.

3. **Envision the End Game.** The only thing that Schnabel had was this high-risk, high-reward vision. His firm didn't own any of the parcels, nor did it have the resources to acquire them. To solve that problem, he had to imagine who might be the ultimate purchaser if he could pull off each separate acquisition. In strategic terms, this kind of thinking is called backward mapping. It's a matter of starting analysis with the final objective and then reasoning back, step-by-step, to uncover paths for getting there.

Schnabel identified a likely prospect right across the street: First National City Bank, as it was then called. The bank was outgrowing its present offices and looked with envy at the spectacular headquarters of its downtown rival, Chase Manhattan Bank. Schnabel approached First National City Bank cold. After months of internal meetings, the bank gave its go-ahead.

Proceeding discreetly was essential, however. If the various neighborhood owners learned about a deep-pocket buyer, they would hold out for top dollar. Competitors could swoop in too. Schnabel set up a straw holding company, Lexman Realty. He was listed as vice president, and his boss as president, but the identity of the sole stock-holder—the bank—was not public record.

4.   **Make Learning a Priority.** Having conceived his grand strategy, Schnabel had to go back to square one and choose which owner to approach first. The physical map of Manhattan is precise, but the map of possible deals on a single city block is complex. To get his bearings, Schnabel had to start moving, just like our snowbound soldiers in the Alps. It wasn't a matter of proceeding methodically from one property to its immediate neighbor. Instead, he needed to find vantage points that would give him a realistic sense of possibilities.

Schnabel decided to hold off on the Lexington Avenue parcels, as important as they were. They would be the most expensive, and if he were to make a move there—right across from the bank—other real estate people might sense what he was attempting. It seemed safer and cheaper to begin around the corner on Fifty-third Street.

For his initial probe, Schnabel chose a four-story building that housed a gourmet restaurant on the first floor. He negotiated a buy-out of the operator's lease but then was shocked to learn that the landlord had just contracted to sell the property to one Manny Duell, a man described in the Alpern and Durst book as a "sometimes developer and professional holdout." Somehow Duell had gotten wind of the project and claimed to have contracts to buy the abutting buildings as well.

5.   **Adapt When You Have To.** Having an early competitor on the block threatened to derail Schnabel's entire plan, but the bank encouraged him to see if it could buy out Duell. After some bargaining, they arrived at an acceptable price for the three properties—a result that made Duell millions of dollars of profit on contracts that he had held for only a few months at most.

Settling on the price wasn't the hardest part, however. As Schnabel slid the check over to Duell, he added, "Manny, just one thing. If you want me to take over these contracts, I need to know you are going to stay off the block from this point on. I don't want you popping up on the other side with more contracts. I want this to be good-bye, Manny."

Duell promised to disappear, but Schnabel persisted, saying that he didn't want to see Manny's partner, cousins, or anyone else fronting for him. Duell swore once more that he'd stay out of the way.

"I believe you, Manny," replied Schnabel. "As a token of your good faith, I'm sure you won't mind signing over to me a three-hundred-thousand-dollar mortgage on one of the buildings you own. Maybe that nice one at 530 Sixth Avenue. We'll put it in escrow. If you stay off the block for eighteen months, it reverts to you."

According to Hellman's account, Duell ranted that he would never do such a thing, but all the while, he couldn't take his eyes off the big check with all the zeros and his name on it. Schnabel waited until the seller calmed down and yielded to his demand for security.

Schnabel worked on multiple levels. He was pushing forward with his grand plan of assembling the block. But he was also hammering out deals with individual owners, adapting to circumstances as they became apparent. Closing the first purchase was more work than he had anticipated, though it was better to discover potential obstacles early. He also inoculated himself against further incursions, at least by Duell. The experience underscored the importance of moving quickly before others learned of his plans.

In subsequent cases, money wasn't always the obstacle. Schnabel's next move, for example, was acquiring a Hungarian restaurant on Lexington Avenue. He guessed that the owner, Eva Trefner, might be seeking to retire after having operated the place for twenty years. He was right, but she was also concerned about what would happen to her loyal staff. Schnabel promised to keep the place open for at least another year, so that sale went through smoothly.

6. **Think Like a Competitor.** It was important that Schnabel not overpay in any of these transactions. He owed it to his client to be prudent with its money. There were also strategic considerations. The more

properties he acquired, the more costly it would be to be stymied by holdouts. There was the risk he could reach a point where he'd have to pay big premiums to acquire the last few pieces of the puzzle.

Schnabel also had to worry about the downside of possible competition. Secrecy was one line of defense. In addition, he sequenced his acquisitions, hopping around the block like a Monopoly player bent on controlling key portions of the game board. Schnabel thus turned his attention to Fifty-fourth Street, where he started acquiring brownstones. He also approached the pastor of St. Peter's—his original client—and floated the possibility that its property would be worth much more as part of a package than as a stand-alone.

The church was intrigued by the financial benefits but was concerned, as Hellman recounts it, that "no horrors be perpetrated on residential tenants who were forced off the block." Schnabel pledged that this wouldn't happen, and worked out an elaborate condominium arrangement that would allow the church to rebuild a bigger structure on the same corner, largely outside the footprint of the office tower.

7. **Be Multilingual.** Dealings with some other owners differed from the hard-nosed bargaining with Manny Duell. Schnabel kept his word with the church, of course. And his colleague Charles McArthur arranged moving plans for two elderly sisters, Julia and Alyce Belora, providing them with first-class tickets to their new home in California. It's another example of how the more-for-me, less-for-you view of negotiation doesn't capture the richness of many real-life situations. Some sellers put a high value on Schnabel's courtesy and integrity in ways that were independent of price.

Timing was a key factor in other cases. Schnabel's colleague Charles McArthur met a reclusive bachelor who insisted that he would never sell. This wasn't Manny Duell holding out for top dollar. There was no room for agreement at any price. Nevertheless, McArthur kept visiting and once brought slides of his recent European trip. Finally, after two years of quiet courtship, McArthur felt it was time to press the issue.

"We'll draw up a contract," he told the owner. "The line for purchase price will be blank. We'll say yes or no. If we say no, Tom, I promise you'll never be bothered again." The owner then wrote down $850,000 on the form. The bank—which was funding the acquisitions—gave its approval, and the owner bought himself a handsome brownstone farther downtown.

Think about how this worked both at the outset and then again at the end. For months and months, McArthur held off, recognizing that it was not yet time to negotiate. And when the time seemed ripe, he moved delicately. He didn't make an offer, nor did he ask for a demand, but in handing over the contract, he signaled that the time to do business had come. Leaving the purchase price open was a sign of the respect and trust that had grown between the two men. McArthur sensed that Tom would reciprocate this gesture. (By contrast, neither he nor Schnabel would have ever given Manny that kind of control.)

Other pieces fell into place, some because of creativity and patience on the brokers' part, others due to haggling. Sometimes it was both. According to Hellman's account, the big prize on Fifty-fourth Street was the Medical Chambers building, owned by forty doctors. Most were in high tax brackets and unlikely to be tempted by cash. Schnabel proposed a swap for a better building. The doctors fired their board for even considering it.

Their new board rebuffed a $4 million offer and even rejected having a new building constructed to their specifications. Once again there was no apparent room for agreement. This time Studley solved the problem not by relationship building but through creativity. The Medical Chambers was a stock company. It could merge with the bank and thus give the doctors shares in Citi. They wouldn't pay taxes until they chose to sell—and then it would be at the lower capital gains rate. Out of nowhere, enormous room for agreement suddenly blossomed.

8. **Guard Your Exit Option.** In hindsight, stories such as the Citibank acquisition suggest a certain inevitability, as if each step inexorably

led to the next. But Schnabel and his colleagues might have been just as savvy and resourceful yet still have failed due to factors beyond their control. In an alternative universe, Manny Duell might have refused to stay off the block. Had that happened, Schnabel's firm would have faced a tough choice: Should it quit the project that it had just started or engage in a race to tie up other properties? With deeper pockets and perhaps more skill, it might be able to secure enough parcels to prevent Duell or anyone else from controlling the block. On the other hand, holdouts like him could demand exorbitant prices for their remaining properties.

Just walking away might have been easier. All that the brokers had put into the venture was their own time—and the money the bank had spent to buy out the tenant's lease. If his firm had stepped out, maybe Duell would have stepped in. Everything could have turned out very differently, not because of anything our protagonists did but because of seemingly minor parties. It's impossible to plan for every zig and zag that a negotiation might take. Depending on your luck, maybe you'll run into your own version of Manny Duell, or maybe you won't. Practical strategy must give you multiple options along the way.

Schnabel chose to make his first probe on Fifty-third Street, where properties were cheaper. He protected himself from being blocked by holdouts elsewhere by not getting in too deep. He guarded the option of reselling the early acquisitions to people who might be interested in them as stand-alones or who were more optimistic about pulling together the whole block.

Backward mapping can take you only so far, however. It's a powerful way of envisioning *one* possible route to your destination, but it can't reveal all the potential detours along the way. As a result, you need to keep a sharp eye out for exit options and half-a-loaf solutions that may be better than none. That's true whether you're competing against other buyers in a marketplace or searching for a path to a fruitful partnership. In deal making and dispute resolution, discretion sometimes trumps valor.

9. **Always Be Closing.** Seasoned climbers say that the summit isn't the only place on the mountain. Sometimes in negotiation you have to backtrack. Schnabel's toughest negotiation came at the end. It required hard bargaining over a shoddy corner building owned by an estate that leased ground floor space to an optometrist and a liquor store. Schnabel agreed to pay the executrix a premium for the property, rationalizing that it was worth it to complete the entire deal. At the closing, though, she slyly informed him that she had recently extended the commercial leases by a full twelve years. According to Hellman, Schnabel was furious. "He was trapped; the assemblage was too far along now to stop, and the executrix knew it."

She had sold the valuable lease rights, reaping additional money for the heirs of the estate. The buyer was Sam Salerno. He would regularly stroll the sidewalk, glance over to the existing bank headquarters, and then watch, Hellman says, "as, one by one, the wrecker ball took down the buildings on the block. He did not look like a man in a hurry to sell out his lease."

Schnabel and his client were all in at this point, and Salerno knew it, but the bank acted as if it were in no rush to buy. It seemed prepared to build around him, if need be. And so, in full view of the public, the bank and this streetwise operator played out a game of chicken. The bank knew that Salerno didn't have any other viable buyer. He was all in too. Eventually somebody blinked, and the bank bought out the lease rights for $385,000.

Where this transaction fit into the whole sequence of acquisitions was critical. By the time Salerno appeared, the bank controlled enough properties that it could proceed without him, if necessary, even though that wouldn't be ideal. Secrecy was no longer a factor. Indeed, the fact that Salerno knew the bank had a fallback made it *less* likely that it would have to use it.

Schnabel's shrewd sequencing also took into account the value of early probing and learning. His initial deals weren't just ends in themselves. They helped him garner information and resources that would set up a successful end game. Along the way, he was ever mindful of possible exits and alternatives if things didn't go as hoped.

Thinking through the possible upside and downside of a negotiation takes something of a split personality. It's as if you're building a yacht to cruise the world while also stocking a life raft with provisions. You need optimism, even daring, to undertake negotiations that others might pass up as fruitless, yet at the same time, you must accept the reality that achieving success is never fully within your control.

Assembling the Citibank block proved a big success for the bank and the Studley firm that negotiated all the acquisitions. It took five years of hard work, some luck, and $40 million. At the time, it was the highest-priced land purchase in New York City history. Clearing the site and erecting the tower took years as well. Almost a decade passed between the day that Schnabel first ambled around the block and when the new Citibank Center opened in 1977.

Don Schnabel's negotiating skill got the ball rolling. Charles McArthur and other colleagues in the Studley firm played big roles in executing the project. Together they had the imagination to see that the obstacle to one deal—a simple, stand-alone sale of St. Peter's Church—bore the seeds of a much more profitable set of transactions. If the value of the church's property was insufficient in itself, the answer was to couple it with many others. Quite literally, they generated economies of scale.

THE COST OF INFLEXIBILITY

The Citibank story is exhibit A in the case for adaptive negotiation strategy. The nine underlying principles I've covered don't guarantee success, but they move the odds in the right direction. You can see that by looking at what can happen when the precepts are ignored. Just as that new tower was opening, another developer was attempting a land assembly in Atlantic City, New Jersey, a hundred miles to the south as the gull flies. Unlike Studley, however, Richard Bloom let everyone know what he was doing from the start.

New Jersey had passed legislation authorizing casinos. Atlantic City, an old resort town that had seen better days, was poised to take off. Bloom wanted to put together the last potentially valuable oceanfront block. It was comprised of seventy-two private houses, plus a few store-fronts and businesses near the boardwalk itself. Rather than trying to acquire the residential properties secretly, one by one, he boldly sought to get them in one fell swoop.

Bloom announced to the whole neighborhood that he would pay $100,000 per house—two or three times the typical stand-alone value. But there was a catch: each deal would be contingent on everyone else agreeing to sell. He hoped this offer would turn the holdout problem on its head. Any owner who thought about trying to haggle for more would be pressured by neighbors fearful of losing their windfall. "It's like having fourteen salesmen on the block at all times," said Bloom.

At first blush, his strategy looked clever. People liked its transparency. Yes, Bloom would get rich—he was upfront about that—but so would they. And everybody would be treated the same, whether or not they had just given their place a fresh coat of paint. It was only the land that mattered. After all, every structure would soon be torn down, be it shabby or spotless.

This open approach had risks, of course. To protect himself from other developers who might jump in with sweeter offers, Bloom imposed a strict deadline. Either he'd get a quick yes from everyone, or he'd walk away. He also wasn't worried about the neighbors trying to do the assembly themselves. They didn't have an organization, and relationships among them weren't universally good. "If they had tried to do that," he said later, "they'd still be trying to pick a chairman."

As it happened, his problem lay elsewhere. Bloom had many takers, but there also were several owners who weren't keen to move. For some of them, $100,000 wasn't going to change their way of life. Others had principal homes elsewhere. They didn't feel the peer pressure to sell—or weren't bothered by it. Bloom succeeded in getting more than 90 percent of the owners to sign up, but this wasn't a game of horseshoes. Coming close wasn't good enough.

In the end, the simplicity of his strategy was both a strength and a weakness. By making a one-size-fits-all offer, Bloom couldn't adapt to the needs and demands of particular owners. The kind of value-creating solutions we saw with the Citibank example (such as the tax deal with the doctors and pampering the elderly sisters) were not available. He tried to salvage the project, saying that he was willing to pay more for certain houses, but appeasing holdouts risked unsettling deals he had already made.

Nevertheless, Bloom did some things right. He had a clear goal and a plausible plan for achieving it. Perhaps it was a long shot, but if it had come through, his payoff would have been big. On the prospect matrix, it was in the *chancy* box, but there was minimal downside. Bloom anticipated possible competition and shielded himself from it. His downfall was his plan's rigidity. Once he set it in motion, he learned little about various owners' priorities. Moreover, he could bargain only in the language of cash. To his credit, though, he gave himself a cheap out. All he lost was his time and effort.

The Walt Disney Company should have made the same decision far sooner when it was pushing a new $650 million theme park thirty-five miles west of Washington, DC. It was the 1990s, and the company was flush with success. Disneyland in California was spectacularly profitable, and Disney World in Florida was even more so. Disney's only regret was that it hadn't acquired even more adjoining land in its earlier projects, given the local development booms they had launched.

Its new park was to have a historical theme and be called Disney's America. Through secret negotiations (much like those for Citibank), it had already acquired the three thousand acres it needed. The company had also quietly lined up support from local, state, and federal officials. Having tied up the land and corralled most of the politicians, Disney went public with its plans in 1993. The problem was that its chosen site was four miles from the Manassas National Battlefield Park, where the Civil War Battles of Bull Run took place. The tract also abutted a dozen notable towns, as well as more than two dozen lesser-known battlefields and historic districts. Not surprisingly, preservationists and environmentalists voiced concern about increased traffic and other adverse impacts on local communities.

Disney countered with a massive public relations campaign that further mobilized opposition. Proponents praised the park for combining education and entertainment, citing a Lewis and Clark white-water raft ride and a Depression-era country fair. One Disney spokesman sparked a firestorm by heralding a planned ride that would "make you feel what it was like to be a slave or what it was to like to escape through the Underground Railroad."

Historians such as David McCullough and Shelby Foote condemned the project. Disney countered that those people were merely fronting for rich members of the Washington establishment who didn't want their country estates invaded by common tourists. CEO Michael Eisner sabotaged his own efforts repeatedly with comments such as this: "Over the years, I've visited my son at Georgetown University, and I learned that he and most of his fellow students . . . have never been to a Civil War battlefield . . . I attended many history classes in my life . . . and I didn't learn anything."

Eisner's arrogant stance made great copy for fund-raising appeals by preservationist groups. Editorialists across the country quoted his remark that "the First Amendment gives you the right to be plastic." All its prior secret dealings didn't help, either. Politicians who had gotten on the Disney's America bandwagon earlier looked for ways to gingerly slip off it.

Even within the company, top people began to think it was time to kill the project. Regulatory fights were costing the company money. More important, the controversy was distracting management and tarnishing the Disney reputation. Eisner was resolute, however, telling reporters, "If people think we will back off, they are mistaken." He said that the opposition "just makes me more excited about the project." Eventually even he had to capitulate. Eisner had fallen into the trap of believing that past is prologue. Sticking with an approach that had succeeded in Anaheim and Orlando, he was blind to the reality that this was a different time and place. He was slow to learn and still slower to adapt.

AGILITY

It's easy to render that verdict after the fact, of course. The fair test of strategy isn't whether it succeeds or fails in a particular case. Luck can tilt the outcome one way or another. But sound strategy should anticipate a fan of possibilities. Negotiators need to be open to latent opportunities (as was Schnabel in New York) as well as to pitfalls of the kind that doomed Disney in Virginia.

We can only speculate what would have happened if its team had used Gary Klein's premortem technique early in the planning process. Just driving around northern Virginia with the thought in mind that something *will* go badly might have made the Disney people realize that this time they weren't in the orange groves of Florida or California. If they had foreseen possible opposition, they might have addressed it by revising the design or finding a less controversial site—or perhaps by junking the plan before it sparked so much costly controversy.

Being an agile learner takes a special mind-set. On the one hand, you need a measure of commitment and a sense of direction. You negotiate to achieve certain ends, after all, not just to solve an intellectual puzzle. But on the other hand, you need a constant willingness to reevaluate your prospects and priorities. You have to be willing to walk away when your hopes don't square with reality.

It's easy to fall in love with your plans. The more effort you put into making them, the more seductive they become. But your counterparts may be unreasonable. They may have a better offer. Their personal style may drive you nuts. Too bad. That's how it is sometimes. Effective negotiators cope with uncertainty and chaos. Great ones thrive on it.

KEY POINTS

- Don't get trapped by prior success; past isn't always prologue.
- Tune your approach to fit the circumstances and the style of the person with whom you're dealing.
- Remember that deal making isn't just about dollars and cents; relationship building is essential.
- Make sure that your strategy aligns with clients and colleagues.
- Give yourself wiggle room, or you may get stuck.

PART 2

Improvising

Some situations are like playing chess while mountain climbing.

—AMBASSADOR RICHARD HOLBROOKE

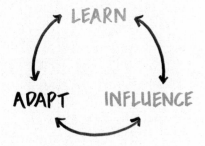

[5] Presence of Mind

Picture two ultracompetent people, both accomplished in their respective fields. One gets a huge rush out of negotiating. The other is paralyzed by the mere thought of it.

First, there's Donald Dell, the pioneering sports marketer and agent. Back when he was just starting out, Dell was in a tense negotiation with the maker of Head tennis rackets, endorsed by one of his star clients, Arthur Ashe. The company wanted to stop paying the 5 percent royalties on all sales. Dell and Ashe wanted to keep the payments flowing.

Dell was meeting with Head's marketing team when the door flew open and the chairman stormed in. "Goddamn it!" he screamed. "This is outrageous. He's making ten times what I'm making, and I'm chairman of this company."

The room went silent. Would Dell cave in or blow up the deal by answering in kind? Everyone turned to see how he'd respond. After a brief pause, Dell tilted his head, smiled, and said, "But Pierre, Arthur has a much better serve than you do."

The tension broke, and people laughed and got back to business. They tweaked the royalty schedule and preserved a business relationship that was beneficial for both sides. Dell was quick with a joke. Even more important, he was poised in the face of high emotion. And his own ease and good humor relaxed everyone else.

Then there's Chris Robbins, an emergency room physician in a big city hospital. Chris is exactly the kind of doctor I'd want if I were wheeled in on a stretcher: calm and focused amidst all the stress. But that's true only in the ER. That composure falls apart when it comes to negotiating. Chris craved a spot in a highly selective clinical training program but was tied up in knots about even asking for the two-month leave it required. Such requests are unusual, and, given current staffing problems, there was a risk of appearing disloyal to the ER team. The answer could be no. The prospect of a confrontation was so intimidating that Chris never raised the issue.

People like Chris are phobic about negotiation. They'll do anything to avoid pushing or being pushed. They're neither competitive nor cooperative. In psychological terms, they're avoiders. If they can satisfy their minimum needs, they'll say yes just to cut short the stress of dealing with people who have different agendas and styles. It's an expensive aversion.

I remember a participant in an executive program who bristled at the thought of haggling with a car salesman. "I just pay the sticker price," she announced. "I've got better things to do with my time than play some foolish game." I asked if she realized what she was passing up. "Maybe you're rolling in money," I said. "But in just fifteen minutes, you might knock down the price by a couple of thousand dollars. If you were willing to play a little hardball, wouldn't your favorite charity welcome that cash?" I saw a trace of panic in her eyes.

Most people fall somewhere between the extremes of loving negotiation and loathing it. They don't relish tough encounters, but they don't run from them, either. They see negotiation as an unavoidable part of business and personal life, an obstacle course they have to run to get work done. At a break in a recent negotiation workshop, I heard two participants trade horror stories about their own recent negotiations. One guy admitted that he had messed up a deal by losing his temper. "I was bending over backward with my customer, giving concession after concession. Nevertheless, he accused me of playing bait and switch and demanded even more. He sure knew how to hit my hot button."

"You and I must be fire and ice," laughed his colleague. "In my case, I just froze up. The minute we started, all the preparation I'd done, every number I'd run, everything just flew right out the window. And the more I realized that I was blowing it, the worse things got."

Most of us could tell similar stories about losing our footing in negotiation, at least once in a while. Slipups don't have to involve fiery outbursts or going blank. Even a momentary lack of focus at a key point can spell trouble. Indeed, throwing other people off stride is the point of hardball ploys. Tom Wolfe's novel *A Man in Full* describes a negotiation between a bank and a real estate developer who has fallen on hard times. (As research for the book, Wolfe sat in on such meetings.) These so-called work-out deals involve restructuring the financial terms of huge loans. In practice they're often about lenders' attempts to shake every last dime out of borrowers' pockets before they fall into bankruptcy.

In Wolfe's account, this particular developer had been given royal treatment back when times were good, but now he finds himself summoned to a claustrophobic room. The Danish pastries on the sideboard are stale. The only available drink is warm orange juice served in flimsy plastic cups, the same size as for urine specimens. The developer knows the game being played, but as the bank forces him to hand over one asset after another—first one property, and then another, and finally his private plane—he starts to perspire. By the time the meeting is over, he's a broken man with saddlebags of sweat under each arm.

How should you cope with the hot and cold feelings that negotiation often provokes? You won't find many answers in standard texts. Indeed, many negotiation books tiptoe around the topic of emotion. The classic *Getting to Yes* earnestly advises "separating the people from the problem," which some readers took to mean focusing one's attention solely on substantive issues. But negotiation is about more than money or terms and conditions. The people you deal with want to feel respected as individuals. They want their ideas to be appreciated and their status acknowledged as well. Later in his career, Roger Fisher and psychologist Daniel Shapiro coauthored a sequel to *Getting to Yes* called *Beyond Reason: Using Emotions as You Negotiate*. Roger and Dan warn that if you ignore other parties' core emotional concerns, you risk stalemate even if your offers ostensibly meet their tangible interests.

That's only part of the story, though. Your passions both reflect and influence your relationships with people. You may feel warmly toward one person, while someone else makes your blood boil. And then there are people like Chris, who get the chills just thinking about negotiation. Those responses can either help or hinder your search for agreement, depending on how you understand, channel, and learn from them.

Feelings color perceptions and influence behavior. You can be up or down, tense or relaxed, depending on the day and the particular circumstances. Studies even show that seemingly irrelevant factors (whether it's sunny or rainy, if the room in which you're negotiating has been freshly cleaned, and whether you're standing tall or hunched over) all can tilt your emotional outlook. And, of course, much depends on the mood of your particular counterparts.

Having emotions is one thing. **The problem is that *when your emotions have you*, they can derail the negotiation process instead of being useful signals that help you orient to the situation at hand.** It's a big mistake simply to let feelings wash over you. Instead, you should put them to creative use. According to an old adage, "We see things not as they are, but as *we* are." Being upbeat and confident can't guarantee success, of course, but it does help. The alternative—having low expectations—is often self-fulfilling. Worry about slipping up breeds caution and distrust. Anxiety may not doom you to failure, but it's often a needless burden.

Even if you have Donald Dell's poise, it's important to understand how emotions impact your counterparts. It's rarely in your interest to confirm their worst fears. Even debt collectors like those in Tom Wolfe's novel have to sense how hard they can press without provoking an explosion or a walkout that leaves everyone worse off. In more collaborative negotiations, you need to know how to encourage others to be open to your arguments and ideas.

Like Wolfe's developer, you won't always be in a strong position. Nor can you dictate whom you deal with or how they'll treat you. External circumstances may be beyond your control as well. But you can manage your emotional responses to those challenges. Much of the pressure that people feel in negotiation is self-imposed. It is a self-defeating attitude, one that with practice you can discard.

MASTERING PARADOX

People such as Donald Dell love high-wire negotiations. Like star athletes, they rise to the occasion, especially when the stakes are high and the competition intense. "I live for such moments," Dell says of the Arthur Ashe–Head deal. Some of these remarkable people have PhDs or professional degrees. Others never finished high school. Many boast years of experience, but there are also gifted novices. These great negotiators share one common trait: keen presence of mind. That's how people like George Mitchell and Lakhdar Brahimi can envision agreement in the midst of bitter conflict.

Their emotional balance is buttressed by tenacity and underlying optimism. They're comfortable with ambiguity, uncertainty, and risk. Averell Harriman, a diplomat from an earlier era, was known as "the crocodile." Once he sank his teeth into a problem, he wouldn't let go. Bruce Wasserstein, the late New York investment banker, treated everything as a negotiation, not just business deals, but where to eat and whether to call if you might be late for a meeting. "This could be quite exhausting," says Laurence Grafstein, who worked with Wasserstein for more than a decade. "After a while, you just began to cave. But then he wouldn't allow you to capitulate, so the negotiation cycle would begin anew." There are other negotiators whose deals don't make the front page but who fit the same profile. Arnaud Karsenti, a young real estate developer and entrepreneur, says, "I love negotiation; the hairier, the better!"

In my consulting and research, I've met, worked with, and studied top negotiators in a wide variety of fields. I've been impressed with their mental makeup, their ability to balance what might seem to be opposing states of mind. I've come to see that to excel, negotiators must be simultaneously:

calm *and* alert,
patient *and* proactive, and
practical *and* creative.

This balancing act isn't a matter of switching from one to the other at different times during a negotiation. The key is being all of these things at once. Nor is it a matter of trade-offs. The goal isn't being a little calm and somewhat alert. A closer look at each of these dualities shows how to reconcile them.

Take poise. It's essential when negotiations get heated. It gives you the emotional wherewithal to defuse tense situations. But vigilance is just as important. It helps you spot early signs that the negotiation is not turning out as hoped.

You likewise need a rich brew of patience and initiative. The former is a well-trumpeted virtue: good things come to those who wait, and haste makes waste. Those adages apply in negotiation. Building trust takes time. Rushing the process can backfire in cultures where what seems like small talk is an important social ritual. And making proposals prematurely, before laying the groundwork, can spur rejection.

But initiative is a virtue too. The thesaurus likens it variously to a plan, inventiveness, and having the upper hand—all of which are decided advantages at the bargaining table. Only by probing do you learn how high up the value ladder you can climb, or when it's time to switch to plan B. If you fail to take the lead, the other side will set the tune.

Then there are the dual goals of practicality and creativity. Master negotiators are hardheaded realists. They realize when they've been stuck with a lemon—but they also know how to make lemonade. When parties are deadlocked over price, for example, a resourceful seller might provide financing to bridge the gap. Maybe forming a joint venture could create profit all around.

On the other hand, being grounded is a plus too. Practical recognition of the other side's needs and constraints helps negotiators focus on workable solutions instead of flights of fancy. It signals when half a loaf is the most you're going to get. Pragmatism also inoculates you against falling in love with a deal and paying more than the top dollar you set initially.

Ideally, you'd like to have all these virtues in full measure, but each pair seems a contradiction. How can you remain calm if you're also on the lookout for danger? But embracing paradox isn't some fanciful New Age notion. You often rely on other professionals to do exactly that. If someone in your family needs a coronary bypass operation, for example, you'd want a heart surgeon who's both calm and alert. Likewise, you hope your children are blessed with teachers who are simultaneously patient and proactive. And if you'd been on board the crippled *Apollo 13* moon mission, you'd have wanted the NASA mission control crew to be practical and creative to the max.

I've seen the same qualities in master negotiators. While each of these three dualities (calm-alert, patient-proactive, practical-creative) is important in its own right, they rest upon and express a deeper pairing of assurance and humility. Those attributes aren't emotions. Rather, they represent a more fundamental way of seeing oneself in relation to others.

The assurance part of the equation is confidence that you can handle the task at hand, given what's reasonably possible. In turn, the humility element accepts that not everything is knowable or subject to your control. Mihaly Csikszentmilhalyi, author of the influential book *Flow: The Psychology of Optimal Experience,* says that the mark of strong individuals is an abiding confidence in having the personal resources to determine their own fate. "In that sense, one would call them self-assured, yet at the same time, their egos seem curiously absent; they are not self-centered." He says that "their energy is typically not bent on dominating their environment as much as on finding a way to function within it harmoniously." It requires recognition that "to succeed, one may have to play by a different set of rules from what one would prefer."

EMOTIONAL BAGGAGE

Several years ago, my colleagues Julianna Pillemer, Kim Leary, and I ran a study of people's thoughts and emotions about negotiation. Julianna is trained in psychology, and Kim is a psychotherapist and psychoanalyst. We were curious: Why do some people love negotiating, while others loathe it?

We were skeptical about whether simply polling subjects about their views would uncover their deep feelings about the process. Telling people to rate themselves is often problematic, and the wording of survey questions can skew results. (For instance, asking about self-confidence puts that idea in subjects' heads.) We also doubted that simple numbers on a 10-point scale could capture the complexity of people's psyches. To get a deeper understanding, we turned to the patented ZMET method developed by our colleague Gerry Zaltman, a sociologist. Drawing on interdisciplinary research from cognitive psychology and affective neuroscience, Gerry and his colleagues believe that people think primarily in images (usually visual), and certainly not in words alone. We dream in moving pictures, after all, not words or spreadsheets.

Their market research firm—Olson Zaltman Associates—studies the underlying structures that frame people's thinking about a given topic. These deep structures are unconscious templates that shape how people process and react to information. They reveal themselves in the ordinary metaphors and descriptions that people use in everyday conversation. Someone who describes negotiation as a waltz, for instance, has a different view of the process than does another person who calls it "a scorpion's mating dance." By exploring such images, we were able to plumb the source of people's complex feelings about negotiation.

The subjects in our study were primarily managers, both men and women, plus a few lawyers. All had fifteen or more years of real-world negotiation experience. We wanted to tap the emotional experience of veterans, not rookies.

Two weeks before our interviews (which ran three to four hours each), we asked subjects to collect a half dozen images that they associated with some aspect of the negotiation process. They could clip pictures from magazines, make photocopies from books, or even draw their own sketches. When they arrived on campus, our trained interviewers asked the subjects how the images they had chosen expressed their thoughts and emotions. We wanted to know the source of those feelings, what triggered them, and how they influenced people's behavior. When we were done, we had days of audiotape and reams of single-spaced transcripts. The pictures that the subjects gave us were the real gems in our trove of data.

I demonstrate a miniversion of the research method in my advanced negotiation course for MBA students. One year my first volunteer was a debonair, seemingly self-assured Frenchman named Thierry, who ultimately graduated near the top of his class. Thierry walked to the front of the room and plunked a photo of a tropical paradise on the overhead projector. "What does that have to do with negotiation?" I wondered.

"Look at that island," he explained. "There's a lot that's pleasant about negotiation. But look at those clouds: there could be a storm brewing. You always have to watch out."

His comment was spontaneous. We didn't put the idea of turmoil into his head. We simply asked him in a neutral way to mull over his thoughts and feelings about negotiation. Despite his outward self-assurance, he harbored concern that tranquil encounters can become turbulent. Prior to coming to class, as he leafed through photos, he read that feeling into this seemingly benign scene.

The older, more experienced negotiators we studied did the same thing, time and time again, and in much greater depth. On the surface, their pictures had nothing to do with negotiation, but for the person who picked the image, it had an element or branch on which their preexisting feelings could perch. Their selections differed, but as with Thierry, they often would point first to something positive in the image and then counter their observation with a strong negative.

In spite of individual differences, the negotiators we interviewed had important commonalities:

- Everyone expressed mixed feelings about negotiation. Those who tended to enjoy the process also spoke about the risk of tripping up or being exploited. Similarly, those who described negotiation as largely an onerous process acknowledged potential silver linings.

- Coping with those conflicting feelings is a challenge in itself. One of our subjects described it this way: "It is a balancing act between the relationship and the task. You want to maximize your opportunity and the relationship you have with that person."

- In the same vein, the unpredictability of negotiation triggered anxiety, especially in respect to the behavior and attitudes of other parties. All our subjects were successful professionally, yet many worried about their own competence and vulnerability. "It's not always clear," said one senior manager, "who is the wizard behind the curtain and who is the charlatan."

- Virtually everyone spoke of the gap between the ideal of win-win negotiation they wished for and what they regarded as the harsh realities of real-world hard bargaining. Even the optimists brought in pictures of alligators and other predators lying in wait.

- Taken together, the swirl of feelings that negotiators experience, the unpredictability of the process, and the tension between aspirations and reality constitute a heavy cognitive and emotional load. Thus, it's small wonder that negotiators find the process stressful.

If you visit our project website, you'll see a sample of images that the participants selected and hear some of their recorded descriptions of what the pictures symbolize. Again and again, you'll find renderings of an isolated negotiator beset by risks and dangers on all sides. What you can't view online, unfortunately, is what our subjects look like in person. They all appear confident and successful. Sitting across from them at the bargaining table, you'd have every reason to believe that you were up against self-possessed negotiators. What they expressed in their ZMET interviews, however, paints a different picture. Some things that particular individuals said were unique to them, but anxiety was commonly triggered by three overlapping concerns:

1. Uncertainty about what counterparts will accept, how best to engage them, and whether agreement is even possible. One person said, "Whenever you are going into any situation where you think you are uncertain, there tends to be anxiety." Another subject spoke of the challenge of anticipating where your target (as he put it) is going to be. "It's chess. It's thinking multiple moves down the line and not attacking the person where they are or addressing just the issue at hand."

2. Worries about the quality of the relationship with counterparts, especially the risk that they might not be ethical, cooperative, or respectful. As one manager put it, "There is posturing in virtually all negotiations. I'm using it in the situation when you have people transparently miscast the facts." Another person chose an image of people appearing to shake hands but actually holding guns. For him, it symbolized how relationships themselves can be counterfeit. "And so it appears to be an act of greeting and cordiality, but in reality it's pointing a gun at somebody. So there's a difference between the appearance and the reality."

3. Performance anxiety, the fear of being outfoxed or appearing foolish. One person's picture featured a city scene with tall buildings lining a street. He noted, "The street is abandoned, and all you see is the pavement. On the pavement is an unlittered pathway, and on either side of the pathway are many banana peels. This image [represents] that I am concerned when entering into negotiations about slipping up." Another worried about self-defeating behavior: "Coming apart would mean losing my temper, losing control of the situation, being unable to think clearly about the options because of whatever the emotional situation is. I feel that if am going to come apart, then everything will come apart." Still another described what he called "an image of somebody weighing their head on a scale to see whether they are worthy or not." Then he added, "That kind of implied doubt wouldn't help our negotiator."

No wonder people approach negotiation warily, not knowing whom to trust or whether they'll succeed. Caution has been bred into us, more strongly with some people than with others. One of our subjects admitted, "I hate confrontation. I don't deal well with other people's anger. I think anger blocks both creativity and understanding because real anger is just such a boiling emotion that it overtakes you. I think that is what is negative about it. It blocks further communication."

Posturing, deception, miscommunication, and confrontation are commonly feared perils of negotiation. Sometimes they're real threats. Other times they are just in our imagination. And that's true for us and for the people with whom we deal.

DOUBLE STANDARDS

Most people in our study saw others as predators in the negotiation jungle and themselves as prey. A few, however, identified with the aggressive side of human nature. One acknowledged the wolf within him. Another saw himself as a rifleman taking aim. But even those who visualized themselves fending off vicious creatures may have revealed more than they realized, projecting onto others their own negative attributes. Listen to how this person merges his impression of other people's motivations with his own self-image:

"Sometimes you can be in negotiations, outfoxed by somebody perhaps not playing fairly. And I think that is a real difficult thing when it occurs. You can have a lack of honesty or you can see that. Sometimes people can play it a little bit unprofessionally; I think that is being outfoxed. I think being crafty and shrewd is playing your side intelligently."

Did you catch that mental shell game? When we're "crafty and shrewd," we're just behaving intelligently. But when others do the same thing, they "lack honesty" and aren't "playing fairly." A double standard is a recipe for righteousness and retribution. When each negotiator sees his own tactics as clever and the other's as evil, tensions escalate, confirming everyone's worst fears.

Even a seemingly small action can trigger a downward spiral. A brusque greeting or an unexpected demand can spark a reaction that this negotiation won't be as easy as hoped. Heart rates may go up a notch, stomach muscles may tighten, and before long, people may lose their composure. Serious negotiation is a physical act. It takes energy, concentration, and stamina. Internal doubts and discomfort are deadweights that can degrade your attention to the unfolding relationship with the other party.

It comes down to who you'd rather be: a well-centered negotiator or one who is anxious and distracted. Either type could start from the same place by extending an offer that he or she thinks is generous, but then be surprised when the other side rejects it. The person who's well balanced will take that reaction in stride and focus on how to be more persuasive. By contrast, the anxious negotiator may start second-guessing himself and worrying about what to do if the deal falls through. With more composure, he could be better focused on making the deal work.

People who bring positive feelings to the table protect themselves against overreacting to slights and setbacks. They are patient and perceptive. The emotions stirred up by negotiation—anxiety and frustration, on the one hand; openness and assurance, on the other—aren't static or transitory. Those feelings morph into trajectories that become the attitudes and inclinations that either facilitate or impede the process of reaching an agreement. Negotiators who can channel the ebb and flow of feelings have a substantial advantage over others who simply let themselves be rocked by them.

PEAK PERFORMANCE

Negotiators can learn a lot about emotional balance and concentration from star athletes and other performers who must be at their best in high-pressure settings. Baseball players describe with awe those days when the pitch coming toward them looks as big as a beach ball. Football coaches praise coolheaded quarterbacks who can pick out an open receiver in the midst of an opposing blitz. And some ice hockey goalies claim that time slows down for them, so that they can casually block a puck flying at them at one hundred miles an hour.

Sports psychologists such as Robert Nideffer link this state of "being in the zone" to the absence of mental distractions. Mihaly Csikszent-milhalyi describes the related concept of flow as total absorption. It's a mental state where "people are so involved in an activity that nothing else seems to matter; the experience itself is so enjoyable that people will do it even at great cost, for the sheer sake of doing it."

It is easy to visualize a cellist, engrossed in his music, or a marathon runner, lungs bursting as she nears the finish line, as being in flow or in the zone. Even a design team, brainstorming ideas for a new product, might have moments when its members are all in sync, free of distractions.

But what of negotiation? Is it possible to imagine a negotiator as deeply absorbed as the cellist or as focused as the marathon runner? Negotiation is an interpersonal process. Keeping up with the exchange of arguments, propositions, and reactions prompts an internal dialogue that can jeopardize your focus on the moment. If you're not self-aware, negotiation can be a hothouse for cultivating thoughts and feelings that subvert concentration.

Athletes (and their fans) know about "choking." Studies suggest that stress cramps working memory, the resource that experts draw upon to excel. In sports, it might be sparked by an external event, such as a spectator throwing something onto the playing field. But often the cause is internal, where a competitor's mind gets tied up with negative thoughts. Pressure to perform in a win-or-lose moment may overwhelm an athlete's senses and cause him or her to freeze. For a tennis player, it may be fear of making a bad shot. For the negotiator, it may be doubt about his ability to get a good deal or win the other person's respect.

W. Timothy Gallwey, author of the classic *Inner Game of Tennis*, describes the dread that some people feel when a ball is hit to their backhand. "Uh-oh," the player says to himself. "You're going to look clumsy again." Gallwey says that this internal critic is much more devastating to performance than hundreds of taunting fans in the grandstand. Likewise, a negotiator who scolds himself or herself for being anxious reinforces self-criticism and compounds the distraction.

Resolving to put aside negative thoughts often does more harm than good, since it takes focus away from playing the game. Gallwey says that telling someone to "keep your eye on the ball" is counterproductive. Instead, more active focusing is required. For tennis, he prescribes the mantra "bounce-hit." That means saying "bounce" to yourself when the ball starts its rebound from the court's surface, and then saying "hit" at the moment the ball makes impact with the strings of the racquet. **This simple exercise constitutes concentration instead of pleading for it.** It displaces internal distractions with outward focus on the relevant environment—in this case, the flight of the ball over the net, on the court, and then onto the face of the racquet.

Let's translate this technique to negotiation. Your entire attention should be focused on what your counterpart is saying and how she is saying it. Not just her words, but her posture and the expression that just flickered across her face. It's akin to watching the tennis ball. You're observing the direction of what is being said, its pace, and its spin. If you're deeply attentive, your mind will be quieted.

Top athletes also are masters of pace and timing. Legendary UCLA basketball coach John Wooden used to tell his players, "Be quick, but don't hurry." The same applies at the bargaining table. When a deadline looms, a caucus or a time-out may provide a moment for reflection and allow participants to regain presence of mind. Even pausing for a second or two before responding can occasion deeper comprehension of what is taking place.

Champion race car driver Jackie Stewart remembers an event where he was going over 150 miles per hour but suddenly sensed the distinct smell of green grass. He immediately eased up on the pedal, knowing that around the corner, out of his sight, one of his rivals must have skidded onto the infield. The best negotiators shift mental gears smoothly, switching back and forth from the micromoments in an exchange to the macroperspective about how the overall process is progressing. By stepping back from minutia this way, they give themselves the chance to check on their own emotional state—whether they are being calm and alert, patient and proactive, and practical and creative.

The best negotiators are also monitoring how things might look to their counterparts. In *Getting Past No: Negotiating Your Way from Confrontation to Cooperation*, Bill Ury emphasizes the importance of being fully present: deeply engaged with the other party while at the same time taking in everything as if one were a detached observer. He calls this process "going to the balcony." It requires the emotional competence to be center stage yet with the viewpoint of a person sitting way up in the last row. Developing that capacity enables you to understand that what you just said may not necessarily be what your negotiating partner heard (or that what you thought you heard wasn't what he or she meant).

THE PRACTICE OF MINDFULNESS

To develop balance and resilience in negotiation, you can also tap the well of mindfulness training. In its most rigorous form, mindfulness is at the heart of the Buddhist practice of *Vipassana* (or "insight") meditation. While other kinds of Buddhist meditation try to clear the mind of conscious thought or direct attention to a single image or idea, insight practitioners seek a nonjudgmental awareness of their passing thoughts and feelings. *Vipassana* followers believe that if our minds are constantly occupied with rehashing the past or anticipating the future, we are never fully alive in the present. They locate themselves in the immediate moment through quiet exercises in which they pay careful attention to their breathing. They become aware of their thinking in a detached, unforced manner.

This rich and subtle philosophy cannot be distilled in a few short paragraphs, and it's beyond the purview of this book to provide a tutorial in the techniques. There are many books available that do so expertly. The purpose here is simply to point to another fruitful method for developing the emotional balance necessary for peak performance.

A monastic life of quiet contemplation is light-years from the multitasking world in which most of us live, of course, yet there is growing interest in pragmatic applications of mindfulness. The General Mills company offers employees mindfulness workshops and yoga sessions. These sessions are aimed partly at reducing stress, but deeper benefits have emerged. The company's deputy general counsel, Janice Marturano, says, "It's about training our minds to be more focused, to see with clarity, to have spaciousness for creativity, and to feel connected." All those traits she names are key assets in negotiation. In the same spirit, Bill George, former CEO of the medical technology company Medtronic, says, "The main business case for meditation is that if you're fully present on the job, you will be more effective as a leader, you will make better decisions, and you will work better with other people." Those, too, are attributes of great negotiators.

It doesn't matter what techniques or practices you use to develop presence of mind. David Hoffman, a Boston-based mediator and coeditor of *Bringing Peace into the Room: How the Personal Qualities of the Mediator Impact the Process of Conflict Resolution,* handles a wide range of cases, including bitter family disputes. He's dedicated to being emotionally balanced and centered, especially in the middle of hot conflict. He realizes that when he is edgy or distracted himself, it amplifies other people's anxieties.

Mindfulness has deep roots. Japanese Zen master Shunryu Suzuki, founder of the first Buddhist monastery in the United States, said, "If your mind is empty, it is always ready for anything; it is open to everything. In the beginner's mind, there are many possibilities; in the expert's mind, there are few." This stance is the antithesis of being on automatic pilot. It requires self-awareness and a willingness to put aside, at least for a time, preconceptions and snap judgments about other parties' behavior and intentions.

Psychologist Ellen Langer describes a Western version of mindfulness that includes constantly seeing things anew. She takes issue with some coaches' notions about helping athletes get into a flow by practicing a skill to "the point of doing it without thinking." Langer believes that overlearning can be dangerous. Imagine an American driver on an

English roadway where traffic flows in the opposite direction. She must "unlearn" her driving instincts and habituate to those of the English.

In negotiation, the practice of mindfulness could involve sensing the first stirrings of one's own anger in a detached way. Then, instead of either nurturing that feeling or trying to suppress it, a mindful negotiator would register the irritation. This process is different from reasoning it through or trying to argue oneself out of the feeling. The point of mindfulness is becoming aware of one's thoughts and feelings without prematurely judging them as valid or inappropriate, useful or dysfunctional. It's accepting their presence and moving on, just as a traveler on a train might take in the passing scene.

As Csikszentmilhalyi says, controlling one's consciousness is not a mere cognitive skill. "At least as much as intelligence," he writes, "it requires a commitment of emotions and will. It is not enough to *know* how to do it; one must do it, consistently, the same way as athletes or musicians who must keep practicing what they know in theory. And this is never easy." But it can be done.

EMOTIONAL PREPARATION

Serious negotiators prepare. They understand the markets in which they function. They run the numbers and read draft contracts. They scout their counterparts and develop a plan B in case things don't go as expected. You can do all that and more, however, and still not be prepared if you haven't readied yourself emotionally.

Six straightforward questions can help you develop a personalized fitness routine. The more thought you give to each one, the more useful this assignment will be. It's essential to be honest with yourself about your temperament, strengths, and shortcomings.

Right now may be a good time to go through this exercise. If you have ten minutes or so, find a pen and paper for making some notes. Slow down a bit as well. (If you're rushed, it might make sense to come back to this exercise when you're not quite as busy.) When you're ready, turn the paper so that it's in landscape format and make a six-cell matrix: three columns across, split into two rows.

As the first two questions are linked, consider them together:

1. What Do You Want to Feel Going into a Negotiation? 2. Why?

Jot down the first emotions that occur to you, then step back and think of others you could add to the list. Now reflect for a moment on why you identified those feelings and make a few notes in box 2. Don't hurry to read the text that's coming next. Make sure that you've given these first two questions some thought before reading about how others have responded. Okay?

I use this six-step exercise in MBA and executive negotiation courses. Typically, when I start out, students say that they want to be relaxed, focused, and confident. Intuitively, people associate those positive emotions with the pathway to agreement.

But then other students chime in on the discussion. It's fine to be calm, they say, but they don't want to be complacent. They want to be alert and maybe a bit on edge, so that they have the energy to drive the process forward. Rather than debate whether it's one or the other, most students come to realize that they need to be both optimistic and watchful. Check the notes that you made in the first two boxes and think about the balance you want to strike among different feelings. Now you're ready for the next question.

3. What Can You Do Beforehand to Put Yourself in Your Ideal Emotional State?

Again, make a few notes on the form.

This question takes people aback if they haven't thought before about manipulating their own emotional state, but they soon come up with practical suggestions. I've heard students say, "It's just like with exams. Don't tense yourself up with last-minute cramming. Give yourself time to decompress."

The same is true in negotiation—and the less time you have to get ready, the more important that advice is. Say that you're at your desk working on your quarterly budget. The phone rings. It's your counterpart in a tough transaction that has dragged on far too long. Your every impulse may be to leap right into that conversation.

It would be smarter, though, to say, "Glad you called. Let me wrap something up here, and I'll get back to you in three minutes flat." Then you could lean back and maybe close your eyes for a moment. Even right now, if you imagine yourself doing that, you may feel how your tension would ease, leaving you better prepared when you return the call.

Other people suggest simple meditation exercises as a way of putting aside distracting thoughts. Visualization, too, may help. Imagine having the right balance of calm and alertness. What will that feel like? Or if you sometimes fault yourself for being impatient, think about what it's like to listen without interrupting. If you are sometimes too withdrawn, picture yourself leaning into the conversation and being more expressive.

Do what you can to minimize distractions beforehand. When you go to an important meeting, the drive may be easy or traffic may be snarled. Circumstances beyond your command will affect your mood—maybe for better, maybe for worse. If it's the latter, bringing that frustration into the room won't be in your best interest. Do what you can to put yourself in the proper state.

Let's say that you're emotionally prepared. Move on to question 4.

4. What Can Throw You off Balance During a Negotiation?

Once again, make a few notes on the exercise form before reading about other people's responses.

Here I'm talking about emotional hot buttons that, if pushed, can make you underperform. These triggers vary from person to person. Insults get under some people's skin but just roll off other people's backs. Likewise, some negotiators have infinite patience, while others get frustrated when talks drag on.

Think back to negotiations where you didn't function at your best. Maybe you lost your temper, maybe not. But if you pride yourself on your self-control, take an honest look at yourself. Are there times that you disengage and withdraw emotionally? Look for patterns and tendencies. Also think about *when* in the process problems seem to arise. Do things go wrong early or more often at the end, when you're trying to close a deal? Candid feedback from negotiation teammates can help.

5. What Can You Do in the Midst of Negotiation to Regain Your Balance?

Again, jot down your own thoughts before reading further.

Problems in negotiation aren't due to just other people's actions, however. They also depend on how you respond. You can't control other people's behavior, but you do have a say over how you react to it. And if you're self-aware, you'll be alert to the first internal signs of annoyance before it blossoms into full-scale anger. But losing your temper isn't the only way to falter; there are more subtle ways of being off your game as well. If a negotiation is dragging on and on, you may lose concentration. Your energy may wane. What then?

One easy answer is taking a break. It works like a reset button, interrupting whatever dysfunctional pattern has emerged. And remember to take a break *before* you actually need it, so that you're constantly performing at the highest level. We are physical beings, after all. Sometimes, of course, you can't leave the room, but when you're feeling weary or irritated, take a deep breath. It's familiar advice because it works. When you're tense or tired, your respiration slows. Reoxygenating the blood does wonders.

Without doing anything different physically, you can also break negative cycles by shifting the conversation. If you've been getting nowhere jostling over the details of a deal, talk about broad principles and concerns. It you're stuck at that level, see if focusing on process issues jump-starts the interaction. These tactical moves may be useful in themselves. More fundamentally, asserting control will help you re-center yourself.

6. What Do You Want to Feel When You're Done?

When I ask this question in classes, some students blurt out "Relieved." That says a lot about the stress they must feel while they're negotiating.

It's understandable, of course. Negotiation is work. It demands concentration, resilience, and creativity in a context where the stakes may be high and outcomes uncertain.

But those who feel that negotiation is an ordeal pay a price twice over. Going into the process, their apprehension makes them defensive and closed minded. And if they are looking at the exit door all the while, they may settle cheap or walk away empty-handed. With a little more time and a lot more positive emotion, they could do much better.

Some MBA and executive students answer "Satisfied." When I probe for what they mean, people speak of being satisfied with the outcome, all things considered, but also feeling satisfied with their own performance. They may have maintained their balance throughout the process, or if they had a setback, they recovered well enough.

Reminding yourself of what you want to feel going into negotiation and then taking simple steps to get into that state is worthwhile. You'll gain a heightened sense of self-efficacy and confidence. Also remember the promotion-priming technique developed by Adam Galinsky and his colleagues that's described in chapter 2. Taking a few minutes to write down the positive behaviors you want to engage in helps you perform at your best in negotiation.

KEY POINTS

- Be simultaneously calm *and* alert, patient *and* proactive, practical *and* creative.
- Diagnose and address the causes of anxiety.
- Know your own hot buttons.
- Don't confirm your counterparts' worst fears.
- Be emotionally prepared to negotiate.

[6] The Swing of Things

Jazz trumpeter Wynton Marsalis says, "The real power of jazz—and the innovation of jazz—is that a group of people can come together and create art, improvised art, and can negotiate their agendas with each other. And that negotiation *is* the art."

Jazz is negotiation? Absolutely. The late Richard Holbrooke, the US envoy who ended the bloody conflict in the former Yugoslavia and more recently tried to forge stability in Pakistan and Afghanistan, said, "Negotiation is like jazz. It is improvisation on a theme. You know where you want to go, but you don't know how to get there. It's not linear."

In a jazz combo, players with different skills and tastes—and competing egos—must negotiate over what and how to play. The marvel is that a quartet of musicians, complete strangers, can jam together to create something new and exciting, all without an apparent plan or tight control over whatever happens next. "The bass—you never know what they're going to do," Marsalis says.

Getting in sync is imperative, whatever the genre or whether the musicians are old friends or rivals. Marsalis explains that it's "like what the UN does. They sit down, and they try to work things out." The Roots have remained on the hip-hop scene for twenty years in spite of the fact that two founders—drummer Ahmir "Questlove" Thompson and emcee Tariq "Black Thought" Trotter—don't get along. When an interviewer recently asked for the secret of the group's long success, Trotter answered, "Two tour buses."

Jazz and hip-hop musicians don't just cope with conflict and uncertainty. They thrive on it by working with whatever the other players
give them, whether those notes are flat or sharp. Once a quartet finds its
groove, Marsalis says, "The four of us can now have a dialogue. We can
now have a conversation. We can speak to each other in the language of
music."

That's just as true when you're negotiating. After all, conducting a
negotiation isn't like leading a symphony orchestra. You can't hand out
sheet music to the other parties, tap your baton, and expect them to follow your lead. Others at the table will have their own preferred styles and
tempos. They may want to be the star soloist and treat you, at best, as an
accompanist.

I'm not just speaking metaphorically. Negotiators who get in a groove
can tackle the toughest problems. It's not a question of being colleagues
or competitors. Even well-intended people often talk past one another.
Nor is good negotiation chemistry a matter of luck. Rather, it depends
on being both internally centered yourself *and* externally aware of other
parties' emotional states.

In both negotiation and jazz, this process of learning, adapting, and
influencing takes place moment to moment in listening and responding.
You reflect, affirm, rebut, reshape, and respond to whatever your counterparts put forth. And as in jazz, it's impossible to anticipate every twist
and turn. Like it or not, you have to improvise right from the start. If
you're threatened unexpectedly, you have to stand up for yourself without escalating tensions. Or if your counterpart surprises you with a generous offer, you need to accept in such a way that he or she doesn't suffer
remorse and pull it back.

As such moments flash by, you are negotiating on multiple levels.
Substantively, you respond to specific demands and offers by saying yes,
no, or maybe. On another level, you are also defining the relationship
as easy or strained, open or closed, cooperative or competitive. On still
another plane, you are setting the tempo and tone of the negotiation
process. And you must do all of this on the fly.

An MBA student was in his final round of interviews at a consulting firm. He had a lot of social polish and glowing references. In earlier rounds, he had demonstrated his technical skills and his knowledge of business generally. The final meeting with the senior partners seemed like a formality; it was just a matter of tweaking the terms of an official offer. Then the head of the firm asked genially, "When was the last time you had to think on your feet?" The question caught the candidate off guard, and he paused. "Well," he said, stroking his chin. "Let me think."

It was an awkward moment for everybody. Right now as you're reading this book, the right answer may have come to you immediately: "Oh, about a half second ago." It's easy to be agile when nothing is on the line, of course. It's a different matter for most people when the personal stakes are high.

Many managers I've surveyed fault themselves for not being more nimble negotiators, especially in coping with belligerent tactics. Many also remember getting stuck when they've had to choose between revealing key information or fudging the facts. "I tend to get rattled when I think I've made a mistake," one person said. "I begin to doubt myself, which makes me second-guess my moves, which hinders my agility."

Such worries are understandable. You can't preprogram yourself to always do and say the right thing. Even in seemingly simple negotiations, you can't know exactly what to do at a particular point until you get there. Let's say that you want to nail down a service contract with a new customer. What's the first thing you should say after the prospect welcomes you to her office, let alone the second or the third? It all depends on how she begins the conversation. She might open in different ways:

Version 1. "Chris, we're looking forward to partnering with you. Let's figure out a deal that works well for both of us."

Version 2. "Good that you could come, Chris. My colleagues have put you on the short list of possible providers for this contract."

Version 3. "It's time for you to fish or cut bait, Chris. We like your proposal, but you've got to come way down in price to beat your competition."

Each statement would warrant a different response. Even if you knew in advance what your counterpart would say, you'd still want to hear her exact words and gauge her attitude. The demand that we drop the price might sound like an obvious bluff. Or the talk about "partnering" could seem insincere. And you won't know how you'll feel yourself—cautious or confident—until you're really there. Only then can you sense if you'll be content settling for half a loaf or pressing for more.

Some negotiators seem to have a natural gift for improvising. The rest of us might wish that negotiation came with a pause button that would let us freeze the action, ponder what the other side meant, and weigh what to say next. Even better would be a replay function, so that we could backtrack and try another response if our initial approach fell flat. Sorry, but there are no such gizmos in the real world. And there aren't do-overs, either. Instead, we have to extemporize.

Standard negotiation books don't offer answers, but you can stretch yourself by borrowing practices from other domains where improvisation is explicitly practiced and taught. Jazz is one such rich resource. You can draw valuable lessons also from theater, psychotherapy, and, as you'll see in the next chapter, even warfare. Musicians, actors, therapists, and soldiers engage in very different enterprises. At the heart of it, though, their agility rests on similar principles.

Improvisation isn't merely a technique. It requires a special mind-set: a blend of unflinching realism about the situation you're in, coupled with a positive belief that you'll muddle through nonetheless. Nor is improvisation simply making up things as you go along. If it were, anyone could sit down at a piano and conjure great jazz. It isn't a blind process of trial and error, either. Improv comedy troupes would be booed off the stage if they randomly tossed out lines, hoping to stumble upon something funny. It certainly isn't waiting passively for something to happen. Even taciturn psychotherapists know when it's time to stop listening to a patient's sorrows and interject a question that sparks insight. Instead, improvisers survive and even prosper because they do three things especially well:

1. They Pay Close Heed.
They have powers of attention that go well beyond active listening.

2. They Know When and How to Influence and Adapt to the People with Whom They Deal.
Jazz musicians call this soloing and comping.

3. They Are Proactive; Even Provocative.
They take considered risks in order to drive the action forward.

PAYING HEED

Improvising starts with paying heed; giving full attention to what others are expressing substantively and emotionally. That involves taking in not only the meaning of words but also tone of voice, facial expressions, and posture. It requires all your senses. Jazz great Herbie Hancock has described the process as being so intense that "sometimes I'm listening with my toes."

Distraction hampers understanding, just like static on the car radio. It's often internal chatter that most interferes with real listening, even in everyday conversation. We've all had awkward moments at parties where our mind wanders instead of focusing on what someone else is saying. "I didn't catch his name," we might tell ourselves, as we tap our mental toes, just waiting for him to stop droning on so that we can tell *our* favorite anecdote. And most of us have been on the other side of such interactions, noting as we are talking how the listener's eyes scan the room for someone more interesting.

Being out of sync is frustrating enough in social situations. In negotiation, it is crippling. Your counterpart may be only in midsentence, but you're already scripting what to say when she's done—if you let her get that far. While you're busy stifling feelings, weighing options, or interpreting something said earlier, the interaction can run away from you.

"Active listening" techniques taught in human relations seminars don't solve the problem. Saying something such as "If I understand you correctly, your concern is . . ." is at best a gesture of acknowledgment, a technique for clarifying factual issues. At worst, it sounds formulaic and patronizing.

Paying heed in negotiation involves turning off one's inner dialogue and absorbing what is happening in the here and now. Doing so is both challenging and liberating. When the other party is putting forth a complex proposal, it's easy to get stuck mentally on a particular point at the cost of missing everything else that follows. Instead, when you hear something troublesome, you should be listening more intently to pick up on other aspects of the offer that might ultimately form the basis of agreement.

As *Flow* author Mihaly Csikszentmilhalyi notes, "It is difficult to notice the environment as long as the attention is mainly focused inward, as long as most of one's psychic energy is absorbed by the concerns and desires of the ego. People who know how to transform stress into enjoyable experience spend very little time thinking about themselves."

Staying in the flow of conversation is easier said than done, though, especially when another person's unexpected behavior upsets your plans. **Thinking that you have to make the perfect response at exactly the right moment only makes matters worse.** The stronger your need to perform flawlessly, the less you're likely to deliver. Letting go of such impulses costs you nothing.

Great improvisers of all types succeed because they stay loose under pressure. That's true for actors onstage, star athletes in clutch situations, and top negotiators, too. Just watch how relaxed the best improv comics are when another performer is holding forth. That other person may be spinning out a bizarre story about an accountant in the Wild West who's lost his abacus, but you'll see no strain or struggle on the listener's face. She's not worrying about when to chime in or what to say. Instead, you'll see only her deep interest in hearing more. Whenever her time comes, she'll have enough material on which to build. By contrast, thrust an amateur up on that same stage, and he'll be bound up in a swirl of paralyzing thoughts: "What am I doing here?" "What would be funny?" "Why can't I think of anything?"

It's easy for negotiators to fall into the same kind of self-defeating be-havior. The other party's mouth may be moving, but you won't hear the words if your own mental wheels are turning too fast. "Is this really their best offer?" you may be thinking. "What am I going to tell my boss?" "Should I come back strong or be more conciliatory?"

Mental tension is debilitating twice over. It puts all your focus on the downside, highlighting everything that could go wrong. It also shifts at-tention away from the other players on the stage. They may be throwing out bits of useful material, but they fall on deaf ears. You must turn off that chatter to improvise successfully.

Sigmund Freud stressed the need for "even, hovering attention," an attitude that takes in everything as it transpires without rushing to judgment. That doesn't mean negotiators should mimic the stereotypi-cal analyst who rarely breaks her silence (and then only to ask, "What makes you say that?"). But many negotiators could learn from therapists' forbearance—their willingness to let certain comments pass while also sensing when the moment is right to offer support or pose a challenge.

Negotiators must be more proactive than therapists, of course, by floating proposals when it's appropriate and drawing lines when neces-sary. But the timing has to be right for each. Trumpeter Miles Davis often said that the biggest challenge in jazz improvisation is maintaining the discipline "*not* to play all the notes you could play, but to wait, hesitate, let the space become a part of the configuration."

You don't need a therapist's or musician's ear to pick up when a new and promising note is sounded in negotiation. George Shultz, in his memoir of his years as Secretary of State in the Ronald Reagan admin-istration, recalls a seemingly small remark made by a Soviet diplomat at the 1986 arms reduction summit in Reykjavik, Iceland. It came in his first meeting with Marshal Sergei Akhromeyev, who was deputy minister of defense (equivalent to the Chairman of the Joint Chiefs of Staff in the United States). US experts on the Soviets had not expected Akhromeyev to be part of the delegation.

Shultz knew that his counterpart had a distinguished military record, but not much beyond that. He was intrigued, therefore, when Akhromeyev casually described himself as being "one of the last of the Mohicans." Shultz asked what he meant by that. The official explained that he was one of the last of the World War II commanders still active in government.

Secretary Shultz, however, had heard something more in the remark, so he pressed further. "In boyhood," Akhromeyev added, "I was raised on the adventure tales of James Fenimore Cooper." Shultz recognized the comment as a positive sign. He took the former general "to be a man with a sense of history and an awareness of the American way" and found him to be "more at ease with himself, more open, more ready for real conversation, than had the professional negotiators of times past with whom we customarily dealt." Akhromeyev ended up chairing the working group and doing most of the talking.

Openness is key to creativity in negotiation. If the parties aren't paying heed to what the other is truly saying, they might as well be mailing form letters back and forth. Breaking an impasse requires a new understanding of the problem and perhaps of the parties' relationship, as was the case with Shultz and Akhromeyev. But that can happen only if at least one of them is paying heed.

LEARNING TO COMP

Strong negotiators aren't shy about taking the lead. They also know when to relinquish it, at least for a while. In jazz, the best solos are exhilarating, but effective comping (accompanying or complementing what the other players are doing) is an essential part of the art as well. It is a group activity, after all, a process of continual give-and-take. Performers who hog the spotlight and don't support the other players aren't invited back for the next gig.

"It is not enough to be an individual virtuoso," says Frank Barrett, author of *Yes to the Mess: Surprising Leadership Lessons from Jazz*. Even as one musician takes the lead, the rest of the players must listen deeply. "They need to interpret others' playing, make instantaneous decisions in regard to harmonic and rhythmic progressions." Barrett speaks with authority as both a professor of organizational behavior at the Naval Postgraduate School and a former member of the Tommy Dorsey Orchestra. "None of this responsiveness can happen unless players are receptive and taking in one another's gestures," he says.

Comping effectively is just as important in negotiation. In the course of the dialogue, each side expects a chance to convince the other of the merits of its position. Usually the parties insist upon it. Letting each other talk is only the first step. If nobody is listening, the conversation goes nowhere.

Even while your counterpart is speaking, you should lean into the conversation and shape his or her behavior. The questions that you pose or even a nod of your head can encourage constructive statements and keep the other party from painting himself into a corner. "Tell me more about that," you might interject if things are going well. Or if you need to get someone back on track, ask, "What could we learn from how other people have solved this problem?"

Once again this goes way beyond so-called active listening. It's not just acknowledging what others have stated but also influencing what they are saying and how they are saying it. Striking the right balance between soloing and comping thus requires awareness of when to step back and when to step in. Annotating each and every thing that someone else says will eventually drive even the most patient person nuts. Letting some things pass, at least for the moment, intensifies the impact of what you say when you do jump in.

According to Barrett, when jazz musicians comp, they agree "to suspend judgment, to trust that whatever the soloist is doing right now will lead to something, to blend into the flow and direction of the idea rather than to break off in an independent direction." For musicians, this means abandoning the illusion of full control over whatever happens next.

Abandoning control and supporting other parties may be a hard pill for type-A negotiators to swallow, but it doesn't require compromising your ultimate objectives. And it has nothing to do with being submissive.

Rather, it simply involves dialing back on the urge to dominate each moment of the transaction. (Paradoxically, that kind of microcontrol actually lessens your power to get where you want to go.) You may exert more influence by following the example of the drummers and bass players, who aren't front and center but who drive the rhythm and tempo of the whole performance.

To understand effective comping, you only have to recall instances of it being done poorly. We've all seen well-intended teammates bump into each other while making a proposal or a sales pitch. Each may interrupt the other to underscore a point or add technical details. Those particular comments may be relevant, but if there's constant butting in, any benefit of having more information is quickly outweighed by the loss of flow and coherence.

Comping isn't politely taking turns, either. Instead, it's finding ways while you're listening to bring out the best in your counterparts, be they allies or antagonists. It's in your interest to coax them to disclose their true priorities instead of concealing them. You're better off as well if you can encourage and augment their tentative attempts at problem solving rather than provoke haggling by contesting their every assertion.

When you're matched with the right people, skillful comping can be transformational. Even if they talk far more than you do, you may guide the conversation by supporting their best ideas and reshaping other ones. In the end, they may feel that you accepted their proposal, when you deftly got them to voice much of what you wanted.

Let's say that the other side tosses out three demands, two of which are out of the question. Your natural reaction may be to focus on what's not workable and why. The other party may then respond in the same spirit and tear apart your arguments. This mode of discourse can deteriorate into a negative exchange where one side brings buckets of paint, the other supplies the brushes, and both end up stuck in opposite corners.

Comping, by contrast, involves picking up a seed of an idea that you can then nourish. A jazz musician doesn't echo what the soloist is doing; rather, he or she selects some piece of it to underscore and develop. In our hypothetical negotiation, that could mean focusing on the one promising theme that the other party put on the table and using that as a scaffold for building more general agreement. That makes much more sense than hammering on all the things that won't work.

A little verbal highlighting may be all that's needed. "Let's focus on that idea for a minute," you might say, or "Maybe we could fold that into what we were talking about earlier." If you're dealing with someone who knows you well, a raised eyebrow might signal "Don't go there," while a tilt of your head could send the message "Maybe now we're getting someplace."

Some negotiators are naturals at letting other parties hold the floor while nevertheless steering the conversation. It's partly listening for glimmers of substantive information from which an agreement can be forged. It's also picking up on people's feelings and comping emotionally—with a shared laugh or a sigh—anything that boosts the positive and disrupts the negative flow.

Comping skills are put to the test when you have to deal with people whose styles and assumptions conflict with your own. Here your ability to bring out the best in others is most important, whether their behavioral bandwidth is large or small. Tough characters who have little flexibility and less smarts may miss or ignore most of your cues. Even so, exerting some small measure of influence is better than beating your head (or theirs) against the wall.

In the end, you have to comp regardless of whether your counterparts are sweethearts or thugs. Even in one-shot, arm's-length deals, rewarding whatever positive things that others express—instead of amplifying the negative—is a pragmatic way to get things done.

BEING PROVOCATIVE

Paying heed is one aspect of improvising. Comping is another. Being provocative is a third. When Ambassador Holbrooke negotiated, he sometimes seemed more like Muhammad Ali than a typical diplomat. "He's yakking and talking. He's jiving," marveled a colleague. Though he added: "The first time you see it, you think it's just bull." In fact, it was Holbrooke's way of pumping himself up and energizing the negotiation process.

Great jazz musicians stir up things as well. Familiar routines and old assumptions have to be disrupted, even though doing so entails risk. Otherwise nothing new can be created. Frank Barrett calls this trait "provocative competence." It tops his list of key principles in improvisation.

Frank uses the word *provocative* in the positive sense of a willingness to abandon the status quo and venture into the unknown, at least partway. For a negotiator, that could be voicing a novel idea or being more (or less) confrontational than usual. Beyond experimenting, it is a way of taking the initiative. Saxophonist John Coltrane said that he deliberately played songs in difficult and unfamiliar keys because it "made me think" instead of just having his fingers play the notes automatically.

Provocation can be aimed at others as well. Clarinetist Benny Goodman's famed Carnegie Hall concert in 1938 began with a dull rendition of "Don't Be That Way." His band was uptight playing in that historic venue before a society audience dressed in tuxedos and evening gowns. Goodman himself was unable to get his musicians to swing, but drummer Gene Krupa galvanized them with a drum solo so wild that jazz critic Phil Schaap calls it "nearly cacophonous." Krupa hit every part of his kit as hard and as fast as he could, "not trying to wake up the crowd," says Schaap, but "trying to wake up the band. He's trying to relax them or scare them beyond their fear."

Fear of mistakes is a great inhibitor in negotiation. It freezes us and makes us brittle. If we fixate on all that could go wrong, it's hard to imagine how things could go right. Stephen Nachmanovitch, author of *Free Play: Improvisation in Life and Art*, connects reluctance to experiment to "fear of being thought a fool (loss of reputation) and fear of actually being a fool (fear of unusual state of mind)."

Fear throws us off balance, not just emotionally but physically. Our muscles tighten and our vision narrows. As Nachmanovitch observes, this literally cramps our style. "If I 'try' to play, I fail; if I force the play, I crush it; if I race, I trip. Anytime I stiffen or brace myself against some error or problem, the very act of bracing would cause the problem to occur."

The answer in both jazz and negotiation is venturing out into unfamiliar waters far enough to be energized and creative, but not so far that you are in over your head. Ed Sarath, former head of the jazz department at the University of Michigan, says that the trick for musicians is to be 80 percent in their comfort zone, 20 percent outside of it. A player who is completely comfortable just recycles past performances.

"I don't like a comfortable person," Miles Davis once said. "I can't be around them if they're just . . . you know. Nothing bounces off them. You get nothing." Davis himself was notorious for making his fellow players *un*comfortable. He actually barred his muscians from practicing together, to keep the group vibrant when it finally got together. The signature cut "So What" from his classic 1959 album *Kind of Blue* was created on the spot and is played in the D-Dorian mode, something the group had never heard of until Davis explained it moments before the recording tape started to roll. Working in that strange mode was scary, but it forced everyone to abandon old conventions and in their place jointly create the bestselling jazz album of all time.

Sarath's 80–20 rule is a good standard for negotiators too. You need the 80 percent so that you can move forward and dampen fears about making irreversible mistakes. But the 20 percent discomfort is just as important. It inoculates you against complacence and heightens your senses so that you're alert for both danger and opportunities.

There are lots of ways to get up to the 80 percent comfort level. The preparation tools covered in part 1 of this book can give you confidence that you're headed in the right direction. The presence of mind techniques described in the prior chapter will help you recognize how far you've gotten.

You will get stuck sometimes. You may lose your train of thought or not have the perfect answer to a tough question. That's bound to happen when you operate on the edge. Trumpeter Tommy Turrentine said that when you're doing a solo and you lose focus, "You better have something to play when you can't think of nothing new, or you'll feel funny laying out all the time." Jazz musicians stockpile familar licks they can fall back on until inspiration kicks back in.

Likewise, as a negotiator, you can minimize the impact of freezing up by having a few stock moves on hand that will buy you time to regain your footing. Shift the conversation to process and treat whatever just occurred as a mutual problem. "Maybe it's just me," you might say, "but it feels as if we're getting lost in the weeds. Let's recap what we've agreed upon so we can put this particular issue in context."

You can also build your confidence by seeking out ideas and techniques beyond your usual experience. If you run a supply chain, for example, read the sports pages to see how pro teams try to balance their payrolls as they negotiate with superstars and journeymen. Or if you're in sports, pay attention to the foreign news and watch how diplomats forge alliances.

Look especially for examples of other people using provocative competence to stir things up. You seldom want to be provocative in the inflammatory sense, but sometimes you have to shock other parties to get their attention. Donald Dell tells about how in the 1970s he tried to dissuade high school basketball star Moses Malone from signing a multimillion-dollar contract to play in the American Basketball Association. At that point, the teenager was the shyest person Dell had ever met. "Almost seven feet tall and all kneecaps and elbows, he couldn't bring himself to look at me."

Dell was getting nowhere trying to explain the unfairness of the contract clause that gave the pro team a perpetual option to extend the deal. Malone was so nervous that he wasn't hearing a word. Dell realized that he had to say something else. "I stopped midsentence, paused for a moment, and then said, 'Moses, have you ever heard of slavery?' His head shot up immediately, and he stared at me intently. 'Because,' I said, 'if you sign this contract, that's like virtual slavery. It could be for the next sixteen years of your life, and I've never seen a contract like this one.'"

It was a risky move, but Malone got the point and was saved from signing a deal that would have cost him tens of millions of dollars over his career.

BENDING THE RULES OF IMPROV

Improv comics bring a jazz mind-set to their work. They speak of the "beats" that set the pace and mark transitions in their performance. Like musicians, they solo and comp. Everything they say adds information that propels the story forward. A comic wouldn't start a skit by merely saying, "Hi," and leaving it at that. Instead, she might open by saying "Brad! I never expected to see you here at the South Pole."

Performers call such an opening an "offer." It gives the other players material to work with. When they build on someone else's offer, comics call that "agreement." Thus, a performer who hears the South Pole line might respond, "Yeah, when my company said it was giving me the southern territory, I was thinking Florida, maybe." With that simple call-and-response, the two are off and running. Their agreement is open ended. It doesn't seal a specific deal. But it serves as a platform on which they can construct their relationship and develop whatever they imagine they're doing on the frozen continent.

You have the same opportunity when you set the stage for negotiation. Your offers, in the broad sense, don't have to be about dollars and cents. They can be suggestions about how to proceed or even more subtle gestures that set the tone for the process. How you comport yourself may send a richer message than the words you use. If you're tight lipped or inscrutable, you're leaving it up to your counterpart to define the interaction. Instead, it's usually in your best interest to provide something for them to respond to.

Some rules of improv comedy don't apply to negotiation literally, yet they still provide useful lessons. One of the precepts, for instance, is "always agree—never negate." In our South Pole example, it would be a cardinal sin to reply, "Antarctica? My name is Angela, and we're in the middle of the Sahara."

A blunt contradiction stops the action onstage. If the players can't agree on who they are and where they're situated, they certainly can't figure out where to go next. No matter how preposterous one person's statement is, the other must accept it and move forward. This ethic gives the skit a loose sense of direction and continuity. Early commitments to role, relationship, and context allow all the players to focus on what's unfolding and put aside the countless options that might have been available at the beginning.

Long before Dick Costolo became CEO of Twitter, he was an improv comic. He still usually answers other people's assertions with "Yes, and . . ." rather than opposing them with the word *but*. Sometimes in negotiation, however, you have to say no loudly. When the other party is demanding the moon, the sun, and the stars, you've got to bring him back to earth. You may also have to draw a clear line in regard to acceptable behavior, whether the transgression is an insult, evasion, or a broken promise. Nevertheless, negotiators have to be smart about when and how to disagree. The word *no* is a verbal stop sign. If someone is being unreasonable, you need to flag her down. But you also have to pave the way to where you want her to go next.

Bill Ury's 2007 book *The Power of a Positive No: Save the Deal, Save the Relationship—And Still Say No* suggests ways of saying no that protect your core interests while still offering counterparts a graceful way to move in a more constructive direction. In some cases, you can make a no sound like a yes. For example, you might say, "Your idea might work provided we could also . . ." Even when you must disagree, it's in your interest to shift the perspective rather than force a counterpart to defend his position. "Look, the reality is that we're not going to see eye to eye on all the details," you might assert, "so instead of rehashing the past, let's find some practical way of moving forward."

Another rule in improv is "Never ask questions." They are a no-no in skits because they make the other person do all the work. If a comic opens a scene by demanding, "What are you doing here?" other players have nothing to build on. They bear all the responsibility for establishing the parties' identities, relationship, and situation. It's as if the conversation hasn't begun at all.

By contrast, questions are essential in negotiation. It's a process of inquiry and exploration, after all. Reaching a durable, value-creating agreement depends on discovering how the parties' true interests can best be dovetailed. But they have to be the right kind of questions. Rhetorical challenges such as "What in the world makes you think your property is worth so much?" make others more entrenched. Asking instead "How can we figure out a reasonable value for the property?" raises the same issue but shifts the focus from a specific number to a mutual search for relevant principles and standards.

Questions aren't the only way to glean information. Often in negotiation, they're not even the best method. Say that a salesperson quotes you a marginally acceptable price. You'd love to know if she's willing to go lower, but asking that question directly would be a mistake, as she wouldn't have any reason to say yes. To learn if there's room to bargain, you might do better by counteroffering or saying something ambiguous like "Ouch. That may be too rich for my blood."

Honoring another rule of improv comedy, "Maintain eye contact," is possible only in face-to-face negotiation, though it's instructive across the board. Steady gaze enables stage performers to pick up cues from their fellow artists—not only their words but also their expressions, gestures, and posture. If each individual is in the same here and now, then the whole troupe is in sync. (Just think how averting your own eyes from someone else who's talking feels like you're stepping back, even if you haven't moved an inch.) Whenever you get lost in your private thoughts and disconnect with others, you squander power to influence them.

Eye contact is a physical form of comping. It's how you tell a counterpart "I'm right here, working with you." In negotiation, it establishes your presence and compels others to take you into account. A slight nod of the head can signal that they're headed in a fruitful direction. A quizzical look may say that you're skeptical or don't understand.

Nonverbal behavior is rich in emotional content. You lose a lot of bandwidth when you have to negotiate long distance by email or phone. As a consequence, those mediums demand special effort to ensure that you are understood correctly. In turn, you need to be careful interpreting other people's written language. You don't want to construe a message as a veiled threat when the words might have been composed hastily. Likewise, when you're on the phone, you don't want to make others feel as if they are talking into the void. Interjections such as "Okay," "How come," and "Let's hold that issue for later" give the conversation color and texture, and also keep you focused and engaged.

You must be emotionally secure and upbeat to make the most of these techniques. I remember conducting an improv exercise in my MBA class almost ten years ago. It was called "instant expert." I would pick out students to perform, and then the rest of the class came up with topics that they'd probably know nothing about.

The first person chosen to stand in front of the room had to give a three-minute talk on haute couture. The guy looked angry and scared. The presentation was a flop. I'm sure that the three minutes felt like an hour to him.

Then I picked a woman in the back row. Her face fell when she was told that she would be an expert on monarch butterflies. But as she strode down the aisle, her expression changed. She stood tall and smiled at her classmates. "I'm so glad to tell you about monarchs," she said. "I'm only sorry that I have only three minutes to describe what I'm passionate about." In her enthusiasm, she was able to dredge up a few facts that she did know about butterflies, and then she embellished her story by describing the joys of scientific discovery. The time flew by, and she got wild applause from her classmates.

"What's your secret?" I asked her. "How did you transform yourself so quickly?"

"My first reaction was being scared because I had been picked," she said. "But then I thought, 'If I've got to do this, I might as well make the best of it.'"

It was a prime example of saying "yes to the mess." And the power of having that attitude has been borne out by recent research by my psychologist colleague Alison Wood Brooks. She has found that if you're feeling anxious, don't try to suppress that emotion. Instead, put yourself on a positive emotional path by transforming that nervous energy into excitement, just as my student did. Alison has found that if your heart is racing, the simple step of saying out loud "I'm excited" can significantly enhance your ability to perform. It's certainly worth a try.

BEING IN (OR OUT OF) SYNC

A powerful way to understand how these improv principles work in negotiation is seeing what happens when they're violated. Take the following exchange between a defense attorney representing an insurance company and a plaintiff's lawyer whose client was injured in an auto accident. It's from an unscripted instructional tape created by Gerry Williams, a pioneer in the negotiation field.

From the start, the plaintiff's lawyer has extended himself by being cooperative and polite, while the blustering defense attorney makes extravagant claims. This segment comes after about forty-five minutes of fruitless back-and-forth.

> **Defense attorney:** We're going to have housewives on that jury. You know how people feel about liquor. The rich, young playboy out for a night of carousing. Don't you think those things are going to cut it down?
>
> **Plaintiff's lawyer:** One question: How do you assess liability here?
>
> **Defense attorney:** Oh, probably about . . . seventy-five percent your boy's fault.
>
> **Plaintiff's lawyer:** If that's your position, I want a judge involved . . . If you are really hung up on that figure, then I say there's no use talking.
>
> **Defense attorney:** We could call it off if you want.
>
> **Plaintiff's lawyer:** I think that's probably wise.

After these parties reached impasse, they were brought into separate rooms, where they privately disclosed their bottom lines. The plaintiff's lawyer said that he would accept $80,000 to settle the case. The defense lawyer was willing to pay $75,000. They had no way of realizing it themselves, but they were only $5,000 apart.

The stalemate might have been averted if the attorneys were more agile. Specifically, if the plaintiff's lawyer had paid closer heed, even in the closing moments of the exchange, he would have picked up on a positive note buried at the end of the defense attorney's harangue.

Look back at the defense lawyer's statement that begins the dialogue. He starts by cartooning the claimant as a playboy out on a wild spree, implying that he doesn't deserve a penny. But then he softens his tone and makes a switch: "Don't you think those things are going to cut it down?" Unfortunately, that comment didn't register with the other lawyer. Had he heard it, he could have responded, "Maybe it would reduce the amount a little. But before we figure out any adjustment, let's calculate a reasonable number for all the damages. Then we can talk about a fair discount for my client's role. Okay?"

It's understandable that the plaintiff's lawyer had given up listening, though, in view of all the hot air the he had heard up to that point. But it's in contentious situations that you especially need to be listening for a positive theme on which you can comp. Writing off somebody as irredeemable is self-fulfilling.

Look also at the different nature of the questions in this short exchange. For all his bluster, the defense lawyer raises a reasonable point: If the injured claimant was partly at fault, shouldn't that reduce his recovery? Had his counterpart heard this invitation, they could have then discussed various ways of calculating responsibility.

Instead, the plaintiff's lawyer leans back in his chair, wags his finger, and with a relaxed smile on his face, poses a different kind of question, one that shuts the door on possible agreement. The query catches the other attorney by surprise. It's the first one put to him in almost an hour of talk. After a little hesitation, he appears to pull a number out of thin air, and it's a ridiculous figure to boot. The plaintiff, eager to end this pointless discussion, then jumps on the 75 percent estimate and lashes it around the other fellow's neck not just once ("If that's your position") but twice ("If you are really hung up on that figure").

The parties in this vignette failed to get in sync. Right to the end, the defense lawyer mistook his counterpart's good manners as a sign of weakness. In turn, the plaintiff's lawyer thought he was dealing with a pettifogger. If just one of them had been more nimble, they might have reached agreement. As it was, however, neither was able to influence or adapt to the other.

The one thing that they had in common was an inability to work outside their respective comfort zones. If the hard-bargaining defense lawyer had been paired with somebody just like him, they likely would have haggled their way to an acceptable number. And if the cooperative plaintiff's attorney had met his clone, they might well have shared information that would have led to a creative agreement.

In real-world negotiation, however, you can't limit yourself to dealing with people who match your own temperament and style. There are rugged individualists who expect others to look after themselves at the bargaining table. Others are relationally oriented. Stretch yourself so that you can deal with both types and everyone in between.

AN APPRECIATIVE MIND-SET

Improvisation rests on having what Frank Barrett calls an appreciative mind-set. Appreciation as he means it doesn't signify the same warm gratitude a parent feels when a grown child calls with birthday wishes. It's a bit closer to appreciation in the sense of broad comprehension, taking into account all aspects of a situation, both good and bad, in a clear-eyed manner. But it's more than that as well. It is an attitude that whatever has befallen you, you can make some good of it, as Barrett says. In other people's eyes, that optimism may seem misplaced or even irrational. Yet it is often useful to believe that somewhere in the trash heap in which you've landed there are bits and pieces of a solution that could be cobbled into a workable deal.

The late investment banker Bruce Wasserstein was known for his brash confidence. His former colleague Laurence Grafstein tells of a time that he was running late for a meeting. His assistant told him the finance minister of Slovakia had been waiting for him in the conference room.

"Arriving well behind schedule, Bruce proceeded to launch into a distinctive, long-winded Wassersteinian monologue about all of the different
issues facing Slovakia's privatization program, corporate sector, and politics generally given its recent separation from the Czech Republic. And
why, of course, Slovakia needed a banker like Bruce to steer it forward.
The guests and his colleagues tried unsuccessfully to interrupt several
times. Finally, the finance minister said, 'Excuse me, Mr. Wasserstein.
We are not from Slovakia. We are from Slovenia.' The way Bruce told
it, the room went silent, with ashen faces around the table. After a brief
pause, Bruce—always a bit faster and more confident than most of us—
answered: 'And that's precisely your strategic dilemma.' What was the
poor Slovenian finance minister to do, other than cave?"

Several years ago, the jazz critic David Hajdu wandered into a
Greenwich Village club where Charles McPherson, a little-known but
highly regarded saxophonist, was leading a band. As Hajdu settled down
at his table, his eyes wandered over to the trumpeter, who was turned away
from the audience and even from the rest of the band. "I couldn't place him,"
Hajdu wrote later. "He looked like an older version of Wynton Marsalis."

Marsalis, by that time, was regarded skeptically by some jazz aficio-
nados who faulted him for being too cautious and conservative. This
trumpeter was dressed stylishly in an Italian-cut suit and had the bur-
nished elegance, as Hajdu put it, of Marsalis and his musician brothers.
But there "was a weight upon him; he didn't smile, and his eyes were
small and affectless." The trumpeter didn't have the "youthful élan that
Wynton Marsalis has always called to mind." But it really was Marsalis,
as became obvious when he played a solo, the plaintive "I Don't Stand
a Ghost of a Chance with You." Hajdu was there, so he should describe
Marsalis's rendition:

> He performed the song in murmurs and sighs, at points nearly talking the
> words in notes. It was a wrenching act of creative expression. When he
> reached the climax, Marsalis played the final phrase, the title statement,
> in declarative tones, allowing each successive note to linger in the air a bit
> longer. "I don't stand . . . a ghost . . . of . . . a chance . . ."

The room was silent until, at the most dramatic point, someone's cell phone went off, blaring a rapid singsong melody in electronic beeps. People started giggling and picking up their drinks. The whole moment—the whole performance—unraveled.

Marsalis paused for a beat, motionless, and his eyebrows arched. I scrawled on a sheet of notepaper, "Magic Ruined." The cell phone offender scooted into the hall as the chatter in the room grew louder. Still frozen at the microphone, Marsalis replayed the silly cell phone melody note for note. Then he repeated it, and began improvising variations on the tune. The audience slowly came back to him. In a few minutes, he resolved the improvisation—which had changed keys once or twice and throttled down to a ballad tempo—and ended up exactly where he had left off: "with . . . you." The ovation was tremendous.

KEY POINTS

- Pay heed. Go beyond active listening.
- Be provocative. Stir things up.
- Venture outside your comfort zone.
- "Comp" in order to evoke the best from your counterparts.
- Say no when necessary, but offer an alternative.
- Develop an appreciative mind-set.

[7] Situational Awareness

American F-86 Sabre jet fighters and North Korean MiG-15s battled fiercely throughout the Korean War. The rival Russian-built plane was faster, soared higher, and was more heavily armed. Nevertheless, American pilots won more than 90 percent of the dogfights.

Military analysts initially chalked up the dominance of the F-86 to pilot superiority, but that was just part of the story. Even after the Russians substituted their own well-trained pilots for the North Korean fliers, the Americans still had a whopping five-to-one advantage in combat. It took the maverick intelligence of John Boyd, an air force colonel and Pentagon gadfly, to recognize what was going on.

Deadly combat may seem an odd topic for this book, especially coming on the heels of a chapter on jazz and improv. Bear with me. Former Israeli prime minister Shimon Peres likened strategic negotiators to hunters. "A good hunter doesn't aim at the bird. If he does, he will miss," he said. "He aims ahead of the bird, anticipating its travel." Foresight is essential in negotiation, both in cases where there are clear winners and losers, and in more collaborative ventures.

Military doctrine can teach us a lot about anticipation and decision making in dynamic, rapidly changing environments. So can competitive games such as chess and basketball. US Marine Corps doctrine defines maneuver warfare as "a state of mind born of a bold will, intellect, initiative, and ruthless opportunism." Will, intellect, and initiative are all negotiation virtues, but what of ruthless opportunism? Negotiation need not—and in most instances *should not*—be "ruthless" on a personal basis. But we shouldn't flinch from tackling tough problems. And we should seize opportunities to innovate.

So back to aerial warfare. Boyd's core interest was military strategy, but he was an eclectic reader well versed in history and philosophy. He was interested in how people make decisions under pressure. *"Machines don't fight wars. Terrain doesn't fight wars,"* he said. *"Humans fight wars. You must get into the minds of humans. That's where battles are won."*

According to biographer Grant Hammond, Boyd was fascinated by what others might see merely as "a confusing and disorderly fur ball of a fight among swarming planes." In the seeming chaos of air-to-air combat, Boyd recognized underlying order. "What initially excited him was that it was limitless," says Hammond. "It could start or end at any altitude, from any direction. It was all azimuth and multidimensional. It was, he would realize, the best way to think about a problem."

Boyd concluded that the success of the American fighter was due to two design factors. First, it had hydraulic controls that enabled it to transition from one activity—climbing, banking, and accelerating—more rapidly than the MiG. Second, the F-86 had a bubble canopy that gave its pilots superior "situational awareness," which allowed them to process information and make decisions more quickly. Each maneuver by the F-86 compounded its edge over its opponent until it achieved dominance.

From this specific example, Boyd formulated a general model of dynamic interaction. He called it the *OODA* loop—a recurring process of Observing, Orienting, Deciding, and Acting. As he saw it, success in any encounter hinges on cycling through this loop faster than the enemy or by disrupting the enemy's ability to connect those activities efficiently.

His full-blown version had dozens of elements. We need only the core features here.

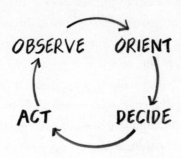

Boyd's model differs starkly from a conventional linear framework in which facts are gathered and analyzed, and then a choice is made. By contrast, actions in his OODA loop stimulate reactions from other parties, which then constitute new data to observe, digest, and further act upon. You can think of his rapid-decision-making process as a wheel within a wheel, running inside the larger strategic cycle of learning, adapting, and influencing that I've stressed throughout the book.

Boyd emphasized two complementary elements of this microlevel learning. *Observing* entails heeding the actions of other parties and assembling that information into a larger mosaic of understanding. *Orienting* then compares what is actually unfolding with prior experience and expectations. Boyd was intent on spotting "mismatches" between expectations, no matter how well-founded, and the resulting reality.

Negotiation is its own kind of fur ball. Offers and demands volley back and forth. What was said just now may contradict whatever was expressed five minutes ago. One issue gets resolved, but then another pops up. At any given moment, it can be hard to know where our counterpart is coming from or who's up and who's down. Even so, there is often underlying order in the chaos of negotiation. But it takes situational awareness to see where we are in the process, and it takes agility to engage other parties effectively.

OBSERVE: WHAT ARE WE LOOKING FOR?

Erin Egan was merely in her midtwenties, but there she was at the bargaining table where a deal worth millions of dollars was being hammered out. She worked for a European industrial giant that deals with General Electric and other megacorporations. It wasn't that Erin was a financial wizard or a precocious engineer. Just a few years earlier, she had graduated with a degree in international affairs from a small liberal arts college. Nor was she highly placed in her organization. Yet her boss soon recognized her uncanny ability to speed-read a room. That's why Erin was often brought along to important negotiations. She wouldn't say anything during the sessions, but when there was a break, the lead negotiator would huddle with her and ask, "Okay, what just happened in there?"

A person like Erin might spot fissures in the other team. "Did you see how their finance person rolled her eyes when the marketing guy was talking?" she'd observe. "They're just not on the same page." Or she might explain why the nos they heard on various proposals could mean different things. "When they refused to lower the front-end payment, they said it flat out and didn't falter. They don't expect to buckle," she could conclude. "But they protested too much about guaranteeing the price for three years. My bet is that they just want us to think they've made a big concession when they finally concede."

It's as if Erin has social sonar, a way of seeing the interpersonal crosscurrents below the surface and the forces that shape their flow. But just as a person with normal vision would struggle to describe color to someone who sees only in shades of gray, Erin can't explain how she spots things that many of us would miss.

Researchers call what Erin does "sense-making." It's the ability to connect the dots and construct a coherent picture. It also requires knowing what constitutes a significant dot and what's irrelevant data. The key lies in looking for relationships among items rather than viewing elements in isolation. In basketball, it's called having court sense. Bob Cousy, the Hall of Fame Boston Celtics player, says, "I just played. The defense tells you what you must do, every time down the floor. For me, it was easy. Maybe that's because I have a vivid imagination."

A clever experiment illustrates how the mind interprets what it sees. Imagine a test where you're given a quick glimpse at a chessboard with randomly placed pieces. You're then asked to re-create the setup from memory. Studies show that most people can perform this task just about as well as an expert player.

But it's a different story if subjects are shown a board from a real game. In that case, masters have near perfect recall, while novices do little better than when the pieces are strewn by chance. Masters succeed because experience has taught them to see the pieces *in relation to one another*. They notice that the white queen is well protected, for example, but also see that a black knight is two moves away from threatening one of her rooks. Those relationships, in turn, are clues to the players' intentions and how the game has developed to that point.

Chess master and writer Graham Burgess says that pattern recognition helps the analytic process and sparks ideas that a player might miss otherwise. "Many blunders, rather than being 'hallucinations' or 'blind spots,' can be explained by the relevant pattern not being recognized." He recalls watching a game where a player seemed to be unlucky, having overlooked something that Graham admits he might have missed as well. But the second time he saw a similar situation, "I would think that they had been a bit careless, and should have seen it coming. Third and fourth time, I would groan, having anticipated the idea a move or two earlier."

Being attentive not only helps us learn about specific moves and strategies but also deepens our pattern recognition skills more generally. As Graham reflects on his own thinking, "Thus, seeing the same idea a few times changed from being something I would not have seen in advance to being an idea I recognized as an inherent possibility in certain types of positions, an idea to be taken into account (to some extent subconsciously) when planning and calculating."

Much of sense-making is context specific and is perfected only through long practice. Newly hatched chicks look like identical balls of yellow fluff to most of us, yet with barely a glance, a professional chicken sexer (I'm not making up this job) can catalog thousands of them a day as males or females. It's a valuable skill, since the earlier the hens can be put on a special diet, the more productive they will be. An expert could point to the subtle differences he sees, but even if we could then recognize them, it would take lots of practice to match the speed and accuracy of the pros.

Military personnel, in turn, try to feel out an enemy's resources and intentions. They speak of identifying surfaces and gaps. Surfaces are hard and solid—the enemy's strengths—while gaps are weak points vulnerable to exploitation. Attacks against surfaces waste energy. Finding or creating gaps enables success.

The opposition will do its best to disguise surfaces and gaps, however, and the passage of time can change their contours. The US Marine Corps's *Warfighting* manual states: "Due to the fluid nature of war, gaps will rarely be permanent and will usually be fleeting. To exploit them demands flexibility and speed."

Negotiation is likewise a process of making sense of a situation and the people on the other side. It takes place on three levels. One is substantive. It's about testing to see what is a real point of resistance and what is a mere bluff. It also involves seeing connections among the issues up for discussion and how your priorities match up with those of other parties. A second level is interpersonal and process focused. It's an appraisal of how well people are engaging one another (or what's getting in the way). The third level is contextual. It's recognizing how larger circumstances influence people's perceptions about their interests and options. Who seems to have the better walkaway? Is time on one person's side rather than on the other's?

Sense-making is thus a holistic linking of microdevelopments and macrotrends. It entails deep engagement with the immediate moment and, at the same time, detached awareness of what came before and what may ensue. Erin's insights about an unfolding negotiation are based on seeing its elements in relation to one another. While the marketing person on the other team was speaking, she was attending to how his own colleagues listened. When she made judgments about which issues were negotiable, they were based on hearing how one *no* compared with another.

ORIENT: HOW SHOULD WE INTERPRET WHAT WE SEE?

Observing and orienting are coupled in Boyd's OODA loop. Although orienting is the second step in the process, it involves reaching back and drawing on experience and expectations to assess what you see in the present.

To get a toehold, you need a theory of the case: a provisional sense of what you could be facing. Does the negotiation present an opportunity for mutual gain, or will it more likely be a toe-to-toe haggle? In transactions that are solely about price, a better result for one party means a worse one for the other, but many more cases have creative potential. Absent strong evidence to the contrary, you should start with the premise that the pie can be expanded through wise trades. The cost of exploring that possibility is small, so don't discard it.

You'll also form expectations about whether your counterpart will be open and trusting, or suspicious and hostile. If you've dealt with the person before, you may have a basis for making a judgment, but bear in mind that his or her circumstances may have changed, for better or worse.

Dealing with a stranger, you may have little to go on, but as a general matter, tilt your expectations toward the optimistic end of the spectrum. A friendly comment is virtually costless. Likewise, disclosing some of your priorities prudently needn't lessen your bargaining power. If such moves aren't reciprocated, you can adjust your approach accordingly.

Others may claim that it's wiser to demonstrate your resolve by starting hard. After softening up the other party, supposedly you can become more cooperative later, if you so desire. I'm skeptical about that approach, however. It gives counterparts little reason to be forthcoming. If you expect someone to be a shark, he's more likely to act like one. Nice doesn't always trump nasty, but consider which approach will give you more flexibility going forward.

The more precisely you define your expectations, positive or negative, the more alert you will be for signs that confirm or contradict those assumptions. In *Streetlights and Shadows: Searching for the Keys to Adaptive Decision Making*, Gary Klein says that complex, ambiguous situations call for having "strong ideas, weakly held." Making a guess forces you to weigh the evidence on hand and see what it would take for you to reverse your judgment. Being specific about your assumptions also reminds you of the risk of being wrong.

Klein adds, "Anticipatory thinking lets us manage our attention so that we are looking in the right places to spot anomalies in the case as they appear." It's not the same thing as prediction. Rather, it's a matter of opening up our minds to various possibilities and how they would manifest themselves.

It's easy to ignore bad news. Consider, for example, this exchange between an airline pilot and his copilot as they waited for the control tower to clear them for takeoff from National Airport outside of Washington, DC, on January 13, 1982. The Air Florida Boeing 737 had been deiced earlier, but flights were backed up, and freezing rain was still falling.

> **Copilot:** Anti-ice?
> **Pilot:** Off. [*This internal device should have been on, but the first officer doesn't challenge him. Later the pilot says, "real cold, real cold."*]
> **Copilot:** Let's check the ice on those tops [wings] again, since we've been sitting here awhile.
> **Captain:** No. I think we get to go in a minute.
> **Copilot:** [*As they are rolling down the runway*] God, look at that thing. That don't seem right, does it? [*Then he repeats the comment, apparently referring to ground speed.*] Uh, that's not right.
> **Pilot:** Yes, there it is, eighty.
> **Copilot:** Naw, I don't think that's right . . . Ah, maybe it is.
> **Pilot:** Hundred and twenty.
> **Copilot:** I don't know. [*There is the sound of the plane straining unsuccessfully to gain altitude.*]
> **Pilot:** Stalling. We're falling.

Copilot: Larry, we're going down!
Captain: I know it.

Those were their last words just before Air Florida flight 90 crashed into the top of a major bridge and plunged into the Potomac River. Both men were killed, along with seventy-six others on board or on the ground. The black box recording is an example of a mismatch between hopes and commitments on the one hand, and grim reality on the other.

National Airport had been closed by heavy snow. Even after it reopened, flights were backed up. The doomed plane had been deiced at the gate, but conditions were so bad that the ground service tow couldn't get traction. Reverse thrust on the engines proved futile as well. Finally, a vehicle with chains got the plane moving. It then had to wait in a long line for almost an hour before getting to the takeoff runway. According to the subsequent National Transportation Safety Board review, the crew was aware of snow and ice buildup.

Why, then, in spite of mounting signs of danger, did the pilot still attempt to take off? The best guess is that he didn't want to prolong what had been a frustrating delay by going back for more deicing. Intent on leaving, he shut out any information that would disrupt his original plan.

He also shut out the fact that he was engaged in a negotiation with his copilot. He didn't hear the latter's remark about the wing as a suggestion to turn back, nor did he understand that questions about the instrument readings were a plea to abort takeoff. The pilot failed to put the pieces together and make sense of the conversation as a whole. And there may also have been failure on the copilot's part to recognize that he would have to be much more insistent to get through to his higher-ranking captain.

Contrast the Potomac case with the miraculous landing of US Airways flight 1549 in New York's Hudson River on January 15, 2009. What was supposed to be a routine flight quickly became an emergency when a bird strike took out both engines minutes after takeoff. The tape of Captain Chesley "Sully" Sullenberger's communication with air-traffic controllers is a riveting example of the tough-mindedness that Colonel Boyd insisted upon.

Sullenberger first reported that he had lost thrust and would return to New York's LaGuardia Airport. Mere seconds later, he was told that a runway was being cleared for him, but the pilot replied, "Unable."

The controller apparently still hadn't grasped the urgency of the situation and offered a different runway. Sullenberger answered, "I'm not sure if we can make any runway. What's over to our right? Anything in New Jersey, maybe Teterboro?"

The controller confirmed Teterboro's availability and identified a runway, but Sullenberger saw that he was losing speed and altitude. "We can't do it," he radioed.

Again the controller's awareness was a beat behind, so he asked, "Okay, which runway would you like at Teterboro?"

"We're gonna be in the Hudson," the pilot replied, his mind fixed on landing the plane safely.

Sullenberger recognized the mismatch between what he expected and the peril he was now facing. As his Airbus A320-216 lost altitude, he just as swiftly accepted that the fallback he would have preferred—landing at Teterboro—wouldn't work either. He wasted no time thinking about what might have been or how he might be second-guessed later. As his alternatives dwindled, his entire attention was directed at doing his best in a harrowing situation. Sullenberger executed a water landing that was smooth enough to keep the aircraft intact and floating. While passengers and crew waited on the wings for rescue boats, the captain himself remained inside to inspect the plane from front to back to make sure that everyone else had exited safely.

DECIDE: WHEN MUST WE CHOOSE?

Observing and orienting set up deciding and acting. But even if you perform the first two steps well, there will likely be ambiguity about how other parties will respond to what you choose to do and say. If you're thinking about making a concession, can you be sure that your counterpart will reciprocate? Or if you issue a threat, will the other side back down or respond in kind?

In their book *Make Your Own Luck: 12 Practical Steps to Taking Smarter Risks in Business*, Eileen Shapiro and Howard Stevenson say that "acting in the face of uncertainty is scary, because you are acting before all the facts are in—though in truth you are always acting before all the facts are in, whether you are doing what you planned to do or making a shift based on new information." Deciding to do one thing can eliminate other possibilities. Either you put the first offer on the table or wait for the other side to lay down its demand, but you can't do both. Psychological research on "loss aversion" shows that trimming options feels painful.

Vacillation is a cardinal sin in the US Marine Corps. According to David Freedman, author of *Corps Business: The 30 Management Principles of the U.S. Marines,* the marines regard it as even "worse than making a mediocre decision, because a mediocre decision, especially if swiftly rendered and executed, at least stands a chance." There's a time to develop your options, but there comes a time to exercise them. The more alternatives you keep open, the more factors there are to analyze and manage. Even the greatest chess players don't contemplate all the eventualities. There are just too many. A player looking forward eight moves would confront more options than there are stars in the galaxy.

Sometimes you can hedge, of course. Even when the US Marines have only a short time to plan for combat, they prepare for both the most likely and the most dangerous courses of action the enemy might take. Having a bump plan in reserve prepares them for the probable turn of events and also the most threatening.

A bias for action is a counterweight to inertia. I'm talking about an inclination, not an ironclad rule to leap before looking. You shouldn't be rash. Sometimes waiting and seeing are best. Nevertheless, your general tendency should be to press ahead even when some important facts are still hazy. The test of that proposition is spelling out when taking action would be *un*wise or premature. Specifically, standing pat makes sense provided that:

- It's costless. That is, if all your options remain open and you won't lose credibility.
- You believe that time is on your side and your options will improve.
- There's a good chance that by learning more, you can make a wiser choice.
- Sleeping on the decision will make you more comfortable with your choice.

On the other hand, the *less* true that one or more of those factors appears to be, the more likely it's time to take a deep breath and move ahead.

Making a decision is invigorating. It deepens commitment and heightens awareness. This is true in many domains. Academy Award winner Russell Crowe is fierce about making choices when creating a movie character for himself: getting down an accent, sensing how the person would move, what he'd wear, and how he'd look. "As [director Martin] Scorsese said, 'Man, you don't get anywhere until you make a decision,'" he once recalled. "So start making decisions quickly, you know. But be open and lucid enough and fluid enough to change your mind if you prove yourself wrong. Okay?"

ACT: WHAT SHOULD WE LEARN BY TAKING ACTION?

Deciding and acting give you the edge in framing choices for your counterparts, rather than their framing the choices for you. Stirring the pot also can dispel uncertainty. Colonel Boyd drew on Napoléon for the proposition that "early tactics, without apparent design, operate in a fluid, adaptable manner to uncover, expand, and exploit adversaries' vulnerabilities and weakness." Smoking out other parties' positions and intentions works, however, only if you are able to make sense of what occurs as a result of your actions.

Jenny Rudolph conducts research at Massachusetts General Hospital on how doctors diagnose problems and prescribe treatment in cases where time is short and information is incomplete and ambiguous. Her findings are both instructive and unsettling. One of her experiments was set in an operating room with residents training to be anesthesiologists. Rather than putting an actual patient at risk, Rudolph used a highly realistic mannequin wired up to monitors that registered simulated pulse, blood pressure, and respiration. The twenty-nine-year-old "patient" had been prepped and sedated for an emergency appendectomy, but suddenly it developed problems breathing.

Rudolph observed the spontaneous decision-making strategies these doctors used. She cataloged four types of practitioners:

1. Stalled.
Two of the thirty-nine doctors in the study didn't know where to begin. Their patients died.

2. Fixated.
Eleven doctors made a quick and sensible diagnosis—only it was wrong in this particular case. They stuck with it even as the patient's condition was deteriorating. These patients died as well.

3. Diagnostic Vagabonds.
Seventeen others avoided this trap. They were open minded but too much so. They jumped from one possibility to another so quickly that they could not identify what treatment was working and what was not. None of their patients survived either.

4. Adaptive Problem Solvers.
The nine remaining doctors initially reached the same conclusion as did the "fixated" group, but unlike them, they treated it as a platform for further testing and not a certainty. Unlike the vagabonds, they didn't drop a diagnosis until there was clear cause for doing so. Seven of the nine adaptive problem solvers found the real cause of the patient's problem before she "expired."

It is sobering that the vast majority of subjects—all smart, well-educated people—were unable to diagnose and treat a problem in a systematic, practical way. There's little evidence that negotiators do much better. Having seen and talked with many of them over the years, my sense is that they fall into similar categories. Some have trouble getting started. They're not stalled, exactly—events may push them along—but they're largely reactive. They don't choose a course of action. Instead, the other party sets the course.

Then there are the fixated types. A negotiation colleague of mine describes such people as "often wrong, never in doubt." Dealing with them is frustrating. They make their plans, charge ahead, and keep on charging even when it should be clear that it's time to change direction. French philosopher Émile Chartier observed, "Nothing is more dangerous than an idea when it is the only one you have."

By contrast, negotiation vagabonds pinball their way through the process. They have no apparent method for choosing a path or weighing alternatives. They overreact to whatever they saw or heard most recently. They may be conciliatory one moment and hostile the next. They may seem poised to say yes to an agreement but at the last minute chase after another deal.

Successful negotiators are flexible but not erratic. They start with a clear hypothesis about how to approach a case but then test it. If their initial assumption is basically sound, each cycle of observing and orienting helps them recalibrate their position so that their strategic and tactical adjustments become progressively smaller. But if their expectations are off the mark, they recognize the mismatch and let them go in the spirit of Gary Klein's advice about having strong ideas held weakly.

If I could pick whom I'd want to deal with in an important negotiation, it would be an adaptive learner. I couldn't hope to dominate or manipulate her—she'd be too smart for that—but she'd be someone with whom I could work. She'd see that I was ready to get down to business. And like Erin Egan, she'd recognize when I really mean no on a given issue and not waste time trying to get me to bend. Instead, the adaptive learner would reorient and look for another way to attack the problem. Of course, I'd have to be at my best too. I wouldn't want to degrade my counterpart's ability to make good decisions—negotiation is different from combat, in this respect—but I'd want my OODA loop to be at least as fast as hers.

It's easy to recite the observe-orient-decide-act mantra, but each step must be executed well. Failing to spot a mismatch subverts the whole process. So does indecision. You have to monitor your own behavior to make sure that it aligns with your intentions. Are you saying no too readily? (Or yes, for that matter?) Are you talking at the expense of listening? Are you too comfortable? Do you need to push harder or risk floating an off-the-wall idea? You may then pledge to be more curious and open minded (or to have more backbone, if that's what is lacking).

It's hard to face up to our own shortcomings, of course, and all too easy to be overconfident about our ability to observe and learn. A leader who ruled his country for more than forty years put it well: "The truly strange thing in your lives is that you not only fail, but you fail to learn your lesson . . . No matter how much your beliefs betray you, this is never accepted by you. You are distinguished by your inability to recognize the truth, no matter how irrefutable."

It is one thing to recognize this truth in the abstract, but it's another to live by it. The writer was the Libyan leader Mu'ammar Gadafi, who several years later refused political asylum even as his regime was collapsing around him. Gaddafi was captured, beaten, and killed by rebel forces.

PLANS VERSUS PLANNING

What happens to strategy if everything is in flux? General Dwight Eisenhower, architect of the D-day invasion that paved the way to an Allied victory in World War II, said famously, "Plans are worthless." What's forgotten is that he added, "Planning is everything."

That's not a contradiction. In any context, a well-conceived planning process sharpens objectives, exposes possible obstacles, and illuminates potential paths, even though the exact route may not be determined until the interaction is well under way. Plans can only be provisional, whether they are for combat, launching a new business, making a deal, or resolving a dispute. In both warfare and negotiation, the fog of uncertainty, unknowns, and changing circumstances make anticipating every possibility impossible. US Marine Corps doctrine states:

"The further ahead we think, the less our actual influence becomes. Therefore, the further ahead we consider, the less precision we should attempt to impose. Looking ahead thus becomes less a matter of influence and more a matter of laying the groundwork for possible future actions. As events approach and our ability to influence them grows, we have already developed an appreciation for the situation and how we want to shape it."

This reality complicates coordination and planning in the military, especially communication between high-level officers who devise strategy and troops in the field who must execute it. A similar challenge occurs in business between senior managers who create marketing campaigns or oversee procurement, and the salespeople and purchasing agents who conduct the actual deals.

The solution in the military has been to distinguish means and ends when giving orders. The Marine Corps's *Warfighting* manual states that every mission has two parts: the task and the intent behind it. "The task denotes *what* is to be done, and sometimes *when* and *where*; the intent explains *why*. Of the two, the *intent* is predominant."

When changed circumstances make a specific task obsolete, soldiers can look to its underlying purpose and devise another way of accomplishing it. "It is this freedom for initiative that permits the high tempo of operations that we desire. Uninhibited by restrictions from above, subordinates can adapt their actions to the changing situation. They inform the commander what they have done, but they do not wait for permission."

Officers are drilled to make their statements of intent clear and concise. For instance, intent might be expressed as "control the bridge in order to prevent the enemy from escaping across the river." An ambiguous statement could be misconstrued to justify an action contrary to what the commander actually meant or leave troops baffled about what to do next. Soldiers are told to ask for clear directions if none have been given.

Karl Weick, a renowned organizational theorist at the University of Michigan, has adapted the concept of commander's intent to leadership in general. Indeed, his distillation of what leaders need to convey instructions is itself a model of clarity:

Situation:	Here's what I think we face.
Task:	Here's what I think we should do.
Intent:	Here's why.
Concerns:	Here's what we should watch for.
Feedback:	Now, talk to me.

Negotiating on behalf of others—your company, organization, or client—is exasperating when people whose interests you're trying to serve can't explain their priorities coherently. While that may be their failing, it can be yours, too, if you don't press for clarification. Likewise, if you ask others to negotiate for you, state your underlying intent so that they can improvise intelligently when circumstances change. To sharpen your description of what you want to achieve, be explicit about what you *don't* want to happen. Often when you negotiate, of course, you will report only to yourself. When selling a house or seeking a new job, don't confuse plans with planning, or short-term means for long-term ends. Remembering your fundamental intent will allow you to employ a robust strategy.

On June 5, 1944, the eve of the Normandy landings, Eisenhower radioed a stirring order to American forces in Britain waiting to cross the treacherous English Channel. "You are about to embark on the great crusade," he said. "The tide has turned! The free men of the world are marching to victory!"

Tucked into his wallet, however, was a second message, which he had scrawled on flimsy notepaper and was holding in reserve. "Our landings in the Cherbourg and Havre area have failed to gain a satisfactory foothold, and I have withdrawn the troops," it said. "If any blame or fault attaches to the attempt, it is mine alone."

Fortunately for the world, Ike never had to deliver that second message, but privately he allowed for the possibility of failure. In spite of unprecedented preparation—the massing of ships, planes, armament, and hundreds of thousands of military personnel—he knew that success was not guaranteed.

LEARNING ON THE GROUND

In conflicts today, soldiers must be prepared both to fight hostile forces and to negotiate with local officials, contractors, and citizens caught in the cross fire. In 1997, Marine Corps general Charles Krulak described the scope of future military missions:

"In one moment in time, our service members will be feeding and clothing displaced refugees, providing humanitarian assistance. In the next moment, they will be holding two warring tribes apart—conducting peacekeeping operations—and, finally, they will be fighting a highly lethal midintensity battle—all in the same day . . . all within three city blocks. It will be what we call the 'three-block war.'"

In 2007 Major Leonard Lira was sent to Iraq for a second tour. The task of his unit—the 2-14 Cavalry—was securing Taji, a town just north of Baghdad. Lira and other senior officers were told to stop the flow of insurgents transporting arms, explosive devices, and suicide bombers. They concluded that security could more likely be achieved by promoting reconciliation in that area rather than using lethal means. One of the army-sponsored projects was improving local irrigation systems so that farmers would have income and city dwellers would have much-needed food. Experts from the US Department of Agriculture engineered an efficient design. Lira's unit had the job of getting local factions to work together to get the system built.

Prior to deployment, members of Lira's unit were given negotiation training. They had been taught about zones of agreement, BATNAs (walkaway options), and other familiar concepts. Staff had also practiced role playing exercises. "Although the training was extensive," Lira said later, "none of it adequately prepared the unit for what it encountered in Iraq."

Lira had initially organized forums to foster collaboration. "All of the tribes made public declarations of reconciliation," he said, "but away from the forum table, they would return to their entrenched positions and try to exclude each other from the local committee." The new irrigation ditches were often blocked or sabotaged. Violent conflicts sometimes ensued.

At first Al Qaeda in Iraq was blamed. It turned out, though, that most of the trouble was caused by certain farmers who were trying to squeeze out competitors by cutting off their water supply. Lira's team had been working with "Negotiation 1.0 tools," as he termed them, but the simple "linear, lockstep, checklist" prescriptions just didn't apply in the complex and fast-changing environment they faced. Lira turned to other frameworks to deal with planning in dynamic contexts. "Once we gained the rest of the story on why the water wasn't flowing," he explained, "we were able to help the local reconciliation council and city government lead a negotiation process to allow the irrigation canals to function correctly."

This change in negotiation strategy exemplifies double-loop learning. It involves rapid OODA assessment of your micromoves and their consequences. But on a second, higher level, it entails critical reflection on whether you are looking at a problem in the right way. Lira had the discipline to dispense with his Negotiation 1.0 tool kit and develop a more sophisticated approach. The negotiation practices of the 2-14 Cavalry became a model for army units elsewhere.

Military negotiators also have to be agile in the moment. In 2003, in the early days of the war in Iraq, Lieutenant Colonel Chris Hughes led a unit of soldiers to meet with Grand Ayatollah Ali al-Sistani in Najaf to help build local support for the American effort. A growing crowd of civilians was anxious about the soldiers' intentions and alarmed that they might be about to violate the sanctity of the nearby mosque. Rumors, perhaps started by agitators, flew quickly that the Americans were there to arrest the ayatollah.

To Dan Baum, a *New Yorker* writer watching on television in the

States, it looked like a disaster in the making. "The Iraqis were shrieking, frantic with rage," he wrote later. "From the way the lens was lurching, the cameraman seemed as frightened as the soldiers. This is it, I thought. A shot will come from somewhere, the Americans will open fire, and the world will witness the My Lai massacre of the Iraq war."

But that didn't happen. Hughes and his soldiers didn't try to force their way down the packed street. Nor was a single shot fired. Instead, Hughes stepped forward, holding his rifle high but pointed downward. "Smile," he said to his troops. "Don't point your weapons at 'em. Relax." He then ordered them to kneel and point their weapons down, as he had done. When the tension abated, he said, "Calmly stand up and move backward. Continue smiling." The soldiers withdrew. Hughes bowed his head slightly to the crowd and let communication with the ayatollah wait for another day.

Hughes hadn't expected to negotiate with an angry mob that day, nor had he ever been taught the specific gesture of having his troops kneel down. But keeping the purpose of his mission paramount—earning the confidence of the ayatollah and his supporters—enabled him to improvise in the moment. The mosque was the holiest Shia shrine in Iraq. Violence there could incite massive opposition to the US-led coalition. "It was a very deliberate turn," Hughes explained later. "If somebody shot a round in the air, there was going to be some sort of massacre." Chris Hughes (now a general) observed the escalating scene, reoriented himself, and acted with patience, respect, and resolve.

KEY POINTS

- Observe, orient, decide, and act—again and again and again.
- Watch out for mismatches between what you expected and what's actually unfolding.
- Have a bias for action from start to finish.
- Prepare for what's most likely to transpire and for what would be most challenging.

PART 3

Managing the Process

Consider Northern Ireland, where the ancient conflict known as the Troubles ended, when longtime enemies came together to form a power-sharing government. This was almost eight hundred years after Britain began its domination of Ireland, eighty-six years after the partition of Ireland, thirty-eight years after the British Army formally began its most recent mission in Ireland, eleven years after the peace talks began, and nine years after the peace agreement was signed. In the negotiations which led up to that agreement, we had seven hundred days of failure and one day of success.

—SENATOR GEORGE MITCHELL, SPECIAL ENVOY TO NORTHERN IRELAND

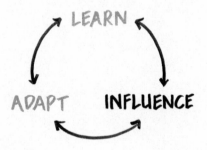

[8] Openings

Katie Stevenson was toying with a career change. She had gone to work for *Hiking* magazine right out of college. The people there were fine, and she enjoyed the mix of editorial and administrative work. The pay was ridiculously low, however, and there was little prospect for advancement.

A self-described geek, Katie developed a web-hosting business on the side to supplement her income. Within a couple of years, it required full-time attention, so she left the magazine. When her new venture continued to grow, she hired freelancers to handle some of the work. The money was better, though not great, and the hours proved grueling.

As a result, Katie looked into an opening at Pullman Press, a small publishing company she admired. She doubted that the job would be a step up, though, as the firm was advertising for an information technology specialist to upgrade its internal network and automated ordering system. Katie had the necessary technical skill, but she wanted a position with more management responsibility and creative potential.

She went ahead with an interview nevertheless, thinking that she'd at least expand her contacts. As it happened, Katie hit it off with the Pullman people. She was frank about her reluctance to take a backroom job and went on to describe what she wanted to do: namely, find a place where she could use social media to deliver content and tap into online communities.

The Pullman team was excited about her ideas and impressed by her obvious ability to implement them. Midway through, Katie realized that instead of the casual getting-to-know-you chat she had expected, she was in an important negotiation. Butterflies stirred in her stomach. This new job they were scoping seemed almost too good to be true. "I wish I wasn't so casual," she told herself. "I'd better not mess this up."

Katie's mood tumbled, but everybody else still looked relaxed and pleased. She thought to herself that it was easy to be agreeable so long as everything was broad brush, but working out the details would be tricky. Turning the job into a more senior position than was advertised would raise organizational issues. Who'd report to whom? What resources would be shifted into this new initiative? Soon they'd have to tackle the awkward matter of money.

Everything worked out eventually. It took three follow-up meetings, but Katie got a terrific job at Pullman, where she is prospering. But now, five years later, she still describes her first realization that she was in a negotiation as feeling as if "a cloud was passing over the sun." To that point, the conversation had been warm and easy. Suddenly she felt a chill.

It was the same people in the same room, exploring the same possibilities. The only change was all in Katie's head. Having a job on the line cast the conversation in shadows. When it seemed that there was nothing to lose, she'd been herself. When the stakes got higher, she started worrying about the impression she was making. "How hard can I push on pay," she asked herself, "when I don't have a clue what these guys are getting?" Sure, the Pullman people all seemed congenial, but did some of them have private agendas?

The irony, of course, is that Katie had gotten that far by being open, engaged, and confident. Had she been guarded and anxious from the start, the possibility of creating a new position might never have arisen. **Paradoxically, seeing something as a negotiation can make it harder to reach agreement.** It colors our perceptions of people and influences how we relate to them. That's true whether a negotiation emerges from a conversation, as it did with Katie, or our intent from the outset is making a deal. The impressions and attitudes that are triggered when we realize we are negotiating can have lasting impact on the process— sometimes for the better, though often for the worse. Yes, it's possible to get off to a poor start and regain our balance later. And we can begin well but run out of energy. But openings matter. Negotiation is challenging enough without making it harder on ourselves by starting on the wrong foot.

WHO, WHAT, AND HOW

This chapter offers a fine-grained analysis of openings. We'll pay special attention to the dance of negotiation, how what one person says influences whatever his counterpart says next. In the early moments, three important things take place—engaging, framing, and norming—and they happen simultaneously.

Engaging defines the *who* of negotiation. It's about identity, roles, and relationships. As social psychologists and neuroscientists have demonstrated, we form judgments of other people ultrafast (just as they do of us). On a visceral level, we label someone as friend or foe. We also measure power and status. At the first hello, we reckon whether dealing with them is going to be easy or hard. The less we know about particular people, the more our impressions are driven by our personality and circumstance. The nature of negotiation in particular can tilt us toward negative assessments. If we're unsure about whether to trust another party, we may read ambiguous comments and behavior as hostile.

ENGAGING: DEFINING THE RELATIONSHIP
FRIEND OR FOE?
EASY OR HARD?
UP OR DOWN?

Framing, in turn, is the *what* of negotiation. It's the way the parties define the task. Are we pursuing a partnership, resolving a conflict, or simply haggling? Is this a matter of high principle or is it run of the mill? Such questions can't be answered unilaterally. They often must be negotiated, though this is rarely done explicitly. The *who* of negotiation—how the parties see each other relationally—is bound up in *what* they think they are addressing.

FRAMING: DEFINING THE TASK

A WIN-LOSE CONTEST?
A COLLABORATIVE EFFORT?
SOMETHING IN BETWEEN?

Finally, norming is the *how* of negotiation. It's the way that parties establish the tone and pace of the process. The *how* is likewise tightly linked to the *who* and the *what*, the manner in which parties relate to one another and define the task at hand. How people actually interact sometimes doesn't square with their intentions or self-image. Mismatches undermine performance.

NORMING: DEFINING THE PROCESS

HAGGLE GAME?
CREATIVE EXPLORATION?
WAIT-AND-SEE?

You negotiate *how to negotiate* each and every time you sit down at the bargaining table. That was brought home to me by a project a colleague and I did several years ago. We videotaped real estate professionals negotiating a long-term deal involving a shopping center about to be built. Participants played the role of either the local developer or a national retailer who might anchor the new mall. We stipulated that most provisions in the agreement had been worked out, but the parties were still deadlocked over the use, assignment, and subletting provisions. The developer wanted strict control over how the leased space would be used, so that the anchor tenant wouldn't compete with smaller stores in the mall. In turn, the tenant insisted on having flexibility to adapt to changing market conditions. Our participants had been called in to try to bridge this gap.

My colleague and I sought to analyze how negotiators tackle tough issues over the contract language that would define the parties' respective rights and responsibilities. We wanted people to be themselves, so our instructions were simple: Figure out what you want to get, we told them, and figure out how to get it.

What follows are verbatim transcripts of the opening moments of two separate pairs of professionals negotiating the same lease. As you'll see, sometimes one party will interrupt the other. Other times a speaker will begin with one thought and then jump to another, without completing his sentence smoothly. That's the way that people talk. More important, you'll also see that the two pairs negotiated very differently. Reading text on the printed page isn't the same as hearing tone of voice or seeing body language, of course, but the contrasting dialogue is striking.

Their different approaches can't be explained by culture. These four participants were all white middle-aged male lawyers from the Boston area. Instead, the key variable was how they viewed the negotiation process—specifically, the way that they managed the *who, what,* and *how* of opening. We took participants to an on-campus studio and had them sit at a small, round table. Then we flipped on the cameras and left the room. They took it from there. Here's the first pair:

Tenant A: Welcome to my office.

Developer A: How are you, John? [*Half standing to shake the tenant's hand.*]

Tenant A: Just fine. Good to see you again.

Developer A: You have nice offices here.

Tenant A: Thank you, thank you. You ought to come out here more often.

Developer A: Very impressive. Listen, I understand you have a meeting in about forty-five minutes, so we should try to get through these clauses as quickly as we can.

Tenant A: Uh-hmm.

Developer A: Frankly, I understand these are the only clauses left to finalize in the deal. It's important to us to get it closed. We're ready to start construction.

Tenant A: Uh-hmm.

Developer A: We have everything set, all our permits, land all under control. Ah, and obviously you're the key tenant. We need you.

Tenant A: Well, we're well aware of that.

Developer A: I know that. On the other hand, if we can't do a deal, we're going to have to look for somebody else. But I see no reason we can't reach agreement on these two clauses. I guess as a starting point, you've managed to . . . [*pause*] Did you draft this lease?

Tenant A: I had a hand in it, but our senior corporate counsel did the yeoman's work.

Developer A: Boy, I must say they've come up with the shortest use-and-assignment-and-subletting clause I've ever seen. And ah . . .

Tenant A: Oh, I've seen 'em shorter, but that's all right.

Developer A: Well, maybe if you eliminated it entirely, it would have been the only thing, but—

Tenant A: I'd be glad to.

Developer A: Well . . .

Tenant A: Why don't we do that, then we can all go home and go to lunch.

Developer A: I think that we'd have a good lease. The only problem is I don't think it would be financeable, and I don't think we'd get any other tenants. And we don't want you in there freestanding. You don't want to be in there freestanding. So I think there's . . . I'm sure you've before . . . you've done lots of other deals where there are satellite tenants and have responded to their needs. We've certainly done a lot of other deals that way. This is going to be a spectacular regional mall. So let's try to get into it and see if we can't reach agreement.

Tenant A: You know what our position is. You and I aren't going to argue as to what's financeable or not, but if you think that you can finance a lease with a blackout clause, then the use-and-assignment clause isn't going to cause any more problems. I wish we shared your enthusiasm for the market. We think it's going to be a good market, but we're not willing to take the risk to the extent that you are. You're the developer. It's a natural risk for you. We're willing to go in and anchor your mall. And as you said, you need us—

Developer A: No question.

Tenant A: —maybe more than we need you.

This conversation was all unscripted. Ostensibly, these negotiators were laying the foundation for a business relationship that would run a decade or more. Yet in a mere two minutes, the developer states that he's ready to have someone else anchor his mall, and the tenant answers that's fine with him. From start to finish, there's a rat-a-tat-tat of aggressive questions and snide comebacks.

When I show the video clip in class, I ask people where it went wrong. Often somebody says it's when the developer talks about finding another tenant. But then someone else usually points out how that comment is a defensive response to the tenant's flatly saying that he's "well aware" that the developer needs him. As one viewer put it, "The poor developer extends an olive branch, but the tenant whacks him with it."

Others go back even earlier, noting that the parties rush through any pleasantries and jump right into talking about the project. A few are turned off by what they hear as a presumptuous tone when the developer claims it's necessary to get through "these clauses as quickly as we can," since they have only forty-five minutes in which to negotiate. These points are all valid. And they're easy to make if we have the luxury of reflection, after stopping the video or rereading the transcript. If we had time to think, we'd hope to be more adroit ourselves.

The problem here is more than the sum of the flippant remarks, however. At the heart of it, neither party seems mindful of where the conversation should go. They get caught up in verbal skirmishing, each one intent on topping whatever the other one just said. And remember, we didn't tell anyone to be antagonistic. These negotiators stumbled into that behavior.

Just look at the long statements that each party makes near the end of the segment. They're odes to negativity. The developer manages to squeeze a quartet of "don't"s into a mere ten seconds and throws in a "problem" for good measure. Predictably, the tenant responds in kind, countering that there's no point in "arguing" whether the lease would be financeable. "You know what our position is," he says.

In this brief opening segment, the parties have resolved the *who* question: they will be foes, and the relationship won't be easy. While they're still jostling over power—who's up and who's down—the prospective tenant seems to be winning the battle. As to framing *what* this negotiation entails, for them it's about whose contract language will prevail. And in regard to setting norms for *how* they will interact, both parties are playing contradict-and-challenge, though neither one may have consciously decided to do so.

This confrontation wasn't inevitable, however. Yes, the participants had tough issues to resolve, but we taped other negotiators who collaborated successfully (again, with no instruction from us). The best of them were natural improvisers. Contrast the interaction between the two we just met and this second pair:

Developer B: Well, Mike, we've given you a tour of the new space. Why don't we see if we can get down to the business at hand that was dumped on both of us in the past two weeks? [*Pause.*]

Tenant B: Well, it looks like we're fairly far along with this lease. At least that's what I was informed, but they leave the tough part for us, Tom.

Developer B: Right, right. That is either a sign of how well we are doing or how poorly we are doing—

Tenant B: [*Laughs.*]

Developer B: —within our respective organizations. One of the things that I did here, and I just want to . . . and you've done enough of these deals all over the country to have a fair sense of where we're coming from, and probably done 'em from both sides. The last response, as I understand it (it may have been the guy on our side who didn't want to take long notes), was, I guess what—we're down to use, assignment, and subletting. Which is it. And got a great response, a good negotiating response last time: company policy.

Tenant B: Right, right, company policy.

Developer B: As I think ought to be indicative of what you and I found in the lease—which is a picture of your leverage . . . If we can work out particular problems you've got, no problem. I just can't, you know, have you run a Chandler Warehouse in there—

Tenant B: Right.

Developer B: —when I've got sixty or seventy tenants counting on your sterling name coming in. What . . . what can you help me with? What sort of thing is behind the company policy line?

Tenant B: Well, the clause that's in the lease right now is, I guess, our standard clause.

Developer B: It's great. I love it from your point of view.

Tenant B: It certainly is a good one. The, ah . . . and it, of course, is designed to give us flexibility, obviously. Our concerns are typical concerns regarding changes in circumstances and having the necessary flexibility. But I understand that you have counterconcerns that make this difficult from your perspective. I guess since I haven't been in the prior negotiations, and I understand you haven't either—

Developer B: Right.

Tenant B: —we probably have to try to understand the concerns of the two parties. And I was interested in what particular problems you foresaw with this clause at this mall. And then maybe we can work through it from there.

I've viewed these clips countless times but am still struck by how different this second opening is. What might sound at first like light banter is, on closer look, the negotiators' way of getting in sync. In the two minutes it took the first pair to get into a tussle, these other two have their suit coats off and are set to solve the practical problems facing their respective companies.

In a sense, both pairs negotiated how they would negotiate, but only the second did this well. They found a way to talk *with* each other, not *at* each other, as in the first case. They did so implicitly. Neither negotiator in the second pair said, "I think we should use a collaborative, problem-solving approach. Don't you agree?" Such a question is off-putting, as it seems to compel just one reasonable answer.

Rather than speaking in the abstract, developer B enacts what he proposes right at the start by characterizing "the business at hand that was dumped on both of us."

His statement presumes that he and his counterpart have much in common and are engaged in the same task. Then, having lobbed the ball into the tenant's court, he stops for a beat and waits to hear the response. After a brief pause, tenant B follows the "Yes, and" rule of improv comics and builds on the opening comment: "Well, it looks like we're fairly far along with this lease. At least that's what I was informed, but they leave the tough part for us, Tom."

Hearing that, developer B grins and adds a "Yes, and" himself by saying, "That is either a sign of how well we are doing or how poorly we are doing within our respective organizations." His crack prompts a knowing laugh from the would-be tenant. In just seconds, they are off and running.

Engaging is inherently a mutual process. In this exchange, the parties have agreed that either they'll play the heroes here, rescuing the deal from disaster, or they'll both be the garbagemen who clean up the mess left by the earlier negotiators. This shared attitude is reinforced by their positive language. (Note, for instance, tenant B's reminder that "we're fairly far along" and developer B's concurrence, "Right, right.")

In the same spirit, these two negotiators call each other Tom and Mike. They also favor the plural *we* to the singular *I* and *you*. By contrast, developer A and tenant A mention each other's name only once, and their use of the singular pronoun widens the gap between them. Each attributes motives to the other. Perhaps developer A is correct when he asserts, "You don't want to be in there freestanding," but nobody likes to be told what he thinks or wants.

Zeroing in on grammar may seem like nitpicking, but the language that we use influences how other people see us. It would be silly to claim that we can win friends and influence strangers just by dropping their names into every other sentence, Dale Carnegie to the contrary. But those pronouns in particular signal how people regard a relationship. *I* and *you* say one thing, while *we* and *us* say quite another.

The second pair of real estate negotiators also swapped flattery and little jokes. More subtly, they mirrored each other's posture and mannerisms. Within moments, they were doing serious work. Whereas the first pair was out of sync from the beginning, trading assertions and challenges back and forth. The one thing that the two agreed on—and agreed upon early—was seeing each other as foes. Once such impressions form, it's hard to discard them.

The two pairs also framed their task (the *what* of negotiation) differently. The first two negotiators acted as if their job was to pound stakes in the ground and defend their positions. (Indeed, the tenant uses that exact word.) They never inquire about underlying interests or disclose their own priorities, for that matter. They soon get into their own kind of sync by falling into a game of me-against-you. It's doubtful that either guy meant to get into a wrestling match. Each may picture himself as a cooperative negotiator but blame the other person for the friction here. If so, each may be half right, as neither one seemed to be thinking, "Is this conversation going where I want it to?"

As for the latter two, I can't say that their collaborative behavior was consciously orchestrated. Maybe yes, maybe no. But in the video, both parties are clearly more attentive to how their relationship is taking shape. The talk about the problem being dumped in both their laps helped establish a bond. It also set up their predecessors as useful foils to play against. In defining the task before them, these negotiators aligned themselves against the problem rather than against each other.

Pair B also attended to a third aspect of openings: establishing norms for going forward, namely the *how* of negotiation. Unlike developer A, who asked bluntly, "Did you draft this lease?" developer B used humor to depersonalize the issues. Note how he dismisses the tenant's original proposal with the remark, "I love it from your point of view" and then asks earnestly, "What sort of thing is behind the company policy line?"

That's when the banter stops and the substantive work begins. Tenant B answers the specific question by explaining that the draft language was designed to give his company flexibility to deal with changes in circumstances. He acknowledges that the developer may have counterconcerns. Then he goes further by suggesting that they lay out the practical interests of the parties before reviewing specific language for the lease: "I guess since I haven't been in the prior negotiations, and I understand you haven't either, we probably have to try to understand the concerns of the two parties."

No one has rattled a saber—or made a concession, for that matter. No one has tried to justify his position. Instead, tenant B continues by inquiring about "what particular problems you foresaw with this clause at this mall. And then maybe we can work through it from here." They are able to advance the process because of what they accomplished in defining the relationship and the task.

Note how the first pair gives almost no attention to process. The two just wing it. The sole exception comes just fifteen seconds after the men sit down. The landlord thanks the tenant for a tour of the latter's offices and then says, "Listen, I understand you have a meeting in about forty-five minutes, so we should try to get through these clauses as quickly as we can."

When I stop the video at a later spot for class discussion, students criticize that remark as being pushy. They feel it comes too soon, before there's been any attempt to build rapport. I ask them what this fellow could do, though, given that time is short and there are important issues to resolve. If you're pressed for time yourself, how should you make that clear at the outset without being provocative?

Viewers have good suggestions. Modest tweaks to the wording might elicit a different response. Saying "we should" sounds as if it's all decided. The word *quickly* might mean "efficiently" to one person but "hurriedly" to another. If the developer were given a second chance, he might have split his comment in two: "I think we have only forty-five minutes today, is that correct?"

Even if the developer is certain on that point, double-checking is courteous. In this instance, it would also prompt a yes from the other side—a word he'd like the other side to get used to saying. With that settled, he could then ask, "Okay, so how can we make best use of the time we've got?" Such a question touches each of the engaging, framing, and norming bases. It invites the other person to connect and implies that they have a common task. It's a first step in articulating a process for getting that task done.

GETTING OFF ON THE RIGHT FOOT

Let's test the engaging → framing → norming model of openings by considering three questions about the friendly pair of negotiations:

1. Don't they duck the power issue? After all, the tenant is in the stronger position.
2. Given their styles, weren't they just lucky to be paired together? Either of them just as well could have been matched up against Mr. You-Need-Us.
3. What specific skills and attitudes explain their success?

By design, there was a power imbalance in this exercise. The prospective tenant could locate its store elsewhere in the region. By contrast, the developer was under pressure to make a deal with a big-name national chain. His financing depended on getting a long-term lease with a creditworthy tenant. That's why the parties were working from the retailer's standard contract language.

The first words out of tenant A's mouth are, "Welcome to my office." Though our participants were in a nondescript studio, he claims it as his own turf, and developer A slips into a subservient role. The host, not terribly gracious, leans way back in his chair and says little. The developer, who seems nervous in most viewers' eyes, fills the awkward silences by motormouthing—which compounds his anxious appearance. Thus, the stage was already set when he says, "We need you."

The second pair doesn't waste time posturing. Both parties are at ease and engaged. The developer finesses the power issue when he refers to the tenant's initial proposal as "a picture of your leverage." Loosely translated, this might mean "Only someone in your position of power would even dare ask for all that." The subtext, of course, would be "Come on, you can throw me some crumbs here."

Underneath the joshing, these parties are also negotiating important aspects of the relationship. But still, why would you ever want to remind the other side that it is up and you are down? In the right circumstances, it can be a smart move. First of all, it establishes credibility. If everyone knows that's how it is, there's little to be gained by pretending otherwise. If you bluff that you've got clout when you really don't, the other side may feel compelled to teach you otherwise by throwing its weight around.

Acknowledging the imbalance expresses your confidence that you can do all right in spite of that fact. When developer B notes his counterpart's leverage, he smiles broadly and emphasizes the word *picture* with an upward, cheerful inflection. He is both granting tenant B's power and signaling that any agreement reached will have to work for him too. He isn't making a threat, but his whole demeanor seems to say that, deal or no deal, the sun will come up tomorrow. By comparison, developer A's comment about finding another tenant seems feeble.

It's easier to express self-assurance in person than over the phone. In this instance, the developer's eyes are wide open. He can register his counterpart's reaction and correct any misimpressions immediately. The same words about leverage written in a text or email might seem snide or resentful, but in the right setting, such moves are risk free. They may encourage the other side to open up and offer more than a noncommittal "um-hmm." And if this particular tenant is in a rotten mood or feels compelled to dominate, developer B hasn't displayed weakness or made any substantive concessions. In fact, his smile and easy manner demonstrate his poise.

How such a comment is received depends on our luck, good or bad, in regard to who's sitting on the other side of the table. In our project, it was a quirk of scheduling that Mike and Tom (the second pair) happened to be matched up. If their calendars had been different, Tom might have been with tenant A (Mr. You-Need-Us). I can only speculate about what would have transpired, but it surely would have been different on both sides of the table.

Suppose that Tom led off, just as he did before, by referring to the business at hand being dumped in their laps. (Recall that he paused at that point and waited for a response.) Perhaps this tenant would have said something unhelpful such as, "What do you mean by that?"

Tom might privately wonder if that remark was meant as a challenge, though he'd be wise not to make much of it so early in the conversation. Rather than being defensive, he could let the remark pass and see if other small talk might draw the tenant into the conversation. Or he could take the question literally, and explain that since they both were new to the negotiation, it would make sense to confirm what issues were already settled and what was left to resolve. If that failed, he could ask, "So, what's the best way we can wrap up what our colleagues were working on?"

Whatever unfolded would depend on both what Tom said and his bearing. My guess is that he would have handled the tough negotiator more successfully. He seems confident, though not threatening. He'd be less likely to invite the testing and put-downs that the nervous developer endured. Nor does he seem to be the type to get bogged down in one-upsmanship.

Negotiations go better, of course, when parties have compatible styles like Mike and Tom. They both pay heed. They also know how to solo and how to comp. (Note how each uses positive words to encourage the other along.) Even their jokes push the negotiation forward. More fundamentally, they say yes to the mess, as jazz expert Frank Barrett would say. They are coming into this case late and with limited information, but they act as if this is a new opening—an opportunity for their respective companies to renegotiate how they will negotiate.

FIRST IMPRESSIONS

We get one chance to make a first impression. New research by my HBS colleague Amy Cuddy suggests that the impression that people typically hope to make may work to their disadvantage.

Amy, a social psychologist, has built upon extensive research on "spontaneous trait inferences," people's impressions when they first see another person's facial features. In seconds, we make assessments on multiple dimensions. Amy focuses on perceptions of warmth and competence, as they comprise 80 percent of our overall evaluation. Our initial judgment is about warmth, specifically whether we believe a person feels warm or cold *toward us*. (This is like the friend-or-foe assessment we mentioned earlier.) It's how we read someone's intentions, positive or negative. A second or so later, we assess her competence, especially her ability to carry out her inclination. Does she have the capacity to do us good or harm?

Amy's studies have revealed a curious paradox. We want others to be concerned about us. Yet we prefer other people to see *us* as competent. In the context of negotiation, competence can mean both holding a strong hand and being skillful at the process.

Now here's the key: people tend to see warmth and competence as inversely related. Thus, if we view the person that we're dealing with as competent, then we assume that he feels *less* warm toward us. That means that the more successful we are in proving our competence, the more distance from others we create. The price of looking supercompetent (our natural impulse) is that we look like foes to other people.

We've just seen how this dynamic plays out verbally, when the first pair of real estate negotiators jostles over position, while the second two endeavor to establish connection. As Amy and others note, similar messages are transmitted through facial expressions and body posture. Indeed, the impact of physical signals may be stronger.

PAIR A   PAIR B

With pair A, you probably don't have to be told that's Mr. You-Need-Us leaning way back on the right. The beleaguered developer is hunched down on the left. With pair B, it's harder to tell who's who—and that's the point. They've teamed up to clean up the mess that their respective predecessors made. (Here it's the developer who's on the right and the tenant seated on the left.) Perhaps their posture is carefully calibrated, but more likely it has happened naturally. Because each side sees the other as warm, they are wholly engaged in a process of reciprocal, reinforcing feedback. Smiles are begetting smiles.

Amy and her colleagues Dana Carney and Andy Yap (both of Columbia University) have significantly advanced our understanding of the biochemical aspect of social interaction. Familiar research on body language has focused on what your expressions, gestures, and posture communicate to other people. Specifically, they have discovered that the way in which you carry yourself not only affects how others see you (confident or vulnerable, for example) but also actually *causes* you to have those feelings, too!

The researchers measured hormone levels of subjects who were told to maintain a particular body position for just a couple of minutes. When people sat or stood in a closed manner, their cortisol level went up. Cortisol is the so-called fight-or-flight hormone, produced by the adrenal glands atop the kidneys. It both results from and activates anxiety.

CLOSED

But when subjects instead assumed the open stances—power poses, as Amy calls them—cortisol went down and testosterone increased for both men and women. Testosterone, the male sex hormone—also produced in smaller quantities by the female ovaries—is associated with confidence and risk taking.

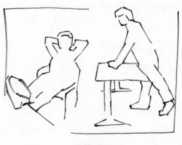

OPEN

Most important, these hormone changes persist and impact behavior. More than fifteen minutes after assuming the power poses, subjects were more likely to roll dice to double a $2 stake. Risk taking is associated with dominance. It's just speculation at this point, but it may have other

positive effects in negotiation. A confident person might be more willing to float a novel solution to a problem, for example. She might also
take the chance of relaxing a bit and feeling more warmly toward her
counterpart.

You can put Amy, Dana, and Andy's insights to work today without
going to the gym or wading through piles of scholarly articles. You just
need to be aware of your body when you prepare to negotiate and throughout the process. Opening up your physical stance can expand your thinking. There may be ripple effects as well. When you feel—and display—an
easy confidence, others may become more comfortable with you.

Circumstances can trigger anxiety, of course. Most of us have no trouble carrying on a casual conversation with a stranger waiting for a bus,
but good luck to us if we were called up from the audience to do exactly
the same thing at an improv comedy club. Every once in a while, the situation is reversed. There is great tension, and then someone dispels it. Just
below the surface of a looming confrontation may lay the seeds for new
understanding and engagement.

On September 16, 2001, Courtney Cowart was heading to Lower
Manhattan on the Lexington Avenue subway line. She was returning to
Ground Zero, where five days earlier, she had escaped a blinding mael-
strom of dust and debris as the World Trade Center collapsed almost on
top of her. Here is her story in her own words.

*Down the steps I went and boarded the first train. There in my car on one
of the benches sat a skinny old wizened Sikh wearing an elaborate gray
silk turban. No one would sit on the same bench with him. His bench
was completely empty, with everyone bunched up on the other side of
the subway car. He sat there alone, perfectly straight and still, without a
sound, but with tears just streaming down his face.*

*As the train decelerated, he reached into his pocket and pulled out a
crumpled dollar bill. Then he stooped over a Hispanic mother with an
infant in her arms sitting by the doors. Into the baby's little fist he gently
tucked the crumpled dollar bill, looking straight into the woman's eyes.
She frowned back and looked at me with a huge question mark on her*

*face and was about to protest when I blurted out urgently, "Don't stop
him. He needs to do this."*

*She was silent for a moment and then replied, "So we know that he
is not cruel?"*

And I said, "Yes. So we know that he is not cruel."

*The doors opened. He stepped out. The doors closed. We looked at each
other, and all of us, every person in that car, burst into tears.*

The anxiety that people bring to new experiences has many sources and
can take many forms. That is also true for its release. The shared anxiety
of the New York subway riders was overwhelming. The sorrow of the
Sikh was different but no less intense. Then something happened.

We cannot know for sure, but something in Cowart's face, perhaps
an open attentiveness, invited the questioning look from the Hispanic
mother. Though the two women had never met, they were connected by
the mother's unspoken plea for help and reassurance. Cowart's spontaneous response could not have been rehearsed. Its urgency had to match the
intensity of the moment. The protective mother who had felt threatened
only an instant earlier was shocked into a new understanding and new relationships with Cowart, the Sikh, and everyone else in that subway car.

Openings are opportunities. They are moments in which mood is
set, issues are framed, and relationships are established. If these moments
are recognized and expressed emotionally, they can be openings to new
understandings and possibilities.

KEY POINTS

- Begin negotiation with an eye to how you want to finish.
- Use opening moments to engage your counterpart, frame the issues, and define the process.
- Don't rush. Small talk reduces tension and builds relationships.
- Avoid small ego battles that can cost you the war.
- Use posture to reduce stress and build your confidence.

[9] Critical Moments

A colleague once told me that if something is cheap and easy to reverse, it's an experiment. But if it's not both those things, it's a commitment. That applies to negotiation. Much of what you may do along the way falls into the no-harm-in-trying category. Being polite at the outset, for example, is costless. If the other side misreads your courtesy as a lack of resolve, you can disabuse them of that notion.

But sometimes you must take a step that could either help or hurt your cause, and there's no easy way to backtrack. If you reveal important information, for example, you can't take it back. Likewise with issuing a take-it-or-leave-it ultimatum. Committing yourself to a strategy is also a critical choice.

Daniel Yin was back on campus for the second module of an HBS executive program for people who run their own companies. He and his brother Steven had founded a high-end publishing firm that puts out gorgeous coffee table art and travel books in another part of the world. For reasons you'll soon understand, I've disguised names here, been vague about the country in which they do business, and converted the currency to US dollars. The rest is true.

Daniel and I met for lunch along with a few of his program classmates. After we exchanged pleasantries, he broke in and said, "First off, I want to thank you, Professor. The negotiation classes you taught proved very helpful to me recently." Everyone likes a compliment, so I smiled, expecting for him to tell me about a recent acquisition or resolution of some copyright claim.

I was startled, however, when he continued, "What I learned was crucial when my brother Steven was kidnapped. I had to negotiate his release. For a whole month, we didn't know if we'd see him alive again."

It never occurred to me that one of my students would use negotiation concepts he learned in my course in such circumstances. But Daniel was convinced that the frameworks we had used in analyzing business transactions applied to his brother's kidnapping case too. In fact, many of the points he made anticipated themes in this book.

Daniel spoke, for example, about the importance of presence of mind. "I had to have the mental discipline to see everything that was happening from a neutral point of view." He also thought hard about BATNAs, "not just for us but for the kidnapper too." The family had no walkaway alternative. It had to negotiate. But Daniel realized that his counterpart had to negotiate as well. "He makes a profit only if he makes a deal."

Daniel also took great care in formulating his offers to influence the kidnapper's perception of deal space. He considered the roles and interests of all the parties, including the police—not all of whom he trusted. Daniel's analysis was impressive, as was his poise in a time of great stress. But Daniel didn't mention how well he handled critical moments in the negotiation. That skill may have been the most important factor in his success.

I'm not talking here about critical choices that can be understood only in hindsight. Those are the province of historians. In 1940 Adolf Hitler's decision to suspend Germany's air assault upon England and attack the Russians on the Eastern Front proved to be a turning point in World War II, though no one could have known that at the time. Instead, I'm focusing on moments where, with appropriate reflection, you should recognize that doing one thing forecloses something else. Your ability to hedge or straddle may be limited at best, but you still must make a decision.

MANAGING CRITICAL MOMENTS

Kidnapping for money has become common in Daniel's country. The professionals who do it are shrewd. They know how to play on people's emotions. After snatching someone, they wait several days before making contact. They want to amp up fear to a point where a family will pay anything to get the victim back safely.

Daniel nevertheless used the time to his own advantage. First, he received a crash course in ransom negotiation from the police. They told him that it's not like the movies. In this country, kidnappers don't state a demand, nor do they impose a deadline. Instead, when they do call, *they insist that the family put the first number on the table.* Right at the outset, Daniel would face a crucial decision: How much to offer for his brother's return? There would be no second chance.

Daniel reviewed his accounts and figured that he could come up with $1 million, maybe somewhat more in a week or two. The fact that Steven was a full partner in the business limited how much Daniel could borrow on his own. He'd pay whatever it took to guarantee his brother's safe release. If that meant financial ruin for the extended Yin family, they would find a way to survive.

The telephone finally rang just before seven on a Sunday evening.

"I have a message from Steven Yin," said the voice on the other end of the line.

"Who is this?" Daniel asked.

"Your brother is all right," said the caller. "He wants you to know how much he appreciated the gold cuff links you gave him for his birthday last week. What else? Oh, the generous toast that you made, about him being both your brother and your best friend—that meant the world to him."

There had been crank calls earlier, but this one was legitimate. Only the immediate family had been at Steven's birthday dinner. And the cuff links were antiques that Daniel had purchased on a recent business trip. Yet in spite of having had the three days to prepare, Daniel was speechless.

"Tell Steven that we are doing as well as we can," he finally said. "Tell him we are praying for him."

Daniel glanced over at a policeman sitting at the dining room table and listening to the conversation through headphones. A tape recorder had clicked on the instant the phone had rung. He gestured for Daniel to continue.

"What do you want us to do?"

"I'll make this quick. I've already invested a lot in preserving the safety of your brother. I paid people well to treat him with respect; to be careful. I thought you should know that before telling me: What you are going to pay?"

Daniel loved his brother and was sitting on a lot of cash. What should he do?

"We can pay you fifty thousand dollars right now," Daniel told the kidnapper.

"That's ridiculous," was the response. "You'll have to do much better than that." The telephone line went dead.

Daniel had a good explanation for his lowball number. He had anticipated that his first offer would be a critical move, one that would shape his broader strategy. He thought hard about the long-term consequences of his answer. While preparing for the negotiation, he realized that his first offer, no matter how lavish, would not secure Steven's release. The kidnapper would reject it, confident that he could get more.

With that in mind, Daniel reconsidered his objectives. "My paramount goal at that point was to simply keep the conversation going," he explained. The $50,000 figure probably was less than the kidnapper expected, yet it was a starting point—that's what Daniel meant by adding the words "right now."

One of his program classmates asked, "Weren't you taking a big risk with your brother's life?" Daniel didn't think so. In fact, he worried more about the risk of making a high offer. If he had started with $500,000, the kidnapper might have assumed that the family could pay ten times that. In laying out his first number, Daniel was already thinking about the end game.

Daniel and the police listened to the tape of the first call over and over again. "This is good," said the head detective. "We know this guy. He's done at least eight kidnappings this year." Daniel stifled the impulse to ask why, after so many times, the police still hadn't made an arrest. Instead, he merely asked, "It's good?"

"Oh yes," said the detective. "He's very professional. He knows what he's doing. Now, if it were some amateur, someone who doesn't know how to play the game, it would be very different." To Daniel, the situation was by no means a game, yet he was thinking like a chess player himself. There would be further moves, he told himself, trying to draw some comfort from the kidnapper's closing words. This was the beginning of the bargaining, not the end.

The second phone call came the next evening. "You have a prosperous business, Mr. Yin," the kidnapper said. "Don't insult me with any more low offers. You can easily pay many times what you said."

"Sir," replied Daniel. "You know what is happening in the economy. Things are bad, our credit line is gone. It's not our fault. It's happening to everyone."

"Well, sell your big Mercedes, then," said the kidnapper. Daniel thought he heard a trace of exasperation. "It's not mine to sell," Daniel answered. "The bank is about to repossess it."

"Make me another offer," the caller said over the crackle of the cell phone.

"I can find sixty thousand dollars," said Daniel. "Maybe sixty-five."

"That's not enough," said the kidnapper, hanging up.

Once Daniel had committed to his strategy, he didn't falter. He focused on influencing the kidnapper's perceptions. "I wanted to keep him interested but at the same time really anchor his expectations," Daniel said. "I was very careful to be consistent, increasing my offers only a little at a time."

The negotiations dragged on for three weeks. In each of the daily calls, Daniel would pose a personal question that only his brother could answer. Next time, the kidnapper would need to have the appropriate answer to prove that Steven was still alive. It was an arduous process.

Something needed to be done to bring it to a close. By day twenty-five, Daniel had offered $78,000, and still the kidnapper insisted on more. "Call me back tomorrow," said Daniel. "I may have another option." This time he was the one to hang up.

When Daniel got the call next evening, he claimed that he had contacted a loan shark, an underworld figure who could provide another $20,000. "That gets us into the nineties," the kidnapper said. "That's better, but it's still not enough."

"You don't understand," said Daniel. "I haven't borrowed the money from him yet. The moment that I do, we owe interest of one percent per day."

"That's your problem," said the kidnapper.

"Actually, it's a problem for both of us," Daniel said. "If I've got to pay interest, it will come out of any money I borrow. So if we keep negotiating, the loan shark is going to cut into the amount that you get. There's no way around it."

"Let me think about it," said the caller.

"Of course," said Daniel, "but the commitment he gave me is good only until noon tomorrow. I either have to take the money then, or he'll lend it to other people."

The kidnapper hung up but called back in five minutes with a counteroffer. "Make the amount an even one hundred thousand, and we have a deal," he said.

"I can do that," said Daniel after a deliberate pause.

Daniel got instructions on making the transfer for his brother. The money would be in cash, of course, small bills. The police promised not to interfere. They also assured Daniel that if the family paid the ransom, the kidnapper would keep his word. "Don't worry about that," said the detective. "He knows that if he doesn't deliver, we'll tell anyone dealing with him in the future not to pay."

Thirty minutes after Daniel passed a duffel bag to a stranger, a gray van drove past the Yins' downtown office, and Steven was pushed out on the street, blindfolded. The public was told that he had managed to escape. The authorities didn't want to encourage more kidnappings.

The whole negotiation took almost a month, but Daniel felt that time was on his side. He increased his offers, though only a little each time. There was enough on the table to protect Steven from harm, but not enough for the kidnapper to keep this game with the Yins going. Maybe he could find someone else to grab whose family wouldn't be so patient and disciplined.

That's not how Daniel felt privately, of course. "It was so stressful, so emotional," he says. "I had to dedicate myself to being very focused about strategy." The kidnapper initially controlled the pace of the negotiations and communication, but Daniel's bold action was what brought the process to a successful close. He knew he couldn't make a take-it-or-leave-it offer. There was too much at stake. So he concocted the loan shark story as a way to dangle an attractive offer, but only for a short time. "I wanted to create a deadline," he said, "but one that would just be arbitrary, because he could call my bluff."

It wasn't a card that he could have easily played again if it didn't work this time. The mythical loan brought the package to a little less than $100,000. Without it, they were still in the high seventies. Psychologically, it could be hard for the kidnapper to take a big step backward. As Daniel expected, the kidnapper came back for a small sweetener to make it a six-figure deal. If satisfying the kidnapper's ego was necessary, that was okay with Daniel. Many moments in this negotiation were important, but two especially. The first was imposed on Daniel when the kidnapper insisted that he make the first offer. But at the close, it was Daniel who forced the issue and restored Steven to the family. "Emotionally, I wanted to resolve this right away," he told us, "but rationally, I knew that if I tried to rush things, panicking would only make things worse."

Few of us will face the choices that Daniel confronted, but his experience illustrates principles that apply to critical moments in negotiation across the board:

1. Use Tactical Moves to Execute Strategy.
Daniel's low first offer established a slow but steady path to agreement.

2. Be Decisive in the Face of Risk.

All of Daniel's alternatives entailed risk. He believed that the prospect of getting some money would keep the kidnapper from acting rashly.

3. Focus on Your Ultimate Objective, Not Necessarily the Immediate Consequences of Your Decision.

Daniel knew that his first offer would not be accepted.

4. Be Consistent.

Once Daniel committed to this approach, he had to stay with it. If he had doubled his offer midway in the talks, the kidnapper might have held out for even more.

5. Be Prepared to Force Agreement, but Take Care to Time Your Moves Well.

Daniel's patient bargaining set up his closing gambit.

CONFRONTING TOUGH ISSUES

Lakhdar Brahimi is the UN diplomat who "navigates by sight." He is always well prepared, but he keeps his eyes (and mind) wide open for new and better information. He triages as he searches for the elements of a workable deal by sorting issues into three areas.

His upper zone is out of reach. It contains any item that's nonnegotiable for the other side. "You don't need to waste your time asking for it," Brahimi says. "You will not get it." Down at the bottom are things that you can get "free of charge," as he puts it. "And it will be really stupid to pay for something that is there for the taking." In the middle area are the points that are open to negotiation.

"So don't lose your time asking for the impossible," he concludes. "Don't waste your resources paying for what is free. Concentrate on that area where give-and-take is possible."

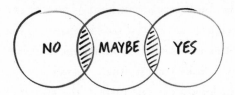

Brahimi's triage model can help you focus your energy where it will do the most good. But the signage in the negotiation landscape is poor. There aren't obvious boundaries between yes, maybe, and no. And those boundaries are in shades of gray and can move as you generate options and relationships evolve.

At any given moment, though, you should have a rough sense of which issues are the toughest. Testing that line is a critical moment in negotiation. If you veto something that's crucial to those on the other side, it could be a deal breaker. Even if it's not, they may feel the need to ask for something they know that you want.

Think carefully about what you mean in saying no, as well as how and when to express it. A *true no* is required when there is a line you simply won't cross even if that results in an impasse. Your position could be based on principle: such as a refusal to pay a kickback as the price of winning a contract. Or it could be based on the practical fact that you can get a better deal elsewhere. By contrast, a *strategic no* rules out a proposal that you actually could live with, but you expect that the other side will improve it if you hold out. It's a matter of gauging your counterparts' baseline, as explained in chapter 2. It comes down to weighing risk and reward. The more room you think they have to move, the more confidently you can say no. You'll win if their purported take-it-or-leave-it offer proves to be a bluff. If you're wrong, though, it could cost you the deal.

In some cases, you can afford to take that chance. In others, not. You can try to hedge, of course. Rather than rejecting a demand by saying "There's no way I'm ever paying that much," you could soften your stance and respond, "Oh. I didn't plan on paying so much." The first version ties you to the mast. The second gives you wiggle room in case the other side doesn't budge. But because this kind of no isn't as emphatic, it may not be as convincing.

A variant of this approach is a *pliable no*. It rejects the demand as things stand, but it links your ultimate answer to other issues. For instance, you might look a car salesman in the eye and give a flat no to his "last, best offer," but then add that you'd meet the price provided he includes an extended warranty.

My colleague Bill Ury observes that when you say no to others, you're really affirming something that's important to you. He gives the example of an employee whose boss asks him to sacrifice weekend time with his family in order to complete yet another last-minute assignment. Always yielding to such demands isn't the answer. Nor is simply refusing and leaving it at that.

Instead, Bill recommends what he calls a yes-no-yes. The employee might start by saying that being a good parent is important to him. (That's the yes to his own priorities.) The subsequent no nixes the request that he work that particular Saturday. But right after that, he could add a second yes. He could suggest, for example, that going forward, they discuss a flextime system in which occasional weekend work would be matched by his leaving early some weekdays to pick up his children from school.

Bill describes this technique in his book *The Power of a Positive No*. This pairing of yeses and nos complements the concept of surfaces and gaps in negotiation (the idea adapted from the military strategy we saw earlier). Your counterparts need to know where you draw the line on important issues. If they don't, they have every reason to keep pushing beyond that. In walling off certain areas, though, it's in your interest to open doors to other possibilities that may serve their needs, at least in part.

Some negotiators don't have any trouble saying no. Instead, the problem is coaxing them to say yes. This is especially true with disputes. (Recall the expensive fight among co-op neighbors over $902 window bars.) People may privately wish they could go back and have a fresh start. Often that's hard, but it's not impossible.

FROM NO TO YES

For years, the Humane Society battled with the trade association of the major egg-producing companies in the United States. The society opposed factory farming in general, and, in particular, the practice of caging hundreds of thousands of birds into a single chicken house. It spent millions on lawsuits against the producers. The companies fought back just as vigorously. The only apparent leverage that each side had was the ability to inflict costs on the other. The society never achieved a victory in court, while the egg producers couldn't shake the bad publicity the litigation was causing.

But then something happened. In the summer of 2011, Gene Gregory, head of the trade organization, used an intermediary to send a message to Wayne Pacelle, president of the Humane Society. "Can we just talk?" he asked.

This proved to be a critical moment. The two longtime adversaries met privately. They agreed that the legal battles in state after state were getting them nowhere, so they decided on a different tack. Together they would lobby Congress for stricter federal regulation of poultry farms. That clearly was a victory for the Humane Society, but it was also a win for the producers. Uniform regulations would simplify operations for the big companies and level the field for competitors.

Gregory's decision to reach out to Pacelle might have backfired if the Humane Society took it as a sign that the producers were losing resolve and could be beaten down with more litigation. Pacelle, in turn, took a risk in collaborating with an organization long seen as "the enemy." Unlike the warring co-op owners, though, these two realized that they had wasted resources digging themselves into a hole. The time had come to fashion a ladder and climb out.

The two men didn't become friends, but they have developed mutual respect. Gregory understands that Pacelle isn't trying to put his members out of business. "I've found him to be a man of his word," he says, "and it doesn't have to be his way or no way." For his part, Pacelle has come to understand the economic pressures confronting farmers. "They were, kind of, in a race with others in a competitive environment to build efficiencies." By forging this unexpected relationship, Gregory and Pacelle reframed their objectives. Instead of inflicting costs on each other, they found ways to help advance each other's agenda. Their adamant nos became pragmatic yeses.

Sometimes it takes an outsider to break a deadlock. In September 1999 Senator George Mitchell returned to Belfast. A year earlier, he had helped Protestants and Catholics reach the Good Friday Agreement to end sectarian bloodshed in Northern Ireland, but the parties had been slow in implementing the terms. Meeting with the key parties yet again, he said:

"You know why I love opera? When I go home and put on *La Bohème*, I know Rodolfo's going to sing the same words every time, and it gets me prepared to come back to Belfast, because the thing I know is that I'm going to have to sit here and listen to you guys saying the same thing over and over again, every time."

According to the *New York Times*, "His listeners were men with no history of enjoying being made fun of. But they laughed." Mitchell wouldn't have made such a crack in his first mediation session, nor likely even in his twentieth. But after years of listening to the parties rehash old grudges, it was time to prod them to talk seriously about the future.

MOVES, TURNS, AND POWER PLAYS

Negotiation is often about more than money or specific terms and conditions. It can also be about who's running the show. The transaction of power usually takes place below the surface or between the lines of what is said, but it can be as important as the substance itself.

Lisa Tschorn was meeting with her boss Stuart Wells about a long-overdue raise and promotion. They'd had a similar talk more than a year earlier that prompted only a small bump in salary. At that time, Stuart had acknowledged Lisa's diligence and intelligence but said she needed more seasoning to demonstrate "real spark and initiative."

This time Lisa felt she was ready. She had worked hard the previous twelve months. Early in the conversation, she reminded her boss with justifiable pride about a new product launch that she had headed. But he brushed aside her point by saying, "Lisa, you did a good job, but you were working alongside Clark and Frank. You're not claiming all the credit, are you?" With that sharp comment, Stuart both dismissed her best argument and belittled her personally.

What's the best way to deal with real-time challenges like that? Deborah Kolb and Judith Williams, coauthors of *Everyday Negotiation: Navigating the Hidden Agendas in Bargaining*, catalog four types of possible responses: correcting, diverting, interrupting, and naming. We can think of these as a negotiator's version of the stock riffs that jazz masters use when they get stuck in the middle of an improvisation.

A *correcting* move takes issue with an assertion and presents a different way of seeing things. Lisa might respond by saying, "Yes, I appreciated Clark and Frank's help, but check with them, and they'll tell you I did the lion's share of the work."

It takes backbone to contradict one's boss, of course, but solid preparation can bolster confidence. If Lisa had thought beforehand about both the most likely and the most challenging things that could happen (just as the US Marines do in planning for battle), she might well have anticipated her boss's cutting remark. And with that in mind, she could have taken the added step of making sure that her two colleagues would back her up.

A *diverting* move is a variant on this approach. It seeks to depersonalize the conversation by focusing on the substance of the problem. Rather than rising to the bait, Lisa could remind her boss of the revenue the new product is generating and document all the effort she invested to make it succeed.

Other times an *interrupting* move is best. Even a short break can give everyone a chance to settle down and regain perspective. When that's not possible, other process moves can have the same effect. For example, Lisa might take a breath and say, "Let's step back for a moment and see what we agree on. You know that we talked about a promotion a year ago, and just now you acknowledged I'm doing a good job. So how do we figure out the best way to move forward?"

Kolb and Williams recommend a *naming* move for certain cases. It's a direct statement that you recognize the power play and won't put up with it. This is a high-risk response, though. You may be 100 percent right, but it puts your counterpart in a position where he may think his only choice is caving in or counterattacking. If somebody angers you, however, don't suffer silently. For both your sakes, give the person a chance to self-correct before you tune out him or her or storm out the door.

What you say should be matched by how you carry yourself. Remember the real estate negotiation from the chapter on openings—specifically, how the second developer got his prospective tenant to consider adjustments in its standard lease? He mentioned that when his company had asked about revisions earlier, it had gotten "a good negotiating response last time: company policy." This developer called out the company-policy tactic but did so with a broad smile and a wave of the hand, as if he were sweeping it away. The message was that he wasn't rattled, nor had he taken offense. His whole manner conveyed that he knew how the game was played.

Well-timed moves and turns can redirect the negotiation process and create an environment for constructive problem solving. The hard part is successfully advocating one's own social position while also striving for genuine connection with the other side. Not every demand or sarcastic remark needs to be challenged, but if too many pass without resistance, there is the risk that preconceptions will be confirmed and roles ratified.

My colleague Gerry Williams videotaped experienced family lawyers trying to work out a separation agreement. In this unscripted simulation, Gerry asked the female attorney (Chris) to represent a husband whose wife had run off with the local tennis pro. He had a male attorney (David) represent the wife. The two lawyers were told to handle the case just as they would in real life.

Chris: I think this is a case with a lot of young children and two young people who have a lot of needs. I think if we can work something out at this juncture without getting ourselves into a litigation stance, we can do a favor for both our clients.

David: Well, I think it's a good idea, Mrs. Brougham. May I call you Chris? Is that your first name?

Chris: That will be fine.

David: I think we had a case together a few years ago. Do you recall?

Chris: Yes, I remember.

David: I appreciate your offer to sit down and visit about this matter. We had a fun time before, but I didn't get to know you that well. How long have you been practicing?

Chris: About five years.

David: I see. Do you do a lot of domestic relations work?

Chris: Enough. It keeps me busy.

David: How long have you known Tom? Has he been an old client?

Chris: No. Tom was referred to me by another divorce client.

David: I see. Did you do any work for the Smiths prior to this time?

Chris: Not in this area. I had some contacts with Tom in connection with an investment that he was considering a few years back, but it never came to fruition.

David: Did you meet Barbara at this time?

Chris begins the conversation by welcoming David, but he then seizes control even though he has the far weaker case. He peppers her with questions, vetting her experience rather than exploring the matter at hand. He has a wide smile, but his tone is patronizing. Nevertheless, Chris maintains her poise. Her posture is straight. Her expression doesn't falter. She gives short, polite answers to his questions (though David is so quick with the next one, he doesn't seem to be listening).

In my class, I stop the video at this point and ask my students how these negotiators are doing. Almost everyone criticizes Chris, men and women alike. They grant that she's focused and businesslike, but they think she's dancing to David's tune. "What should she do about it?" I ask. Many think she's already put herself in a bad position by letting him dominate. Some say that she should call him out, or else it will be a nonstop interrogation. Others wonder if she's capable of standing up to him.

Almost everyone agrees that Chris must turn around the interaction, or things will go badly for her and her client. I remind viewers that we have the advantage of the pause button. Chris had to respond in real time. Then I resume the video just after David's question about whether she had recently met Barbara.

> **Chris:** No. I have not met Barbara yet. I assume that she's been into your office to see you?
>
> **David:** Yes. She came in to see me. She was referred to me by a brother of hers who's been a good client of mine for years. He's a politician, but Barbara is a lot different personality than he is.
>
> **Chris:** Well, yes. She had received the complaint, I assume, by the time she saw you?

It's easy to miss Chris's diverting move because she executes it so smoothly, but Chris changes the direction of the conversation 180 degrees. Look at how she answers his question about Barbara but then adds a question of her own. It's a way to reassert control, by both interrupting the process and changing the subject. It's not a naming move. It says nothing about David's behavior, but it breaks his rhythm.

Then see how she solidifies her control by asking a second, more pointed question. It reminds David of the legal complaint that has been filed against his client for abandoning her husband and their children. Without embarrassing David, Chris is telling him that she has the upper hand. His smile disappears. He slouches a bit. His expression turns serious. You can almost see his dawning realization that his glib patter doesn't work with Chris. Her no-nonsense manner carries a message about the professional respect that Chris expects David to show her.

The interaction between the two is a microexample of the learning, adapting, and influencing model that I've emphasized throughout the book. Here it's Chris who is doing the influencing. But to David's credit, he reads her signal and adjusts accordingly. After acknowledging that his client has received notice of the suit, he continues:

> **David:** And she was rather distraught and depressed when she came in, but I managed to get some salient facts from her. And I think that we're at a point where we can talk about some matters and see if there's any solution to any of the problems.

In a quick pivot, David got down to business, thanks to Chris's lead. Her move was perfectly timed. She wasn't hypersensitive about his manner. Chris waited until he was out of oxygen and then put a stop to his rapid-fire interrogation. She couldn't know whether he was trying to dominate the process or was simply awkward dealing with women. Whatever his motivation, the conversation wasn't going where she wanted it to, so she took charge—and did it so subtly that David may not have realized what happened.

Kolb and Williams call dances like this "shadow negotiation." It's enacted in a broader social context and is about defining power, roles, and relationships. Specific transactions often implicate larger issues, especially within organizations. Those advantaged by unstated rules and norms have little reason to change them. Others burdened by them grow frustrated. Pressure can build up below the surface of a conversation. Someone who feels disrespected will respond with shame and even anger.

Was what he just said a put-down, you may ask yourself, or just a poor attempt at humor? Coping with that ambiguity requires awareness of your own feelings as well as those of your counterparts. Effective moves and turns at critical moments aren't just about what you say, but how and when you say it.

Critical moments arise when parties aren't working well on one or more of these levels. Dogged attention to the substantive issues may mask their real conflict or misunderstanding. For example, two negotiators might be haggling about the terms of sale for a small business. Their fight over the wording of a noncompete clause may have more to do with the founder-seller's need for the new owner's respect than with financial considerations. Both parties will be stymied, however, if they restrict themselves to using legal jargon as a proxy for dealing with underlying personal issues.

OUTBURSTS AND RESCUES

Bill Gates and Steve Jobs had a complex relationship. They were rivals, of course, both in the marketplace and in the public spotlight. But their two companies did substantial business together even as they competed for customers and acclaim. Microsoft actually wrote important software for some Apple devices. Jobs biographer Walter Isaacson likens the relationship at times to "a scorpion dance, with both sides circling warily, knowing that a sting by either could cause problems for both."

Tension between the two men came to a head when Microsoft was preparing to launch Windows. Jobs felt that the new product blatantly copied Apple's graphic operating system. He was furious, even though both Microsoft and Apple had borrowed liberally from an operating system developed earlier at Xerox, PARC. Jobs summoned Gates to a meeting. In front of Apple's top management team, Jobs excoriated him, shouting, "You're ripping us off! I trusted you, and now you're stealing from us!"

Gates just sat there, however, and then offered another way to look at it. "I think it's more like we both had this rich neighbor named Xerox, and I broke into his house to steal the TV set and found out you had already stolen it." Gates's response is a classic correction move. Perhaps it was spontaneous. Or, knowing Jobs's mercurial temperament, maybe Gates had it up his sleeve ready to play at the right moment. Rather than fall into the trap of defending himself, Gates cheerfully admitted to being a thief but differed on who it was that he had stolen from. He also reminded Jobs that he had been in on the same heist as well.

Jobs's anger abated somewhat. Later the two men met privately, and Gates demonstrated the new operating system. Jobs was scornful about its design (with some justification) but recognized that he had little legal standing to thwart its release. But Gates's composure earlier was just as important in preserving the business relationship. Gates says of himself, "I'm good at when people are emotional, I'm kind of less emotional."

It's one thing to defuse a tense situation that's not of your own making. But what if you're the person who did or said something foolish? Two things may be needed to set things right: a lot of brass and a friend like Kramer, the goofy neighbor on the old *Seinfeld* show.

Years ago, a young comic named David had the coveted but highly demanding job of writing for *Saturday Night Live.* New material had to be cranked out each week, and the rehearsal schedule was brutal. Much of what got written ended up in the wastebasket. Like many comics, David had a big ego plus insecurities to match. He lobbied hard for his material. Sometimes too hard.

David had gone through a bad streak. The producers had scrapped a half dozen of his sketches. The last one was cut after dress rehearsal. Five minutes before airtime, David accosted Dick Ebersol, the executive producer, in the control room. Ebersol was already wearing his headphones and was intent on the imminent broadcast. Nevertheless, David lit into him, telling him everything that was wrong with the show. Then in a flare of temper, he quit. By the time he got home, David regretted his outburst. His next-door neighbor told him he was stupid for quitting a well-paying job that other writers would kill for.

"What can I do?" David moaned.

"Pretend it never happened," his neighbor said.

Monday morning, David showed up for the writers' meeting. His colleagues were too shocked by his arrival to say anything. It wasn't their place to challenge him (and they probably wondered what was going to happen next). Then Dick Ebersol came in. The writers' room was just as it had been every Monday in the past. Ebersol shot David a funny look but never said a word.

The punch line? Sometimes situations that seem irreversible actually aren't. It's just that we're so involved emotionally we can't see a way out. That's when we need a fresh perspective from a friend or colleague who's more daring than we are ourselves.

There's a postscript to this particular case. The David here is the comic Larry David, who later became the fabulously successful producer of *Seinfeld* and then the creator and star of *Curb Your Enthusiasm*. The real-life neighbor who advised him to act as though his tantrum never happened became the model for Jerry Seinfeld's fictional neighbor, Kramer. If this story seems familiar, maybe it's because Larry David later exploited it as a gag in one of his *Seinfeld* shows.

KEY POINTS

- Recognize what can—and cannot—be accomplished at any given moment.
- Know how to say no without ending the negotiation.
- Use moves and turns to shift power imbalances.
- Set up the end game.

[10] Closing

A couple of years ago, a colleague of mine was being wooed by a well-regarded university (not my own, incidentally). We'll call him Ben Evans to spare him embarrassment. Ben was flattered that Arundel University (also a pseudonym) was interested in him and excited about the prospect of moving back East.

There still were some issues to be worked out, though. Arundel's usual practice was to have lateral hires come in as visitors for a year before being given a permanent position. "Sorry," said Ben, "but you know my work well, and I'm not comfortable with being on probation." Arundel made an exception and agreed to grant him tenure right from the start.

Then there was salary. Arundel's scale was lower than he had expected. Ben pushed hard for the upper end of the range and won that too. Getting an increase in his research budget proved more difficult, but he made headway there as well.

"Are we all done?" asked the dean when that was resolved.

"Just one more thing," said Ben. "This is a big move for my wife and me. She'll have to wind down her present job and find something new near Arundel. We'd like to delay our arrival for a year." There was silence on the other end of the line, and then the dean said, "Let me get back to you on that."

That was around noon on a Wednesday. Thursday came and went.

Late Friday morning, the doorbell rang. Ben signed for a FedEx delivery and then opened the white cardboard mailer. Inside was a standard business-size envelope that contained a two-sentence letter:

> *Dear Professor Evans,*
>
> *We are withdrawing our offer for a faculty position at Arundel University. We wish you well in your academic career.*
>
>

Yours truly,
Dean J. Joseph Gibson
>

Ben was stunned. Everything had gone so well, with Arundel agreeing to most of what he'd asked for. And for him, the start time wasn't a deal breaker. He just wanted to raise the issue. If being on board this coming September was that important to Arundel, he'd find a way to manage it. Why didn't the dean just say no? Ben phoned a friend on the faculty and asked how he could salvage the deal. "It's over, Ben," the friend said. "I tried to stick up for you, but people have moved on. As somebody else put it, if you were like this during courtship, marriage was going to be hell."

Ben didn't land in the gutter. He has his old job and continues to do great work. But he still kicks himself for blowing what would have been a major step up professionally. He wishes he had taken the original offer without saying a peep. That may be an overreaction, though. After all, he did convert a look-see visitorship into a tenure offer. And he got a bump in salary as well. The deal fell apart only after he asked for still more.

When are you done in negotiation? If we're not making progress and you have an attractive alternative within your reach, then it's easy to know that it's time to walk away. But it's harder to know whether to wrap it up when negotiation is going well. If you get a satisfactory offer, do we take it or press for more? The art of knowing when to say yes—and how to say it—is essential to negotiation success. So is knowing how to get a yes from the other side.

WHEN TO SAY YES

The only way to know how far you can go without exploding a deal is by going a little farther than that. Short of that point, you're operating in a gray area. It's like driving on the interstate. If the posted limit is sixty-five miles per hour, you almost certainly can go sixty-eight without getting ticketed. You're probably okay at seventy-two as well, though you should keep your eyes open for patrol cars. At seventy-five miles per hour or more, you could be pushing your luck.

It's actually harder in negotiation. Whatever signs are posted are hard to read and may be in a language that's difficult to grasp. Ben spoke to the dean long distance, but even if they had met face-to-face, they still could have been far apart in respect to what was said and what was meant. Ben felt that he was floating practical questions. No harm in asking, he told himself. On the other end of the line, however, his inquiries sounded like demands, each one more presumptuous than the last.

Ben admits that much of the blame for having killed the deal lies with him. He thought only about the upside of sweetening the package, without considering how things looked from the other side. Maybe the dean had risen up through the ranks and worked hard to earn the perks that Ben expected to be handed to him. Other Arundel faculty members may have already resented an outsider getting a better deal than they had themselves.

But the dean bears responsibility for the stalemate too. He may have been stunned by Ben's audacity. Perhaps he's someone who has trouble saying no. Ben heard the question "Are we done?" literally, taking it as an invitation to add yet another demand to the mix. But the dean may have meant, "Watch it, my friend, you're testing my patience." Ben was treading close to the edge but missed the subtle warning.

From where you sit, your counterparts' baseline will always seem fuzzy. You can't count on them to give you clear signals, so you have to allow for different possibilities. A back-of-the-envelope decision tree would have helped Ben clarify his choice. One option—a sure thing—

would be accepting Arundel's already handsome offer. The other possibility—counteroffering—could lead to an outcome that could be better, worse, or the same, depending entirely on the dean's reaction.

Calculating exact odds for those eventualities is impossible, but Ben knew that deferring his arrival for a year was far from a sure thing. Most likely, he'd get a flat no. Also, as proved to be the case, his request could be the last straw for the university. Even without attaching percentages, however, sketching the alternatives would have underscored how little there was to gain compared with all that could be (and ultimately was) lost.

That's not to say you should never push. The downside of counteroffering might not be so stark in other situations. But whenever you ask someone on the other side to improve her offer, there's a decent chance that she'll ask for something else in return. Before dragging out a negotiation, therefore, you should have reason to believe that it's worth the risk. Having a good walkaway option enables you to push harder, of course. If you're car shopping, for instance, and are stalemated at one dealership, it's easy to try somewhere else. But cases such as Ben's call for caution. **When someone hands you a tasty piece of cake, with rich frosting to boot, think twice about asking for sprinkles on top.** What you stand to gain on the margin may be dwarfed by what you could lose.

Several years ago, a small company—call it Brims—paid $225,000 for downtown land in a Northern California coastal community. It planned to build a coffee shop that would serve the local market as well as a growing number of tourists. But the owner of the abutting property fought the development, not wanting to lose the harbor views from his bed-and-breakfast, the Westerly.

After failing to block a building permit, the Westerly owner offered to buy the disputed lot from Brims for what it had put into the project: the initial purchase price plus its preliminary development costs, for a total of about $250,000. He said that the figure would "make Brims whole and spare them the risk of litigation." Brims felt the legal claims were groundless. It rejected the proposal out of hand, without making a counterproposal.

The Westerly owner went to court but lost his bid for a restraining order and failed on other fronts as well. Two months after making his initial proposal, he approached Brims's lawyer about reopening negotiations. "Look," she replied. "You didn't offer nearly enough to tempt my clients last time, and all you've done since then is make them angrier." If he wanted the property, she told him not to be "cute," as she put it. "Give us your best offer, and we'll give you either a yes or a no."

The next day, the man called and offered $500,000—which was more than enough to buy another prime commercial site in town. In fact, there was a property for sale just two blocks away that already had a good-looking building on it. Brims could be up and running well before its scheduled opening.

It looked like a fabulous deal for Brims. It would make money on the project even before selling its first latte. But instead of thanking his lawyer, the local manager told her to counter with a demand for $650,000. "If he's willing to double the money in barely two months," he reasoned, "he must be willing to pay a lot more."

The lawyer was shocked by her client's attitude. She reminded him that they had told the Westerly owner that they'd give a thumbs-up or thumbs-down to his best offer. Haggling now could provoke him into pulling it off the table. "Do you really want to take that chance?" The Brims manager relented but still wonders how much better he might have done. Win or lose, second-guessing ourselves comes with the territory.

Now consider the other side of the transaction. The Westerly owner made it harder to close by raising his offer so dramatically. He should have anticipated that it would rev up Brims's expectations. A more measured sequence of proposals would have sent Brims a signal that there were limits to how high he was willing to go. And even if the Westerly felt compelled to make a blowout offer, it should have made clear that it wouldn't consider counteroffers.

The contentious nature of this case amplified miscommunication. The Westerly owner likely thought he could bully Brims into selling, but he had a weak legal case and only aggravated the company. If, instead, he had approached Brims more collaboratively, he might have bought the property for much less. Who knows? By working together, the parties might have found a place for the coffee shop in the B and B, preserved the open space, and gotten a tax write-off by donating the contested lot to the town.

HOW TO SAY YES

Accepting a counterpart's proposal isn't like hitting the Confirm button when you order a sweater online. You often need to convey more than formal assent to the negotiated terms. What needs to be said depends on your objectives. Compare these alternative ways of expressing agreement:

A. Yes. That's terrific! I know you've extended yourself to do this deal. You can count on me to make it work great for you too.

B. All right. I'd hoped to do a little better, but I can make this work. So thank you.

C. Excellent. We've got a deal, for sure. I'd really appreciate it, though, if you could help me out on one last item.

D. Good! If you can guarantee delivery by the end of the month, we have a deal.

Example A expresses gratitude. If somebody has made you a generous offer, he knows it. It's important to show him that you know it too. That's an end in itself. It also strengthens relationships and may lead to future collaboration.

Version B is more measured. It suggests that the other party has pushed you close to the limit. Such a message may be prudent if your counterparts are taking the deal back to their client or boss for approval. It makes them look good—and that's in your best interest; otherwise they may be sent back for more. But they also need to know that you're happy enough with the deal to honor your commitments.

Both the first and second examples also include a thank-you. Gratitude should be standard practice in closing, whether the process has been cooperative or acrimonious. If it's been stressful for you, that's likely true for them as well. They must have moved at least a little in your direction for you to come to agreement. If ice hockey players can line up to shake hands after a hard-fought game, you can do the same.

Example C, by contrast, is a hedging tactic. It eliminates the downside risk of blowing the deal but still leaves open some possibility of doing better. It might even increase those odds. Declaring commitment unambiguously transforms the final issue from a precondition to a request for a favor. (It wouldn't hurt to throw in an explicit thanks here as well.)

Ben Evans wishes he had said this to the Arundel dean. As it happened, being reticent may have reduced his influence. Perhaps the dean wouldn't have gone along with delaying Ben's arrival for a full year. But if he was certain that Ben was coming, they might have worked out a reduced fall schedule that would have allowed him to phase in over the course of the year.

Example D is conditional. It's less than full commitment but still expresses enthusiasm. Just as important, it suggests that the negotiations are all but over. Those on the other side will have to decide whether to meet this last condition, of course, but at least they've been told that if they agree, they won't be hit with another one. This last hurdle may be small or large, but framing things this way at least puts the focus on a single issue rather than calling the whole negotiation into question.

A conditional yes puts the decision in the other party's hands, however. He or she will have to weigh whether ratifying the deal—including your modification—is better than testing your resolve by saying no to that last demand. Before making such a statement, consider your next move. If your request for, say, prompt delivery is refused, would that be a deal breaker? If that's the case, say so up front so that the other side doesn't lock itself in as well. But if you'd actually back down, you'll need to find a way to do so without losing face or credibility.

There are other ways to say yes, of course, depending on the situation. The four examples here differ in style and function, but they all are forward looking. They seek to secure agreement and facilitate implementation. Beware of giving grudging acceptance, such as saying "Yes, but you owe me." That sounds like whining. And if that's what you feel, think twice about agreeing. There's little profit in harboring resentment, whether or not you express it.

Ben couldn't utter even this weak form of yes. And each time he brought up another issue, it likely raised doubts on Arundel's part as to whether he truly wanted the job. I still wonder about that myself.

PERSUASION

Salespeople are taught techniques to overcome customers' resistance. Placing a pen on the signature line of a contract is supposedly more effective than just handing it to someone, but who knows if that's true. Likewise, those car salesmen who press a prospect by saying, "Tell me, what do I need to do to put you in this car today?" may repel more people than they win over.

That kind of lore is of dubious value, but there's been useful research on the psychology of decision making, including how framing a proposal influences whether it's accepted or rejected. Studies of so-called loss aversion show that people tend to give greater weight to what we might lose than what we might gain. Therefore, someone pitching a new project to her boss could do better by saying that his veto would mean *losing* $100,000 in annual profit rather than telling him his approval would mean *gaining* exactly the same amount. Other experiments demonstrate the power of reciprocity. People repay small favors handsomely. Charities send out packets of personalized address labels because those token gifts generate bigger contributions.

Sheena Iyengar of Columbia Business School has done fascinating research that shows how giving people too many options can backfire. Whether it's buying jam in a gourmet shop or choosing among retirement plans at work, the bigger the array of items to select from, the *less likely* it is that people will pick any of them. Thus, you may increase the odds of closing a deal if you give your counterpart the choice between A and B rather than offer an alphabet soup of possibilities.

This emerging science offers important lessons for negotiators, but it is far from being the whole story when it comes to persuasion. To convince someone to see what you're offering more positively, you've got to match what you do and say to her particular concerns and perceptions, both those she's expressed and those beneath the surface. People's reasons for saying no (or not saying yes as soon as you'd like) fall into several categories:

1. Substance.
Your counterpart may not see the full value of what you're proposing (or the inadequacy of what she's offered).

2. Options.
She may believe she'd be better off with the status quo or by dealing with somebody else.

3. Timing.
She may think that time is on her side.

4. Process.
She is uncertain about whether you're being sufficiently open or fair.

5. Commitment.
She may doubt your willingness or capacity to deliver on what you've promised.

6. Identity.
She may feel that you don't respect her (or worry that if you fast-talk her into saying yes, she won't respect herself).

In negotiation, people typically focus on the first three items—substance, options, and timing—to build a utilitarian case for saying yes. How those issues are explained and framed clearly matters. But negotiation also requires being persuasive on a personal level. Concerns about process, commitment, and identity can stifle people's willingness to hear you on the substantive merits. Judgments about your openness, reliability, and respect aren't made in an instant. And they aren't based on sales gambits or the particular words you choose in extending an offer. Rather, they depend on how you relate to other parties throughout a negotiation.

Former New York City detective Dominick Misino has been conducting high-wire hostage negotiations since the 1970s. He has a natural gift for connecting with other people, even in dire situations. His frequent successes are all the more remarkable considering how little he has to offer someone in return for a peaceful surrender. He can't promise clemency or a getaway car.

Much of what makes Misino successful resonates with the central themes in this book, notably his presence of mind and emotional attunement. "Top negotiators are excellent listeners," he says. Misino is always asking questions, trying to build rapport. When he asks hostage takers to tell their side of things, he gets back an earful. "I hear every instance of when the other guy has ever been wronged." When they tell him that they've never been cared for or that they've been framed, Misino is nonjudgmental. "The way I look at it, all of it is true—to him. And that's what matters."

Misino also listens to himself. He says that hostage negotiators have to be aware of the "noise" in their own minds. "Believe me, even if you don't know what's going on inside your head, the other guy will," he notes. "You need to know your hot buttons and limitations." Early in a conversation, he typically asks if the person wants to hear the unvarnished truth. The answer is almost always yes. (When somebody is in a standoff with police snipers, he observes, "Who in his right mind would have wanted to be lied to?") But then Misino will attach a condition. The guy has to promise not to hurt anyone even if he hears things he doesn't like. Nine out of ten times, such promises are kept. "These people may be the outcasts of society," he says, "but they do have a code of honor."

To deepen trust, Misino adds, "You use every possible opportunity to agree with your adversary and to get him to agree with you." He deliberately uses the plural pronoun (as in "*We* can work this out"), to "alleviate the bad guy's isolation and paranoia." In this context Misino doesn't comment. He doesn't argue. Instead, he just takes one simple step after another without explaining where he is headed—though he knows that surrender is the only option. Misino's key insight about the whole process is stated so simply, it's easy to slip right past it, so I've italicized it for emphasis: *"A successful negotiation is a series of small agreements."*

For him, persuasion isn't about carrots and sticks, charm, or bluster. It's about relational understanding. By being respectful, he elicits respect in return. By listening closely, he teaches the other person to listen to him. In the end, Misino can offer only respect, empathy, and safety. Surprisingly, those often prove sufficient.

But let's take this back to everyday negotiation. How could someone expect to get you to say yes and close a deal if, throughout the process, he's challenged your every assertion, rebuffed your conciliatory gestures, and shown no understanding of or respect for your point of view? In the face of all that, no matter how eloquent his closing argument or clever his framing, you'd likely turn down his proposal—maybe even if it tops what you'll get by walking away.

The same applies when you're looking to get a yes from others. Relying on a set of tricks and gambits to close deals is inconsistent with building a relationship in which people feel secure enough to say yes. To paraphrase Misino, we ultimately forge agreement by working out small understandings all along the way.

LAST-MINUTE BLOWUPS

Even everyday transactions can be emotionally charged. The sale of a $3 million Greenwich Village brownstone almost fell apart because of a dispute over a used washing machine that the sellers had removed from the premises two days before the closing. According to Stephen Raphael, the lawyer representing the owners, it wasn't worth fighting over, "but the buyers had already felt pressured to up their offer and to concede many things, and this was the last straw."

At the closing, the sellers still refused to replace the machine. One of the buyers ripped up the seven-figure check for the balance due, put a match to the scraps, and stomped out of the room. The sellers finally relented and agreed to reduce the price by $300. The brokers found the angry buyer at a nearby bar, nursing a drink. They coaxed him back, and the deal was done.

In another sale, a buyer tested the sellers' patience by haggling over one item after another. Finally, it was too much. The sellers stormed out in the middle of the closing, returned to their home one last time, and removed every lightbulb from all the fixtures. Wolf Jakubowski, who represented both parties, says, "It wasn't the amount of money that was the issue. It was the principle."

Real estate closings can get violent. Fern Hammond, a New York broker, tells the story of an angry woman who flung the set of house keys at a man's face as hard as she could. "All of a sudden there was blood all over the place," Hammond says. "Everyone was pushing the papers out of the way." And the target of the woman's anger was her own husband! She was furious with him because he had agreed to sell their place for less than she thought it was worth.

When tempers erupt at the end of negotiation, it's often because pressure has been building up along the way. Buying or selling a home is the biggest financial transaction that many people ever undertake. It's usually emotional as well. For sellers, parting with a home is often freighted with memories. For many buyers, the transaction is laden with hopes and worries.

These deals, moreover, are usually conducted at arm's length, through brokers and lawyers. Offers volley back and forth as the parties haggle price, with each side trying to read the intentions of the other. Preliminary agreement may be reached, but then, while the paperwork is being done, there's a dormant period when people have time to brood over their decision. Small wonder, then, that these anxieties tumble out when the parties meet—sometimes for the first time—to close the deal.

Negotiating through intermediaries complicates the process. Brokers and lawyers may contribute expertise, perspective, and credibility, but they complicate communication. It may be unclear who speaks for whom, or who has ultimate authority to approve a deal. When relationships are strained, a tag-team approach may be needed. The first cohort of negotiators may settle some issues but get stuck on others. A new set of negotiators, unburdened by whatever interpersonal issues arose between their predecessors, may be able to wrap things up.

Of course, this can be a bargaining gambit as well. It's a classic move in auto showrooms. You think you've reached a deal, but then there's a bait and switch. You shake hands with the salesman, but then he goes off to confer with his manager. When he finally returns, he wears a hangdog look. "I'm sorry," he'll say, "but my boss says it's gotta be another thousand dollars." He'll quickly add that's really only another $29 in monthly car payments—and in return, he'll toss in the deluxe floor mats for free.

Shame on those who resort to such tired old ploys. Shame on us, too, if we're not prepared for them. Ideally, we should confirm at the outset that we're negotiating with the right person: someone who can make a binding commitment. When that's not possible, we should also hold back something in reserve that we can throw in to close the deal.

LUCK AND PERSISTENCE

Last-minute hang-ups aren't inevitable. **How we negotiate through the process helps set up what happens at the end.** Recall Sandy Ritchie's patient purchase of Bold Island in Maine. For years, he corresponded with its elderly owner. When she was finally ready to sell, Sandy couldn't afford the price set by her lawyer. She overruled that advice, and Sandy is now the owner. It was a long process, of course, but sometimes one simple gesture can make the difference in everyday transactions.

A young couple, the Owens, had their hearts set on a single-family house in a desirable community. When they made their offer, they asked their broker to pass along a handwritten note to the owners, whom they had not met. In the letter, they explained that they were scientists doing cancer research. On weekends, they enjoyed making improvements on their condo, but they were eager to own a real home. Of all the places they had seen, they said, they loved this one the best. They even emphasized that their offer was negotiable.

The Owens got the house for the price they offered originally. At the closing, they met the sellers, who told them that they were moved by their note. "They said a couple of times that they loved the letter," the husband recalled. "I don't think they felt they were just selling it to an anonymous buyer."

Relationships matter in business negotiations too. Jerry Weintraub, the Hollywood music and movie producer, courted Elvis Presley's manager, "Colonel" Tom Parker, calling him almost daily for a full year in hopes of taking the King of Rock and Roll on a concert tour. Weintraub was young and didn't have much of a track record, but his persistence and charm eventually prevailed. Parker agreed to let Weintraub put together Presley's first tour in almost a decade. After the final show, the Colonel spotted Weintraub backstage and told him to follow him. They had to talk.

The Colonel was trailed by a big guy lugging two large suitcases. The three of them went through a warren of tunnels to a little door leading to an electrical closet. Inside was a bunch of machinery and a table with a lightbulb dangling above it. The Colonel told the other guy to put down the bags and get lost. "I need to talk to Jerry alone."

He then had Jerry put the bags on the table and open them. The cases were stuffed with cash. It was money from the sale of T-shirts and concessions. Jerry said he had nothing to do with that; his deal was only for a share of the ticket revenue from the shows. The Colonel and Elvis were giving him half of that, which Jerry felt was already lavish, but Parker insisted on giving him more. "When I have a partner, I have a partner. Now pile up that money." Here's how Weintraub describes the scene:

"It was a mountain of bills, some stained with ketchup, some stained with chives, stacked on the table. The Colonel said, 'Stand back,' then raised his cane and brought it down hard on the pile, dividing it into two big piles, which he pushed apart with the cane, saying, 'That side yours, this side mine. Is that fair?'"

Elvis's tour was a huge success. It also made Weintraub's career. In a mere six weeks, he went from being just another young, ambitious promoter to somebody with a name, a track record, and—thanks to Colonel Parker—$1 million in his pocket.

May we all be so lucky when we close deals. Weintraub was fortunate to be working with a kindred spirit. The Colonel relished the spark and hustle of show business as much as he did. Parker and Elvis already had a ton of money, so they could afford to be generous. And Weintraub had earned their trust because of how hard he had worked on their behalf.

But Weintraub also knew how to say yes. In fact, he first expressed his gratitude by saying no: it was too much money, he said; way beyond what he expected. To the Colonel, though, the fifty-fifty split wasn't about dollars and cents. It was about their relationship. When the Colonel asked if the concession split was fair, Jerry answered, "It's more than fair."

We began this chapter by seeing how my friend Ben blew his negotiations with Arundel University. We'll close with another contract story. In the early 1970s, teams in the fledgling World Hockey Association were trying to gain credibility by luring big-name players from the long-dominant National Hockey League. The Philadelphia Blazers had their sights on Derek Sanderson, a former NHL rookie of the year and flashy center on the Boston Bruins.

Sanderson was happy where he was but felt there'd be no harm in finding out what he was worth on the market. He was currently earning $75,000 a year from Boston. The Blazers offered him $2.3 million for three years. "I was stunned," Sanderson remembers.

A friend he had brought to the meeting with him whispered, "Take it. Take it!" But Sanderson just sat there. "Actually, we could make that $2.6 million," the general manger said. ("That's when I knew I had them,"

Sanderson recalls now.) Still, he didn't accept. Instead, he said, "It would be awfully hard to leave the Bruins. It was my lifelong dream to play in the NHL."

The Blazers' offer jumped to $3 million, and Sanderson still wasn't done. "I'll need a limo for my girlfriend, of course," he added. The team said yes to that and even agreed to hire Sanderson's father as a scout. Sanderson finally ran out of asks. He signed a deal that made him the highest-paid pro athlete in the world at the time, even topping Pelé, the legendary Brazilian soccer star. Was Sanderson smart in pressing for more, or just lucky that he didn't exasperate Blazers management to a point where it would sign a better player for less?

In coming to agreement, you have to balance risk and reward. The harder you press, the more you may gain—but also the more you stand to lose. In theory, decision-making models can pinpoint the crossover point where the net payoff becomes negative. Such formulas aren't much practical use in real negotiation, however, since estimates of messing up a deal are only rough guesses. With some items, there may be no harm in asking, while others shouldn't even be broached. In between those extremes, however, the pros and cons will be fuzzy.

It's safe to start from the premise that whatever you've been offered, you can likely do better. That's not always true, but it's a fair bet. It's possible—but not probable—that you've magically landed on a package that is the absolute best that your counterpart can do for you. It's also possible—though not certain—that there are no further ways to expand the pie through creative trades.

The probability that there's more to be gained, however, doesn't necessarily mean you should keep negotiating. Oil tycoon J. P. Getty is credited with saying, "You must never try to make all the money that's in a deal. Let the other fellow make some money too, because if you have a reputation for always making all the money, you won't make many deals." Likewise, there's an advantage to keeping things clear and simple instead of fashioning elaborate provisions.

Whether your instinct is to close the deal or keep dealing, give yourself time to have second thoughts. You can sketch a decision tree (like the ones in chapter 2) and test your assumptions. If you're inclined to press for more, what's the evidence for believing that there's plenty left to win? Likewise, what's your basis for thinking that there's no harm in asking? Conversely, if you're ready to shake hands on a deal, why do you think that you've done about the best you can?

Even in cases where relationships and reputations aren't important, be smart about how hard you press. Asking someone to sweeten an offer is one thing. It's another to make a demand that requires him to lose face. Emotionally intelligent negotiators sense when they're pushing too hard and pull back before a proposed deal collapses.

Now a postscript on Sanderson, who pushed, and then pushed some more, and ended up with what was then the fattest contract in the history of sports. His good luck continued, though in an odd way. Sanderson was injured when the new hockey season began, so he got off to a slow start. The Philly team was woeful, attendance was worse, and the owners were in a financial jam. After Sanderson had played only eight games, they bought out his contract for $1 million. He went back to the Bruins a much richer man. Once again Sanderson was a lucky negotiator, as the Blazers folded just a few years later—though that's not quite the end of this story.

By Sanderson's own admission, he was too young to handle the money. He craved the celebrity spotlight, partied hard, drank too much, and did drugs. His on-ice performance suffered, and his career trailed off. He squandered his money and ended up sleeping on a New York City park bench. For all his brashness and immaturity, though, Sanderson had made good friends along the way. His former Bruins teammate Bobby Orr checked him into rehab and paid the bill. Sanderson overcame his addictions, and he got into broadcasting and financial advising. He has been sober for many years.

The moral of the story? What seems like a good outcome in the short term might prove worse for you later on (as it did for Sanderson for a while). But still later, what seemed bad may turn good again (as it eventually did for him as well). Nobody can plan for such vicissitudes. That's why you're doubly lucky when you have good friends.

┌─ KEY POINTS ──┐

 ■ Take care not to push too far.

 ■ Pick the right way to say yes.

 ■ When others say no, probe for the underlying reason.

 ■ Anticipate last-minute blowups.

 ■ To conclude a negotiation smoothly, begin that same way.

└──┘

PART FOUR

Mastery

You need, I think, to be at the same time arrogant, because you want to solve problems that look insolvable, but you also need to be very, very humble.

—UN DIPLOMAT LAKHDAR BRAHIMI

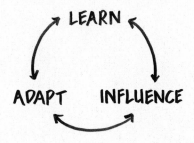

[11] Silk Purses

A major publishing house signed a contract with a respected author for a biography of Franklin Roosevelt. The writer threw himself into the project, delving into official documents and personal papers. He spent months in the library at Roosevelt's Hudson River estate in Hyde Park, New York, immersed in his subject's life and family.

The deadline for the manuscript came and went, as did an extended date. At long last, the author delivered his draft. It was a magnificent narrative, rich with insight, especially about the complex relationship between the thirty-third president and the first lady.

There was only one problem. The finished book was over 1,400 pages long. The publisher admired the writing but was convinced that the massive tome would intimidate even serious readers. The author was told that he had to make cuts. Drastic ones. He refused. Having poured years of effort into the book, he wasn't about to trash half his work. Stalemated, the parties tore up their contract, and the author repaid his advance. The writer then contacted another house, W. W. Norton & Company. It also was concerned about the length of the draft, but its editors saw a simple solution. They just cut it in two.

The first volume, titled *Eleanor and Franklin*, was still more than 700 pages, but it won both the Pulitzer Prize and the National Book Award for its author, Joseph Lash. His sequel, *Eleanor: The Years Alone*, was a bestseller as well. Decades later, both volumes are still in print.

Why didn't the editors at the first publisher spot this obvious solution? After all, they read the same manuscript and were dealing with an author that they liked and respected. Yet they saw as irreconcilable their own need for a shorter book and his refusal to make cuts. The second publisher had the creativity to recognize that instead of being a problem, the length of the draft was an opportunity. A single creative idea can spell the difference between a deal and no deal, as with Lash and the two publishers. It can also turn a good deal into a great one. Creativity is important in all sorts of fields, of course, from business and diplomacy to sports and the arts themselves.

Being inventive in negotiation is especially hard, however. We marvel at how a solitary sculptor can look at a rough block of marble and somehow imagine the finished figure lurking within. But it would be even more daunting if there were two sculptors—strangers—each with a hammer and a chisel, trying to fashion something valuable out of the raw material in front of them. Both might be masters of their craft, but each would have his or her own vision of what the final piece should look like. Each would also have a favored way of working and would want credit for the result. That's the challenge in negotiation.

In the 1990s, Stevens Aviation, a sales and maintenance company, began using the slogan "Plane Smart" in its ads. A couple of years later, Southwest Airlines launched its "Just Plane Smart" campaign, prompting Stevens to claim trademark infringement. The companies could have spent hundreds of thousands of dollars in litigation costs, but Stevens chairman Kurt Herwald proposed a different idea: he'd arm-wrestle Southwest CEO Herb Kelleher. The winner would get the rights, and the loser would have to donate to a charity of the other's choice. Kelleher lost the two-out-of-three match and sent a $10,000 check to the Muscular Dystrophy Association. Herwald, in turn, generously allowed Southwest to keep using its slogan. Both companies got great publicity from the stunt. Herwald said later that it was a factor in the subsequent threefold growth of his company's business.

FROM LEMONS TO LEMONADE

People like Kelleher and Herwald have a knack for coming up with creative ways to reach agreement. It may seem like magic when they pull rabbits out of hats, but psychological research shows that attitude has a lot to do with it. Recent studies by Evan Polman and Kyle Emich, from Cornell University and New York University, respectively, found that people were more creative solving problems for others than when asked to solve the same problems for themselves. In the movie *Heist*, the criminal mastermind (played by Gene Hackman) denies that he's very smart. "I tried to imagine a fella smarter than myself. Then I tried to think, 'What would he do?'" **Psychological distance opens up the imagination. Instead of fixating on what may block our goals, stepping back allows us to see a way around obstacles.**

Puzzle Number I

The real estate market is soft. You've had a For Sale sign on the front lawn for three months without getting a nibble. Finally, a prospective buyer appears, Jones, who's willing to pay close to your asking price. But there's a catch: Jones wants to make the deal contingent on the sale of his own property.

You refuse, understandably. You don't want to take your house off the market and depend on Jones's luck—good or bad—in unloading the other place. Jones, in turn, doesn't want to run the risk of owning two homes. Tweaking the price one way or another won't solve the underlying problem. Nor will seller financing. What should you do?

Any good book on negotiation explains how value is generated by trading on differences. If the owner of a painting *likes* what she has but someone else really *loves* it, they should make a deal. Negotiators have come to understand this, at least intuitively. In fact, all successful negotiations create value. Say that I'm about to trade in my car for $8,000, while across town, you're ready to pay $10,000 for the same model in identical condition. If we find each other through Craigslist and make a private deal, we'll both be better off. Basically, $2,000 worth of value is created. The only question is how much of that will be profit to me and what will be savings to you.

If we're limited to price, our negotiation within that range is said to be "distributive," or zero sum. That is, any dollar gain that goes into one party's pocket comes out of the other one's. A price of $8,100 would be great for you, while $9,900 works much better for me. As a result, we may haggle. But either of those numbers—and every one in between—would leave each of us better off than no deal.

When negotiators speak of value creation, however, they usually mean finding outcomes that improve their mutual welfare, so that one person's gains don't come at the other's expense. Joint benefit arises from trading on different priorities, expectations, time horizons, or attitudes toward risk. Just as differences of opinion make horse races, they're also the sources of value in negotiation. Here are some quick examples.

Valuation Differences.
Two diners may like pie à la mode, for example, but if one is crazy about ice cream and the other adores pie, each should eat what he loves best and then swap plates.

Economies of Scale.
Likewise, ramping a deal up or down can create value. Delivering a larger order may not cost a supplier much more than handling a small one. A buyer thus may get a better per-unit price (and the seller, more profit) by doubling the order.

Time Horizons.
Tweaking the time element is another source of value. In the sports world, a long-term contract may provide security for the player while letting the team lock in his salary at today's rates.

Differing Expectations.
Value is also created anytime that a pessimist sells to an optimist. If I think I've expanded my business to its limit, while you see a bright future, you should buy it.

Risk Tolerance.
Even if people have identical expectations, value can also be created by allocating risk wisely. A wildcatter may agree that the chances are good that he's found a productive oil well, but he might worry about being wiped out if it's a bust. A big company, with a portfolio of investments, is better positioned to bear that risk.

A pair of negotiators will weigh these factors differently. And this is good news, since differences can create value. With wise trades, parties can bridge gaps and break impasses. Even where there's room for agreement on price alone, creativity can enhance value for everyone.

It's one thing to appreciate this idea in the abstract but another to apply it in practice. Just think back to puzzle number 1, where your home buyer wants to make his purchase contingent on the sale of his own property. It's a common problem. Maybe you've figured out a solution, maybe not. Here's one possibility: you might solve the impasse by tweaking the structure of the contract.

Specifically, you could accept the offer, contingent on Jones's sale, provided that you add a twist allowing you to keep your house on the market notwithstanding the provisional deal. If another buyer makes you an offer before Jones sells his own house, he or she would then have forty-eight hours to match that price and close the deal. If not, your new buyer would get your house.

This arrangement isn't perfect, but it's better for both parties than no agreement at all. It lets you have it both ways: you keep alive the chance of selling to Jones but without losing the opportunity to deal with someone else. (Other prospective buyers shouldn't be deterred from bidding, since the forty-eight-hour deadline will quickly let them know if the house is available.) Jones comes out ahead too. Given a little more time, he may be able to sell his own home and then buy yours, no strings attached. Of course, if you find a buyer before he does, Jones will have to make his choice. If he then walks away, he's no worse off than doing so today.

OVERCOMING BARRIERS

Roger Fisher, coauthor of the classic *Getting to Yes*, was fond of saying, "Solutions aren't the answer." Process, he would regularly remind us, is paramount.

Puzzle Number 2

You've successfully launched a small real estate brokerage and want to grow the enterprise. You'd love to recruit a superstar salesperson with the visibility and contacts to bring in lots of new business. Having such a person on board also would help you hire other top-notch people. But how do you induce a major league player to take a step down and play in the minors?

For every example of a clever way to salvage a deal or resolve a conflict, there are needless stalemates that could have been avoided if only someone had looked at the problem from another angle. Strategic behavior often blocks that view. Negotiators frequently bluff, using high demands, low offers, ultimatums, and artificial deadlines. These gambits work sometimes, particularly if the other party is naïve or desperate, but hardball tactics smother creativity. People withhold information, fearful it will be exploited. That leaves everyone in the dark. If no one grasps the parties' interests, their chances of stumbling upon a good solution are slim. Even negotiators who see potential for expanding the pie may jostle over who gets what slice. Invoking mantras about dealing with "interests, not positions" is all well and good, but fair-minded people will nevertheless want to advance their own agendas.

The barriers to creativity are greater when negotiators are acting on behalf of their organizations or clients. Standardized contracts and company policies constrain salespeople's ability to tailor deals that meet the needs of specific customers. A procurement officer may work overtime to nail down an agreement with a key supplier only to be second-guessed by a senior manager who wasn't at the table but somehow thinks that their buyer should have gotten a lower price. Inability to reach internal consensus over priorities also hobbles creative negotiation with outside parties.

Company-to-company transactions can likewise breed an us-versus-them mentality that exacerbates people's natural tendency to be self-righteous about what they think they deserve. Seeing a problem from someone else's point of view is hard enough. In a group setting, expressing appreciation for an outsider's interests can seem downright disloyal to your colleagues.

The second puzzle, the one about a fledgling firm trying to recruit a superstar, was described by journalist Rob Walker in *Inc.* magazine. To solve that problem, New York real estate broker Barbara Corcoran focused on the *process* of negotiation rather than the substantive terms of the deal. The day before the candidate was to appear, she asked her best, most loyal salespeople to dress up for the visit.

When the sales diva arrived the next afternoon, "acting deservedly self-important," Corcoran groveled and ushered her guest into the conference room, where her team was assembled. "Here are some of the people who work here," she said. "They'll tell you what's good about the company." And then Corcoran left. The superstar met with the group for almost two hours. That night, she called Corcoran and accepted the job, declaring that meeting the staff convinced her that she couldn't work anyplace else.

After that, Corcoran landed a string of other talented people. Her company grew rapidly. "That wouldn't have happened," she says, "if I hadn't closed the deal with my first high-end salesperson." Corcoran succeeded not because of *what* she negotiated but *how* she negotiated. Instead of dealing with the dollars and cents of compensation, she made relationships paramount. Her fresh approach turned what might have seemed like a weakness—having a small team of younger people—into an asset.

Enlisting her employees as allies was farsighted as well. Instead of feeling upstaged by the arrival of a big-name salesperson, they understood their stake in hiring her. The negotiation process itself demonstrated that everyone was in this together, which built a foundation for future collaboration and mentoring.

BREAKING DEADLOCKS

Being creative in negotiation depends on the attitude you bring to the task. Focusing on whatever it is that won't work can blind you to solutions that will.

Puzzle Number 3

In 1995 the Dayton Accords had quelled the bloody conflict in the former Yugoslavia. Even after the agreement was signed, however, violence continued in contested regions. Serbian gunmen were shooting at cars with Bosnian-issued license plates that didn't use the Cyrillic alphabet. With relationships still bitter, Bosnian officials certainly weren't going to adopt the Serbian system, nor would Serbs accept the Bosnians' modern Latin alphabet. Cyrillic type differs from the Latin type used in the book you're now holding. Any suggestions?

А   Б   В   Г   Д   Ђ   Е   Ж   З   И   Ј

К   Л   Љ   М   Н   Њ   О   П   Р   С   Т

Ћ   У   Ф   Х   Ц   Ч   Џ   Ш

Strategic behavior is a formidable obstacle to creativity. Organizational constraints are another. Mind-set is the biggest of all. And that's one thing over which we have real control. The phrase "thinking outside the box" has itself become a cliché. Nevertheless, testing boundaries and turning problems upside down is imperative in negotiation. Joseph Lash's first publisher missed an opportunity because it was stuck inside the box of thinking in terms of a single volume. That's what the original contract specified, so it seemed that the only options were either having the author radically cut his draft or junking the project. The second publisher wasn't encumbered by that assumption; hence, it could recognize the much better alternative of turning one book into two.

It's easy to scoff at other people's lack of imagination, but by definition, it's impossible to spot our own blind spots. Psychologists say it's easy to fall prey to "naïve realism": the ability to see holes in other people's thinking while being blithely ignorant of our own lapses. We're all vulnerable to the powerful cognitive and social forces that constrain creativity.

Pessimism is self-fulfilling. People who believe in the mythical fixed pie, as Harvard Business School professor Max Bazerman calls it, see negotiation strictly in win-lose terms. For them, differences over value, expectations, and other issues are evidence of conflict, not material for constructive trades, so they don't bother to look for joint gains.

At the other extreme are the dreamy optimists who believe that luck is somehow always on their side. No matter how long the odds, they're convinced a great deal is right around the corner. There's danger in that kind of optimism as well. Doubling down after losing five times in a row in roulette, because "the law of averages" means that you're bound to win next time, is a ticket to financial ruin.

Stephen Nachmanovitch, improv expert and author of *Free Play: Improvisation in Life and Art*, says that to be creative, our minds must embody two inner characters: a muse who proposes and an editor who disposes. "The editor criticizes, shapes, and organizes the raw material that the free play of the muse has generated." He warns, however, that if the critical part of our brains kicks in too soon, "our muse gets edited right out of existence."

It helps to be optimistic while negotiating. That means believing that with a little more effort and imagination, we can solve a problem that at first may seem intractable. The late actress Ruth Gordon (star of the classic black comedy *Harold and Maude*) had the motto "Never face facts." She said that other people are always telling you what isn't possible. Her advice was to forget about them and make things happen.

People who are admirably unreasonable like Ruth Gordon relish the challenge of solving a problem that would stump others. It's akin to what organizational behavior expert Frank Barrett describes as having an appreciative mind-set, or, in the vernacular, saying yes to the mess. That means having a clear-eyed view of whatever we confront, while still believing that there's something that we can make of it. French anthropologist Claude Lévi-Strauss called it bricolage. In the United States, it's called MacGyvering (a nod to the 1980s action-adventure TV series *MacGyver*): improvising a solution with a few pieces of junk, some duct tape, and a Swiss Army knife. A healthy defiance of reality is contagious. It can encourage other parties to roll up their sleeves and help search for agreement. But it has to be tempered, of course, by the recognition that not everything is negotiable.

The divide between the Bosnians and the Serbians stretches back for centuries. It was unthinkable that either side would buckle under and accept the other's alphabet for its license plates, yet the late American diplomat Richard Holbrooke mediated a truce. Unburdened by their bloody history, he saw a simple solution: just use the ten letters the two languages have in common.

А   Б   В   Г   Д   Ђ   Е   Ж   З   И   Ј

К   Л   Љ   М   Н   Њ   О   П   Р   С   Т

Ћ   У   Ф   Х   Ц   Ч   Џ   Ш

A blend of optimism and skepticism can be leavened with a playful attitude. Recall the demeanor of Ambassador Holbrooke "yakking, talking, and jiving" during the middle of the Balkan peace talks. According to Nachmanovitch, "Play is the free spirit of exploration." Its mood, he adds, "can be impish or supremely solemn." The lesson for negotiators is that creativity requires shaking up and reordering what we know.

Our best ideas don't often come from lockstep analysis. Rather, it's through a process of juggling different possibilities, taking elements from each, and fashioning them into a novel solution. Scrabble players naturally shuffle letters in their rack. It's not nervousness. They're looking for a sequence that sparks a new idea. And *spark* is the right word: recent studies using functional magnetic resonance imaging (fMRI) scans show how Tetris game players' brains light up when they actively flip shapes on a video screen.

Great scientists engage in playful thinking as well. Albert Einstein said that many of his dazzling insights came from what he called "combinatorial play." He was a visual thinker who toyed with images in his head. Contemplating relativity, for example, he conjured a picture of himself riding a beam of light and carrying a clock. Sometimes great ideas may seem to come in a flash. The nineteenth-century German scientist Friedrich Kekule claimed that the hexagonal chemical structure of the benzene ring came to him in a daydream of six intertwined snakes. Of course, before he had that vision, he had been studying carbon bonds for years. He just had to make the right connections.

We can't simply wait for inspiration to strike. We have to keep working our ideas. Creative negotiators work both top down and bottom up, inductively and deductively. They play around with concepts and rules of thumb, wondering out loud how adding more issues to the mix could generate more value. If a comprehensive solution doesn't materialize, they break down the problem into smaller parts. When asked how he thought about complex diplomatic challenges, President Bill Clinton likened them to crossword puzzles: "You start with what you know the answer to and work from that. A lot of problems are like that. You have to find some aspect of it that you understand and build on it until you can unravel the mystery that you're trying to solve." Small victories move us forward, bolster our confidence, and expand our influence.

THE POWER OF ANALOGIES

Studies by Leigh Thompson and Dedre Gentner of Northwestern University, along with Jeffrey Loewenstein, now at the University of Illinois, show that familiarity with a negotiation concept doesn't guarantee that people will put it to practical use. The research team looked specifically at contingency clauses: contract terms that can transform differences in expectations into opportunities for mutual gain. For example, an injured baseball player may believe that he is fully healed and will have a great season, while his team is more pessimistic. Rather than arguing about who is right, they would be wise to craft an agreement with a low base salary but big performance bonuses. This contingency clause would reward the player appropriately if he is as healthy as he thinks he is but protect the team if he isn't.

The researchers presented this concept to subjects using two familiar pedagogical methods. One group read about trading on different expectations and then did a negotiation exercise in which that was a possible solution. Almost all of its members missed the latent opportunity. Reading about the principle was insufficient.

A second group was introduced to contingency clauses by actually doing a simulation that also had this potential and then debriefing its experience. Unfortunately, when these subjects were given a second simulation, set in a different context but with the same value-creating opportunity, *they missed it too.* It's as if after having had a lesson in preparing chocolate pudding, they were no better than novices when it came to making vanilla.

But the researchers weren't done. They tested two additional ways of introducing people to how contingency clauses can be used to generate value. A third group of subjects watched a video of people using this approach. (We'll get back to them in a bit.) A fourth group did a "warm-up analysis" in which people who were paired up to negotiate first read two different cases in which contingency clauses were used and then *compared* them. The researchers told them to look for parallels and share their impressions with each other.

This method did the trick. The fourth group was twice as likely to be creative as the first two were. These subjects applied what they had read and talked about in their own negotiations. The specific instructions about how to talk were critical, however. Still other subjects were given the same minicases and merely asked to discuss if they were successful negotiations. This control group didn't really learn to be creative either. Its performance was no better than that of people who did the simulation without any kind of introductory training in making comparisons.

What about group three, the subjects who watched a video of negotiators making good use of a contingency clause? Good news. Afterward, they handled the simulation creatively, too. But here's something quirky: when they were debriefed, they had no words to describe what they'd done or explanation of why they did it. Their learning was implicit. They became better negotiators without even knowing it.

We can read the message of the studies as being half empty or half full. The downside is that learning concepts and analyzing experience are necessary but insufficient in respect to becoming more creative negotiators. The upside is that we can improve, provided we take the added step of ruminating about comparisons between what we're doing now and what we've seen before. This analogical thinking is related to Colonel John Boyd's OODA loop model, the ongoing process of orienting ourselves by comparing what's unfolding before us with what we expected initially.

The fact that not many people think this way is actually encouraging. It's something we can do better if we attend to it seriously. While we're negotiating, our minds should turn over clever solutions we've seen elsewhere, no matter how far afield they might seem. We may find lessons, links, or combinations that could be helpful today. As you read about examples—in this book and elsewhere—stop and ask yourself: "Where have I seen that before?" "How could I have used that approach in deals that slipped through my fingers?" "How can I expand my know-how going forward?"

COLLABORATION

We've already noted that creativity is a challenge in negotiation because it involves multiple parties, each with his or her own agenda and style. Two heads can be better than one in other settings. A married couple can always finish a crossword faster than either spouse could alone. One may know science, while the other knows literature. But their real advantage comes from reciprocal contribution: the way that one person's answers help fill in the blanks for the other. You should strive for the same kind of collaboration in negotiation.

That's true even if you are the smartest person in the room and can see the ultimate solution long before it's apparent to others. Rushing things is often folly. Many years ago, the chief labor negotiator for General Electric, Lemuel Boulware, got himself in legal trouble trying to bypass the traditional bargaining process by simply putting his best—and final—offer on the table right at the start of talks.

He had run all the numbers, analyzed wages in comparable companies, and put together what he thought was a fair and reasonable compensation package. Perhaps it was. Who knows? But, no surprise, the union officials balked. They insisted that crafting a collective bargaining agreement must be mutual, and the courts agreed. Boulware's approach, even if sincere, blocked the union from advancing any of its ideas—perhaps to both sides' detriment.

The chances of an idea being accepted improve if both parties have a hand in developing the deal, especially if other stakeholders need to endorse it. Screenwriter-producer Robert Kosberg is called the "king of the pitch" in Hollywood. To sell an idea to a studio, he says, "You want the listener to become your collaborator so by the time he goes to pitch it to his boss, it's his story, and he has a vested interest. He's no longer pitching Bob Kosberg's project. He's pitching his project, and I'm lucky if my name gets mentioned."

In the best of all worlds, your willingness to toy with problems may inspire your counterpart to take a fresh look at the possibilities. The classic book *Getting to Yes* tells us to "invent before you judge." Premature criticism stifles brainstorming, its authors advise. When people are intent on poking holes in one another's proposals, they miss the seeds of other, more promising ideas.

A dialogue where both parties are building solutions, not tearing them down, will be peppered with comments such as "Just thinking out loud," "How can we go to school on what others have done?," "This may be off the wall, but," and "Wouldn't it be great if we could . . . ?" In negotiation, that kind of interchange requires a high level of comfort, openness, and trust.

Parties need to feel free to play with options that test the boundaries of practicality; otherwise they limit their options. However, brainstorming can happen only if there's a mutual understanding that floating ideas is not the same as making an offer. Even with good intentions, it's hard to separate inventing from judging. Whatever ideas are voiced may color perceptions and anchor expectations. Temporarily suspending judgment is helpful but not always possible.

Babson College professor Lakshmi Balachandra has studied potential investors' reactions to almost two hundred pitches by entrepreneurs. The substantive merit of their business plans matters, of course, but interpersonal dynamics often seal the deals. A presenter's poise, passion, and eye contact are in themselves strong predictors of success. Likewise, in negotiation, creative ideas don't sell themselves.

Timing is important as well. We have to resist the impulse to announce our brilliant solution until others understand the problem it addresses. Moreover, proposals are always relative in negotiation. That is, they're weighed against what our counterparts can get elsewhere and, also, what they think they'd gain by pressing us further. There's no magic formula for calculating the perfect moment to introduce a new idea that will bring a negotiation to a fruitful end. That's inevitably an intuitive judgment, one that requires experience and emotional intelligence. When we're assessing whether the time is right, we should consider the following:

- Have we earned our counterpart's confidence?
- In listening to his or her proposals, have we modeled the respect that we want given to our own ideas?

- Does the other side have realistic expectations?
- Have we managed other potential obstacles to agreement, such as strategic behavior and organizational constraints?
- Are there other things that we still could do to increase the odds of acceptance?

Skilled psychotherapists have a keen sense of timing. Judith Coche is a clinician in Philadelphia. A *New York Times* profile noted her ability to intercede between bickering spouses, "pulling out unexpected common threads in the stories the couples were telling, giving the assemblage a whiff of fresh perspective." Sometimes that means putting forth a provocative notion. "Causing the right amount of trouble is an art form," Coche says. She also does what she calls "seeding," putting forth a suggestion but letting it germinate if people aren't quite ready to accept it.

Negotiation likewise has similar ebbs and flows. Proposals ignored or rejected early on can be revisited, revised, and integrated later, when the parties realize that they are stuck. Nachmanovitch says that people often have to pass through such a phase to be truly creative. For negotiators, confronting an impasse may be the equivalent of hitting rock bottom. That's not a pleasant prospect, but it can jolt a person into thinking creatively.

ALIGNING INCENTIVES

We've looked at three puzzles so far in this chapter. The first described an imaginative solution to the problem of selling a home in the midst of a weak market. The second described a clever process for recruiting top talent to a fledgling firm. The third, involving license plates in the Balkans, underscored the importance of having a playful, optimistic mind-set. Here is a final conundrum, which illustrates another important aspect of creativity:

Puzzle Number 4

A neighborhood was alarmed about a landfill operator's application to increase the size of the dump. The residents had long been angry about windblown litter from the site landing all over their lawns. Expanding the facility would only make matters worse, they claimed. They vowed to continue their opposition unless the operator guaranteed payment to an independent contractor who'd clean up future debris to their full satisfaction. The operator refused, convinced that the neighbors would make a sweetheart deal with someone's brother-in-law to fix problems that the landfill hadn't even caused. His business could end up overpaying substantially.

The parties were at an impasse: the operator couldn't get his revised permit, and the neighbors still had trash floating into their yards. How could both sides do better?

The parties here had a long and antagonistic history, with each side imputing bad motives to the other. The lack of trust stymied creative problem solving. Town officials were caught in the middle. They were sympathetic to the abutters but also valued the landfill business, as it provided tax revenue and an important service to other citizens.

When other efforts at peacemaking failed, they hired an outside mediator, an environmental lawyer who had no prior ties to the community. He held a public session where people shot accusations back and forth, and then he met privately with individuals. His goal was to find a solution that would address everyone's core concerns. The landfill wanted to grow; that was obvious. And its neighbors wanted their own properties to be cleaner—much cleaner. The mediator then called together key representatives. He told them that he had come up with a possible solution, but he wanted everyone to hear each of its elements before expressing opposition or support.

"Point one," the mediator said. "At the start of each fiscal year, the landfill will advance one hundred thousand dollars to the town to cover cleanup costs." The owner started to speak. This was more than he was prepared to pay.

But the mediator put up his hand. "Hold on," he said. "Point two. Town officials will control that fund and put the cleanup work out to bid." The neighbors looked at one another. This scenario wasn't quite what they had in mind.

"Point three," the mediator continued. "At the end of the year, whatever's left of the fund will be divided two ways. Half will go back to the landfill operator. The town can spend the other half any way it wants."

A few people smiled. Others looked confused. "Run that last point by us again," somebody said. The mediator explained that whatever was left of the $100,000 would be divided, with the landfill getting a refund, of sorts. The town could spend the other half on the library, a new Little League field, or anything else it needed. Some people looked skeptical, as they were catching up with the idea that the problem that had long confounded them might have a practical solution. It was as if they were looking for holes in the plan and were perplexed that there weren't any.

The up-front guarantee of $100,000 addressed the concerns of even the most pessimistic opponents. In turn, the landfill operator was relieved to see that his exposure would be capped in the worst-case scenario and likely be much lower in the best. After all, the town would now have an incentive to control cleanup costs in order to enjoy a year-end bonus. As for the neighbors, after thinking about it, they actually liked that the landfill could earn back some of its money. Dangling that carrot could make it more careful about keeping trash from blowing off the site in the first place.

It was a simple and elegant solution, one that addressed past problems and created incentives for joint value creation going forward. The only regret was that someone hadn't thought of it earlier. Maybe things had to get bad before they got better. Maybe people would listen only to an outsider with no local political baggage. But often we can't count on a mediator riding in to solve our negotiation problems. Instead, we have to rely on our own creative vision and the capacity to explain it so that it is accepted.

KEY POINTS

- Trade on differences to generate value.
- Be creative about process as well as substance.
- To open up your imagination, step back and see what you'd suggest to someone else in your situation.
- Think analogically. How does the problem at hand compare and contrast with other situations that you've resolved?
- Expand your mental library of creative solutions.

[12] Wicked Learning

Margaret pushed the Down button a third time.

"Go ahead," said Richard with a sweep of his hand. "After you." Margaret looked up, half startled that the elevator was already there. She was too deep in her own thoughts to be embarrassed. "Yes," she said absently.

This was the first time that Margaret and Richard had met, and those were the only words they spoke. This would also be the last time their paths ever crossed. Yet at that particular moment, their fates were intertwined.

Unbeknownst to them, Richard and Margaret had been competing against each other for a lucrative contract with ComTX, a major telecommunications company. Each had survived a review process in which dozens of proposals had been winnowed down to two finalists. They each had worked nonstop this past week, trying to negotiate a winning deal.

And here they were, strangers bumping into each other late on a Friday afternoon, having just left different offices on the forty-fourth floor of ComTX's imposing Midtown tower. One of them had just signed a contract with the communications giant. The other had been thanked politely by a company official but told that another bidder had been selected for the project.

Richard rocked back and forth on the balls of his feet, a grin spreading across his face, as the elevator began its descent. He could feel his tension drain. It was all he could do to keep from whistling. Glancing over at Margaret, he was tempted to ask, "Is everything okay?"

Her brow was furrowed, and she was shaking her head no, as if she were lost in a difficult internal conversation. Margaret took a deep breath, but that didn't seem to do much good. She was consumed by anxiety and self-doubt.

How, then, is it that *Margaret* carried the signed contract in her briefcase, while *Richard* had just been told that his deal was dead?

LEARNING FROM EXPERIENCE

What constitutes success in negotiation? And, for that matter, what is failure?

This story is a parable, though it's surely been enacted countless times in the real world. (All the other examples in this book are based on actual negotiations.) Here Richard walked away empty-handed, yet his spirits were buoyant. He had fought the good fight, he told himself. Time after time, when negotiations with ComTX seemed to be at a dead end, he had found a creative way to keep the dialogue going. Sometimes that meant tweaking his proposal in response to what he'd learned about the client's priorities. At another point, he encouraged someone across the table to become a de facto champion of his bid.

Richard was pleased, in fact, that his proposal had gotten as far as it did. He was confident of his own abilities and those of the team he had assembled, yet this project had always been a stretch. Together they had worked hard on the plan, though their principal goal was getting their name out. Even if they had little prospect of winning the contract, they knew they'd learn a lot just by going through the process. Richard and his colleagues were a bit surprised that they survived the first cut. Later, when told they were one of two finalists, they were astonished.

As implausible as winning had first seemed, some of Richard's partners started to believe that they'd be selected. "Don't count your chickens," he warned. Their presentation was strong, but his new team didn't have much of a track record. And the truth was, he was a bit superstitious, too. The surest way to jinx the deal would be to assume that it was all locked up.

Maybe Richard even knew ComTX better than it knew itself. The company would be tempted by his team's innovative approach, yet in the end, its conservative bureaucracy would feel safer going with a more established outfit. He was the runner-up, the silver medalist, but in his mind, there was little chance his bid would triumph.

That's not to say he didn't try. On the contrary. If Richard was at peace with himself on the elevator, it was because he knew that he had done his best. He had been patient, inventive, and, yes, forceful, too, when necessary. Perhaps Richard could have clinched the deal if he had conceded on each and every point, but there were certain principles he didn't want to compromise.

For instance, he might have snared the contract with ComTX had he been willing to cut costs by squeezing out one of his teammates, but that just didn't sit right with him. Forging a business relationship with ComTX would have been great, but not if that meant swallowing a financial loss or rupturing a relationship. It wasn't as if Richard hadn't gained anything. He had established important contacts and had learned a lot about a promising new market. Already he had ideas for potential projects that were closer to his expertise and might better meet ComTX's needs.

"Give it a rest," Richard told himself. This would be the first weekend in more than a month that he wouldn't be working the phone or redrafting memos. He deserved some time off. Rowing out to his vintage sloop would clear his mind. He could clean the winches, varnish the teak. Or why not go out for a long sail just the way the boat is? Leave the cosmetic work for some other time.

As Richard was mentally casting off and hoisting the main, Margaret's thoughts were still back in the conference room. All the ComTX people had seemed eager. Their enthusiasm was flattering, yes, but maybe their desire to nail down the deal signaled something. Were they desperate? Lots of small firms must have submitted proposals, but perhaps her chief competitors had dropped out at the last minute. Or maybe the ComTX team couldn't agree on any other bidder. If that were the case, Margaret told herself, she should have been steadfast and held out for a better overhead rate.

The ComTX's team clearly valued her work—otherwise it wouldn't have awarded her the job—but Margaret was less convinced that she'd earned her new client's respect as a negotiator. Sitting alone across the table from their team had been a little intimidating, particularly as the talks wore on. The numbers person would quibble about this or that, and then one of its marketing types would take the conversation in a different direction.

ComTX's senior vice president sat opposite Margaret with an inscrutable look on his face, not saying a word. Was this some new negotiation gambit, she wondered: good-cop, mime-cop? Did they practice their roles before each meeting? There was no way of knowing, of course, but Margaret was sure that after every session, they must have dissected everything she said and how she said it.

There were times she had wanted to be more aggressive—to say no forcefully—but she had bitten her tongue. As the only woman in the room, she feared that being tough might come off as being bitchy. Her younger brother could always be a wise guy, quick with a smart comment or put-down, and get away with it. But growing up, she had learned that if she said the same thing, she was accused of having an attitude. At the playground and in a business meeting, there was one code for men and another for women.

"Stop obsessing," she told herself as the elevator descended. "What's done is done." But now her mind turned to the hard work ahead. She'd have to make copies of the signed contract and lead her partners through what it meant, line by line. Margaret knew that she'd have some selling to do. She had promised ComTX a lot, including an ambitious delivery date. She and her colleagues would have to scramble to pull together all the pieces. Margaret expected one person in particular to be critical of commitments she had made on their behalf. "I'm not necessarily disagreeing with the terms," Anne in marketing would say, "but I'm not very happy with the process."

Margaret had tried to keep everyone informed, but she was the one who had to make the hard decisions. Now, of course, she'd have to listen to her colleagues tell her how they would have done things differently. The reward for negotiating the ComTX deal, she thought ruefully, was now having to negotiate with her own people to make it happen. With so much left to do, she probably should cancel dinner with her friend Kim tonight.

MAXIMIZERS AND SATISFICERS

Who would you rather be, Margaret or Richard?

That's not an easy choice. If Margaret is tied up in knots, she's also the one who got the contract. Richard may be mellow, but serenity doesn't pay the rent. He's walking out without a deal, after all. It would be bliss to have it both ways, of course—triumphing at the bargaining table while maintaining peace of mind—but it may be that Margaret's temperament gave her an advantage over Richard.

Back in the "Prospecting" chapter, I mentioned psychologist Barry Schwartz, who adapted a short test that distinguishes people whom he calls maximizers from others who are satisficers. You can find the test in his stimulating book *The Paradox of Choice: Why More Is Less*. Maximizers fret over every decision. At a restaurant, they scrutinize the menu from top to bottom and then back again, weighing the appeal of each item. Even after giving the waiter their order, they wonder if they should have asked for something else. By contrast, satisficers just take a quick glance at the offerings, spot something they like, order it, and don't worry about it further.

Margaret is a poster child for the first category, while Richard probably falls into the second. What's interesting, though, is that these differences are more than mere personality quirks. How people feel about choices—specifically, how much they agonize over them—significantly influences what they achieve in negotiation. As mentioned earlier, there was a catch: maximizers are *less happy* with what they get.

For Margaret, success and discontent may go hand in hand. All that brooding can't be fun, but her relentless self-criticism may have yielded insights that eluded Richard. She doesn't take things at face value. She always wonders what she has overlooked or misread. Those traits left her feeling less happy but may have impelled her to look harder—both at the situation and at herself. She worries about the right things too. After all, it is possible that she left value on the table. And she's right in recognizing how social norms affect what a woman can say and do in negotiation (and elsewhere). She thinks hard about the substantive issues and how she relates to others.

And what should we make of Richard? If an optimist is someone who sees the glass as half full, Richard looks like a guy who has just been handed an empty glass but somehow convinces himself that he isn't really thirsty. He recognizes that negotiation is a learning experience, yet did he grasp the right lessons?

Richard has no regrets, but he may have been blind to opportunities to save the deal. For all he really knows, he may have been oblivious to signals that ComTX was sending. We just can't know whether he was astute, obtuse, or somewhere in between—and neither can he. His positive spin may be exactly right. Then again, it might be only rationalization and self-delusion, exhibit A in a text on cognitive dissonance. If Margaret takes self-criticism to the extreme, perhaps Richard could use more of that trait.

THE FEEDBACK PROBLEM

It's devilishly hard to judge success in negotiation. You may love an agreement you reach or feel lukewarm about it, but either way, results themselves are an imperfect test of how well you've done.

Let's say that you just bought a car at the price you hoped. Isn't that success? Yes, in a sense, but the fact that you achieved your goal doesn't tell you whether with a little more persistence you could have kept another $600 or $700 in your pocket. Maybe your aspirations weren't high enough. Then again, another time you might be disappointed that you paid more than expected. Is that failure? Maybe not, if the seller wouldn't have gone a penny lower. The true, substantive test of negotiation success, then, is how well you do in light of what is possible. The problem, though, is that you never know what the other party might have accepted.

Throughout this book, we've seen how a shroud of fog obscures the negotiation landscape. Even after a deal is done, it presents a serious challenge to effective learning. Were you smart last time or merely lucky? Robin Hogarth, author of *Educating Intuition*, contrasts what he calls *kind* and *wicked* learning environments. A kind environment provides quick and accurate feedback on your actions. It shows you what works and what does not, so that you learn easily from experience and make adjustments.

Imagine a basketball player practicing free throws at the foul line. If the ball goes in smoothly, he should keep on doing what he just did. And if it clanks off the rim, he should experiment—maybe next time trying more knee bend or more arc on the ball. Through trial and error, he'll get reliable feedback: the ball either goes in or it doesn't. He can learn and improve.

Negotiation, on the other hand, is a quintessentially wicked learning environment. If you're not careful, it can teach the wrong lessons. Let's say that you've worked hard to close an important deal but ultimately were stalemated. What should you conclude?

There are lots of plausible explanations. Maybe you were deadlocked because there just wasn't any room for agreement. Perhaps you overplayed your hand, expecting the other side to buckle when it wouldn't. (Or maybe your counterparts misread your resolve.) Or it could have been a failure of creative insight on everyone's part. Perhaps a lack of trust may have been the obstacle. Behind-the-scenes stakeholders may have scuttled the deal. Any and all of those factors could have been in play. You might have caused the impasse or had nothing to do with it.

Explaining success is just as dicey. If we make a great deal, we like to think that it was due to our virtue, charm, and intelligence. In truth, though, it may simply be that we were in the right place at the right time.

How, then, can you tap your experience and improve as a negotiator if you can't know for sure why you've succeeded in some cases and failed in others? Three precepts can sharpen your learning:

1. Beware of mislearning. Admitting that you don't know is better than operating from an erroneous conclusion.
2. Don't confuse satisfaction with success.
3. Remember: it's not all about you.

It's natural to congratulate yourself when you succeed and second-guess your setbacks. Letting go of such judgments isn't easy. But acknowledging uncertainty is far better than clinging to—and acting upon—mistaken assumptions. The most important thing is to avoid mislearning. Just because you were stalemated in a case where you held your ground on an important issue doesn't necessarily mean that you should be more accommodating the next time around. The other side may have been responsible for the deadlock.

Self-assessments must be provisional, since the information on which they are based is necessarily incomplete. People learn from what they see, but not necessarily from what they don't see. The fog of negotiation can't be wished away, but you can guard yourself against being overconfident about what you discern.

A while back, it was time to replace my car, so I returned to a dealership I'd done business with for years. My old salesman had retired, so that evening I found myself talking with his tiresome replacement. He ran through a whole gamut of pressure tactics. If it hadn't been so late and I wasn't busy, it would have been entertaining, but I just wanted to buy a car and get on with my life.

We haggled down to a decent price, but I was so turned off, I said, "Let me think about it. I'll call you in the morning." At that moment, I just didn't want to reward the salesman's behavior. He glared at me and said, "Someone else could snap it up." It was 8:27, and the showroom was closing in three minutes. "I'll take my chances," I replied, but I don't think he caught my sarcasm.

I was planning to call back the next morning and do the deal, either at a little better price or at his number, if need be. But driving home, I mulled over how unpleasant the guy had been. Yes, I liked the car, and yes, the price was acceptable, but the more I thought about it, the less I wanted to do business with him. The next day, I bought the same model elsewhere for the same money. I haven't been back to my old dealership since.

What did this salesman learn from that experience?

My guess is, nothing. Instead, he remembers other times that his pressure tactics seemed to work with customers who paid a fat premium over his bottom line. Yet there's nothing in his feedback system that teaches him about all the deals that he has lost with people like me. To him, I may have looked like just another tire kicker, not somebody who was ready to write him a check (as I actually was). From where I sit, it's easy to recognize his mislearning, but anyone can fall into that trap.

ENDS AND MEANS

We mislearn when we draw hard conclusions from incomplete and ambiguous evidence. We also mislearn when we confuse *what we ultimately obtained* in a negotiation with *how we performed*. As already noted, luck—good and bad—can influence what happens in the course of negotiation.

In the movie *The Verdict*, a down-and-out lawyer played by Paul Newman rejects a settlement offer without even telling his clients. Instead, he takes his chances in court. That's unethical, of course, but movies being movies, he wins dramatically thanks to a surprise witness at the end. Was he smart in refusing to negotiate or merely lucky?

Compare that story with a real-life case involving a blind college student who brought a medical malpractice suit. She accepted a $165,000 settlement, against the advice of her lawyer and family, while the jury was in its third hour of deliberations. It was on the verge of awarding her $900,000. Some of its members burst into tears when they learned that the settlement had rendered their verdict moot. Did the student make a grave mistake?

It might seem that way, but she was philosophical. "I think I made a wise decision," she explained. "Everybody said, 'You've got it won.' But I wasn't sure. They [the insurance company] said they definitely would have appealed and there's a chance I would have lost it all." The only practical test of the wisdom of an agreement depends on what was known and knowable at the time it was made. Subsequent events over which you have no control may make it look better or worse. At first we may love the house we bought and be pleased that we got it at a great price. A year later, when a guy who raises pit bulls moves in next door, we may wish that we had blown it. As the carnival barker says, you place your bet and take your chances.

Even when circumstances turn out as we'd hoped, things we worked hard to get in negotiation can look different after we win them. Dan Gilbert, author of *Stumbling on Happiness*, has found that most of us aren't that good at predicting how we'll feel in the future. We know that positive things will make us happy and that negative ones will make us sad, of course, but we tend to overestimate both the magnitude and duration of our future feelings. We can be similarly myopic when we negotiate. Whatever satisfaction Margaret felt at signing the ComTX deal gave way to regret even as she was leaving the building.

It's healthy to remember that whatever you're seeking to achieve (or avoid) during negotiation may not matter as much to you in the future. That's not invariably true, of course, but the anxiety you feel in the moment often abates—and likewise for exuberance. If you keep that in mind, short-term and long-term considerations may come into sharper focus. The same attitude is important when you look back and try to draw lessons from past experience. You should ask yourself whether certain things you tend to fight for have lasting value. The pleasure of winning small ego battles may be fleeting.

ONE HAND CLAPPING?

To learn from experience, we need a wide-angle lens. Too often we zoom in on details and miss the bigger picture. I see this tendency a lot in my

MBA and executive education courses. When students do simulations, paired up as a buyer and a seller, every person is eager to see how he or she did. Results typically vary widely. Some people sell high, while others buy low, even though everyone was working with the same information. When we dig into analysis, most students tell self-centered stories. Those who snatched up bargains think it was all their own doing. Others who paid more than necessary beat themselves up for making stupid mistakes.

Self-centered comments miss the point, however. Wherever a student ends up is driven as much by what his counterpart did as by his own actions. After all, for every buyer scrutinizing an outcome for clues about what he did right or wrong, there is a seller trying to figure out the same thing for himself.

Negotiation is never about us alone. What ultimately unfolds is a function of each party's attitudes and decisions, not just our own. Asking ourselves, "How did *I* do?" is the wrong question. It's a one-hand-clapping exercise. *Instead, our starting point should be, where did* we *end up and how did* we *get there?*

Posing the question that way focuses attention on how you interacted with your counterpart. It leads you to review more closely how the process unfolded at each stage of the process:

- Recall how you and your counterpart engaged each other when the negotiation began. Was the opening friendly, hostile, or someplace in between? How did the both of you frame the task ahead?

- Likewise for critical moments. Were there transition points where the process could have taken a sharp turn? Were these rifts or breakthroughs? What provoked them, and how were they handled?

- Finally, what brought the negotiation to a close? Is this what you anticipated? If not, could you have planned for it?

It's a matter of dispassionately reconstructing—not judging—what took place. You will do a better job and learn more if you've taken notes along the way. Only after getting the facts down should you turn to evaluating your performance.

Some of my Program on Negotiation colleagues employ the acronyms WWW and WWYDD as debriefing reminders. The first one stands for what worked well. If you handled a prickly exchange deftly or came up with a clever solution, keep those techniques in mind for your next negotiation. Just as important, identify what allowed you to respond effectively. Perhaps it was good preparation, the right kind of emotional balance, or some combination of the two. Building that foundation for future negotiations will help you handle other challenges.

WWYDD is short for what would you do differently. This is an important question, whether you feel snookered or successful. Margaret got halfway there in her ruminating. She worried about the right things, but she should take the further step of playing out what would have happened if she had acted differently. Not being as flippant as her wise-guy brother was smart, but negotiating solo against a formidable team may have been a mistake. Having another set of eyes and ears at the table would have allowed her to calibrate her own impressions.

Don't forget to similarly assess the person you just faced. You probably saw her up close. What did she do well, and what might she have done better? Consider the underlying factors that might explain her attitude and behavior, starting with her perceptions of you. And if you feel that you didn't get a good outcome, there might be consolation in regarding the experience as an instructive demonstration of what effective negotiation entails.

You can do this reflection on your own or as part of a team, if you were negotiating on behalf of your company or organization. People recognize the importance of preparing seriously for negotiation but too often neglect to analyze their experience afterward. It's a lost opportunity for organizations and individuals alike. "After-action reviews" are a matter of course in the military; they should be common practice in negotiation as well.

Think about the car dealership I no longer patronize. Its salesman not only blew that particular deal but also cost the company a longtime customer. And if ComTX didn't debrief after negotiating with Richard and Margaret, it certainly should have. The potential benefits for companies that take a systemic approach to their negotiations are huge, especially if it helps them identify their best negotiators and develop the skills of others. *Built to Win: Creating a World-Class Negotiating Organization* by Hal Movius and Larry Susskind lays out a practical blueprint for enhancing corporate negotiation competence.

I recommend as a further step, conducting an annual review of your negotiation fitness. You likely undergo a regular physical from your doctor, after all. If you're lucky enough to have a nest egg, you check on your investments with your financial advisor. Do the same with your negotiation portfolio: see if you're getting a healthy return on your efforts.

Keep a journal documenting transactions large and small. It should include projects that you'd considered but soon dropped, as well as others that you saw all the way through to agreement. From your planning notes, you might see how you could have better allowed for surprises. You could also compute a success rate. If you reach a deal most every time, you are being awfully agreeable. Have they all panned out? You may discover that you conceded too much in deals that didn't work. Maybe you should get more comfortable with the idea of walking away from the table. Also look for patterns. Are you better at price-driven transactions or ones where it's possible to create joint gain? Work on your weaker suit. That's where you'll have the biggest upside for improvement. And look at your own behavior. If you recognize your hot buttons, you'll be less likely to lose your composure in a heated negotiation.

If need be, you can do this annual exam on your own, though that means being both player and coach. Better still, recruit a friend or colleague for this exercise. It will help you be more discerning and objective. And in returning the favor, you can learn from his or her experience as well.

ARROGANCE AND HUMILITY

Earlier in this book, I spoke of the importance of being modest about how much we can know in negotiation and not treating assumptions as hard facts. I also stressed the need to master paradox. To be effective, negotiators must be both calm and alert, patient and proactive, creative yet fully grounded.

UN diplomat Lakhdar Brahimi describes another, more fundamental duality. "You need, I think, to be at the same time arrogant, because you want to solve problems that look insolvable, but you also need to be very, very humble." Brahimi insists that these two traits aren't contradictory. By arrogance, he means determination, the belief that something "is do-able, even if everybody says it isn't." Just as important, however, "You need to be modest; don't play God."

How could it be otherwise? Nobody is omniscient. Modesty about what will occur is essential. Yet you also need the will to act notwithstanding that uncertainty. Top negotiators such as Brahimi project a certain equanimity. Their comfort with paradox arises from a basic acceptance of what is ultimately within their power and what is not. "Accept failure like it is part of the job," Brahimi says. "And see how much luck you can have and take along with you."

KEY POINTS

- Be a maximizer as you negotiate, but consider how your actions will impact your counterpart's decisions.
- Be a satisficer when you're finished, content with what you've achieved, and focused on the next transaction.
- Deal or no deal, conduct an after-action review. Focus on how you prepared for and managed the negotiation. Were there surprises that you should have seen coming?
- Review your negotiation portfolio so that you can build on your strengths and shore up any weaknesses.
- Accept the luck factor in negotiation. Your results—good or bad—aren't all of your own doing.

[13] Fair Enough

Every time we sit down to negotiate, we implicitly decide what we owe other parties—if anything—in regard to fairness, honesty, or the use of pressure tactics. The hardest questions aren't about right or wrong—rather, they force us to reconcile competing rights and obligations. Often we must deal with people whose values don't match our own.

SCENARIO I: DIVIDING THE PIE

Imagine that you've saved some money and are at a stage in life where you want to buy a vacation home. You're not looking for anything fancy, just a cabin in the woods, far from the city, where you can get away and relax. The real estate market in your area is soft, so you're hopeful that you can find something reasonably priced. After thinking carefully about your baseline, you're prepared to pay around $200,000, though exactly how much you'll spend will depend on the particular place and how it compares with others.

On recent weekends, you've done some prospecting, meeting with real estate agents and looking at properties. These outings were enjoyable at first, but now you're discouraged. Everything that you've liked costs at least $250,000, sometimes more. Even if you negotiate well, a decent place may be beyond your budget. You may have to put this plan on hold.

But on your latest excursion, you spot a hand-painted sign, For Sale by Owner—Inquire Within. You slow down and turn into a gravel drive-way. There it is: a well-maintained cabin nestled among tall pines. Off to one side is a glistening pond.

The elderly owner shows you around the place. You accept her invita-tion to sit down for tea and listen politely to the story of how her family built the cabin almost fifty years ago. You also talk about politics, the latest books, and even sports, yet there's been no mention of price. You're careful about spending money, but this place is by far the best you've seen. Maybe you should stretch your budget.

The owner finally broaches the topic and says, "It's always awkward to talk about money, I know, so I hope you won't be offended if I'm asking too much." It turns out that she is moving back to the city to be closer to her grandchildren. The cost of living is higher there, so she'll need to get every penny that she can garner from this sale. That's why she's not using a broker.

You brace yourself for a number that's way out of your price range. But then you're shocked when she asks only $180,000. As you know from looking at other properties, this figure is way under market value. How do you respond?

I'll sharpen the question. Whatever you decide, there's no downside. You can draft a simple offer to purchase that gives you complete protec-tion if there's any problem with legal title to the property or its physical condition. Likewise, you can write a small, fully refundable check to se-cure the deal. Now, taking all that into account, how would you respond to the owner's $180,000 price?

A. Quickly accept the asking number.
B. Counteroffer with a somewhat lower figure, knowing that you can always agree to the $180,000 if necessary.
C. Inform the owner that you want to buy the cabin, but you believe she has undervalued it.

Take a moment to think about the pros and cons of each of these options. You might do something different, but pick the one that comes closest to what you'd say. Also, note which of the responses seems least desirable. Why?

I've presented this scenario to executive program participants from all over the globe. Opinion on the right thing to do is always sharply divided. Forty-five percent say that they'd quickly agree to the owner's asking price. But 29 percent say that they'd counteroffer. Almost as many (26 percent) say that they'd inform the seller that the price is below market value.

I start case discussion by posting the tally and then ask those people who'd inform the owner that the price is too low to explain their choice. They typically speak in general terms. Taking advantage of an elderly person troubles them, they say. It just feels unfair. I push a bit to see how they define fairness. Would they feel any differently, I ask, if they were certain the person is mentally competent? I remind them that in the conversation over tea, she was well informed about current affairs.

That's not the problem, they reply. What bothers them is that they know the local real estate market much better than the seller does. Bargaining power is unfairly tilted in their favor. When pressed, they acknowledge that there isn't a precise measure of fairness. They see it more as a reasonable range, not an exact number. While they'd be happy to buy at the lower end of that band, the asking price seems far below that here.

I next turn to the group that would make a counteroffer and ask them to respond to the arguments that they just heard about fairness. "Seller beware," some say. For them, it's a logical corollary of the caveat emptor principle. They assert that buyers and sellers both have the responsibility to know what something is worth. Others note that this owner chose to save money by not hiring an expert broker, so if there's any blame, it falls on her shoulders.

People who take this position are on solid legal ground, at least in most Western countries. Courts sometimes invalidate agreements where there has been a mistake, but the misunderstanding must be mutual. If a customer walks into a jewelry store, pays $50 for a Timex watch, but an absent-minded clerk inadvertently hands her a much more valuable Rolex, that wouldn't be what either party intended. There'd be no real meeting of the minds. Other than that, however, courts are leery about second-guessing mistakes about value, especially when the error is unilateral.

Meeting legal requirements is merely a threshold requirement, of course. Moral standards may be more stringent. I challenge the counterofferers by asking, What if this is your family's cabin and the owner is your grandmother? Some stranger comes along and exploits her ignorance about property values. How would you feel then?

A few people get the point. If we believe that an action is morally justified for us but not others, we're applying a double standard. However, most people who'd counteroffer say that they wouldn't criticize another buyer who took advantage, even if they happened to be on the wrong end of that deal. They regard negotiation as an arm's-length process where each party is responsible only for his or her well-being. It's up to others to take care of themselves. ("If I have any problem," said one manager, "it's with Grandma for not checking with me first.")

Debate over this case is always spirited. Usually I can step back and let people challenge one another's reasoning, but I make sure to get the third group into the discussion. These are the middle-ground people who'd simply snap up the owner's asking price. If you don't feel obliged to inform the seller that she has underpriced the property, I ask, why not counteroffer?

It's hard to pin down these people when they answer. Most start by saying that they don't want to risk blowing a great deal. Fine, I say, but that's a pragmatic argument, not a moral one. Moreover, the risk of countering here is low, especially if you do it gently. For example, one could say, "I might be able to make your $180,000 work, but I know I could do it for sure at $160,000."

Even so, there's something else that makes them squeamish about countering. "If the seller is happy," they say, "then I'm happy." They emphasize that it was the owner who put the low number on the table. As they see it, fairness is about process as much as it is about outcome. If the other side undervalues what it's selling, then that wasn't due to anything that the buyer did. By contrast, buyers who actively push for a lower price may share some responsibility for the result. For them, it's the difference between sins of commission and sins of omission.

The three alternative courses of action represent contrasting views of right and wrong in negotiation. Bear in mind that whichever answer you chose was passed over by most people in my survey. Some of them rated it as the worst option (just as whichever alternative option you rated as worst was some people's favorite).

The core problem in this example is inherent in any negotiation. Need we worry about the overall fairness of an agreement? People don't use fancy philosophical language to justify their choices in this scenario, though I'm struck by how firmly they state their conclusions. Minds don't seem to change. Discussion doesn't lead to consensus. If anything, people seem to become more entrenched in their particular views. Some see negotiation as a micromarket: a voluntary process where anyone who feels mistreated can say no and walk away. Others maintain that when we negotiate, we define ourselves in relationship to others. Are we isolated economic agents, they ask, or members of a larger community?

It doesn't have to be one or the other. Even if we have responsibilities for others, we also have the right to advance our own interests. "If we are not for ourselves," asked Hillel the Elder, a Jewish religious leader of the first century, "who will be?" But then he added, "If we are only for ourselves, who are we?"

Being fair requires self-sacrifice. I'm not talking about being fair simply out of reputational concern. Believing that what goes around comes around is fine, but that's just an enlightened view of self-interest. **In the purest sense, fairness means leaving something on the table with no expectation that the favor will be returned or commended. It's a matter of doing so because it feels right.**

Before closing discussion of the case, I come back to the people who'd inform the owner that the property is underpriced. "Exactly how would that work?" I ask with a smile. "How does a buyer talk a seller *up* in negotiation?"

These people admit it could be risky. The owner might decide to retain a broker. Maybe the price of the cabin would get jacked way up. Still, most say they'd rather take that chance than feel guilty later. They also point out that the owner might appreciate the candor and reciprocate by sticking with the initial figure. (Remember how the owner of Bold Island in Maine overruled her lawyer's instruction to increase the price?)

The two parties might determine jointly what's fair—perhaps a number that's higher than the asking price but less than full market value. Or they might find other ways to generate value. If the buyer wouldn't be able to use the property all the time, for instance, maybe she could rent it to the owner's family at a bargain rate. Or if her family could use it free of charge, the negotiators might end up back at the original asking price.

Virtue isn't always rewarded, and fairness may not always be a priority. In this case, though, informing the seller seems like the most promising avenue for expanding the deal space. Snapping up the owner's offer would make the transaction into a zero-sum game. You'd get more. She'd get less. Likewise for countering with a lowball offer. Instead, shining a light on how both parties value what they are trading could reveal opportunity for mutual gain.

SCENARIO 2: THE TRUTH, THE WHOLE TRUTH, OR SOMETHING LIKE THE TRUTH

Now flash forward a few years. Assume that you bought the rustic cabin for an acceptable price. You've enjoyed the place but have learned that a motorcycle track will be built nearby in just a few months. The new facility will meet all environmental and land-use regulations, but there is no doubt that you'll hear the noise, especially on weekends. It's time for you to move on.

You found the old For Sale sign that the prior owner had painted and nailed it to the same tree by the roadside. An eager young couple, driving an expensive car, has toured the property and appears ready to make an offer. One of them asks, "Why would you ever want to sell such a beautiful place?"

Which of the following comes closest to how you'd answer that question? (Again note also which would be least desirable.)

A. "You know, ever since I put up the sign, I've been thinking the same thing myself."
B. "I'm worried that the noise from the new motorcycle track may be disturbing."
C "Oh, I guess it just feels like time to try something new."

Think about what you'd likely say on the spur of the moment. Is it the same answer you'd give if you had anticipated the question beforehand?

More than 60 percent of the people I've surveyed favor the third response: namely, saying that it just feels like the right time to move. Alternatives A and B each garners only 18 percent support. In class discussion, this time I start with the majority, asking them why their try-something-new answer is better than the other two. They zero in on the negative impact of telling the buyers about the motorcycle track. Disclosure could kill the deal or at least knock down the property's value in the buyers' eyes.

This is a results-oriented view of the question. It considers how our actions affect us (see part one of Hillel's aphorism about advocating for ourselves), but it disregards what that statement says about us in relationship to the other party (Hillel's part two). The implicit rule seems to be one of convenience: apparently it's fine to be honest if it doesn't cost us anything (for instance, if we're motivated to sell because we're moving to another part of the country), but not if telling the truth hurts.

The underlying reasoning may be more complex than that, however. When I ask these "try something new" people why they prefer that to feigning second thoughts about selling (as the first answer implies), they say that the latter is an outright lie, whereas their response is not. At first that may seem like hairsplitting. Yes, it is true that you want to go someplace else. But that response is deliberately misleading in that it omits the fact that their decision is triggered by upcoming noise in the area.

Perhaps the distinction is just an alibi, a way that some people salve their conscience. But others might see it as a legitimate tactic for ducking the question; avoiding having to choose between self-interest and obligations to others, at least for the moment. Some people who choose this option maintain that they would never tell an overt lie, but they have no reservations about answering questions as narrowly as possible. If the prospective buyer asked a more direct question ("Are there any potential problems with the property that could give me a concern?"), they'd feel compelled to reveal more information.

There are two lessons here, one for each side of the transaction. For would-be buyers, it's about asking questions the right way. Precision and persistence are essential. Asking general questions in negotiation invites vague answers. Be persistent pinning down details. In turn, sellers who don't want to reveal any more than necessary should be ready for follow-ups. Saying "It's time to try something new" might end the inquiry with some people, but others may continue by asking, "Why? Is there some problem?" Know ahead of time what you will feel obliged to disclose if you're pressed. And remember that being evasive can cost you credibility.

Going back to the second option, only 18 percent of the managers I've surveyed say that they'd mention the new motorcycle track the moment they were asked. (Most of the other respondents ranked this the worst choice.) Nevertheless, this approach may be wise. In fact, it would be legally required in some places.

Specific laws vary from country to country—indeed, from state to state in the United States—but many courts disallow fraudulent transactions. Fraud is commonly defined as an intentional misrepresentation of fact on which someone reasonably relies to his or her detriment. Just because a statement is false doesn't make it fraudulent. It must be deliberately misleading. Moreover, it has to be plausible, cause real harm, and pertain to facts, not subjective opinions. Thus, a salesperson's puffery

("This is the finest automobile ever made") doesn't constitute fraud, even if the vehicle in question is a Yugo. And it's all right, legally at least, to say "I'll never pay a penny to settle this case," even if you know that you could write a big check if you ultimately have to do so.

The elements of fraud are easy to state in the abstract. Applying them in specific cases gets tricky. Proving that a particular seller's statement was intentional can be hard, for example. Likewise for showing reasonable reliance on the buyer's part. Fraud is even harder to establish in negotiations where instead of saying something false, a seller remains silent. Legal rules set the bar low when it comes to truth telling. Most moral principles require a higher standard of conduct. In any event, it makes pragmatic sense to keep well away from any gray area. Lawsuits are costly. So is a reputation for sharp dealing.

It's curious in this scenario that fewer people (18 percent) say that they'd disclose information about the new motorcycle track than the 26 percent in the first case who'd inform the owner that her property was underpriced. If you're willing to tell someone that she's shortchanging herself why not also share secondary information that may (or may not) influence how she values things?

My guess is that context is at work here. At least some of the respondents may have adjusted their answers according to whom they think they are dealing with. They may feel more generous toward a charming older person in apparent need of money than they do toward a younger couple who just arrived in a fancy car. There's nothing inherently wrong with making that distinction, but we should be aware of our biases, whether they lead us to be more or less generous.

When I present the first scenario in class, I take care not to mention gender. Instead, I refer consistently to the owner as the seller or the person. Yet almost invariably, people nevertheless assume that the owner is a woman. Essentially, they paint a mental picture, coloring it in with their own experience and values. We do that in real life as well. Dealing with others, even strangers, we don't start with a blank canvas. We bring in old associations, be they positive or negative.

It would be natural to assume that when we come upon a knotty problem, we analyze it from multiple perspectives and then arrive at a well-reasoned conclusion.

PROBLEM → REASON → JUDGMENT

Recent scientific findings, however, indicate that many of our moral judgments really are visceral. NYU professor Jonathan Haidt puts it succinctly: "Moral reasoning, when it occurs, is usually a post-hoc process in which we search for evidence to support our initial intuitive reaction."

PROBLEM → EMOTION → JUDGMENT → REASON

That's a bold and unsettling claim. It tramples the notion that we are principled actors who reach moral conclusions through a deliberative process. That's not what neuroscientists see, however, when they conduct fMRI scans of subjects being asked to make choices. When people are presented with ethical quandaries, the emotional parts of the brain that register fear, disgust, and empathy fire up before the conscious mind kicks in. Those first reactions color our subsequent thinking. We can concoct justifications for what are actually gut responses. If someone pokes a hole in our rationale, we can come up with another argument without realizing what's actually driving our decisions.

Some emotional responses are sound and praiseworthy, of course. The fleeting thought of cheating somebody may trigger self-contempt or disgust. That's good. So is the compassion we feel for someone who deserves a decent slice of the pie. But our first impressions deserve a second look.

SCENARIO 3: CHOOSING BETWEEN RIGHT AND RIGHT

This time imagine that you've been negotiating the sale of some property owned by your company. After some discussion, the buyer made an attractive offer that you orally accepted and shook hands on. Your boss is pleased with the terms as they stand but has suggested that you tell the buyer that he or she has to improve the price to get the deal approved. "No harm in asking," your boss says.

Which of the following responses comes closest to what you would do? As before, note which option is the least desirable:

A. Tell your boss that you've already given your word to the buyer and that you're uncomfortable going back on it.
B. Do exactly what your boss says. It's a common bargaining tactic, after all.
C. Meet with the buyer and ask if he or she can raise the offer, while making it clear that this isn't a deal breaker.

Our first scenario focused on distributional fairness. The second raised the question of what's required in regard to honesty. This one poses a dilemma of divided loyalties: Do you stand up for your own values or compromise them if that seems to be in the best interest of your employer?

Of the people I've surveyed, 53 percent picked the first answer, choosing to tell their boss that they didn't want to break their word to the buyer. Their answers may be sincere, though I wonder whether that many people would have the nerve to contradict their superior. Still, it's significant that this is many people's first impulse.

It would be nice to believe that you don't have to leave behind your principles when you show up at work, but the problem is more complex than it might first appear. In the prior examples, you were acting on your own behalf. If you chose to be fair and honest, you bore the consequences, specifically the risk of paying more or losing the deal. In this scenario, by contrast, keeping your word could be at your employer's expense.

In the Citibank land assembly, as you may recall, the last piece of the puzzle was a corner property owned by an estate. Don Schnabel had agreed to a premium price to wrap up the project. When they closed the deal, however, he learned that the executrix had just extended the tenants' leases and then sold them to a speculator. This last-minute bait and switch was legal, but it meant that Schnabel didn't get the property free and clear. That move may seem slimy, but the profit from selling the leases went to the heirs' pockets. The executrix could have been more upright in respect to Schnabel, but that would have meant less money for the beneficiaries. She might even argue that she had a fiduciary duty to violate her personal scruples. Of course, that doesn't feel right either.

The best way to avoid this dilemma is defining your scope of authority before negotiating on someone else's behalf. One aspect of authority involves substance; getting clarity on what you can agree to. Sometimes your role may be to scout the landscape and let others reach a final agreement. Other times you may be empowered to commit to a deal within specified limits. But you also need to clarify authority regarding process. Your boss or client has the right to know what you're willing to do on his or her behalf and where your ethical boundaries lie. If you're lucky, your values may be well aligned. But if they want an attack dog, and that's not your style, you owe it to them to resolve that up front.

In the survey, 18 percent of respondents said that they'd do what their boss asked. Perhaps some saw it as a matter of loyalty—or staying in the boss's good graces. And others might have regarded the check-with-my-boss gambit as perfectly acceptable. It's a common practice in auto showrooms, after all.

The third option—broadly hinting to the buyer that he really doesn't have to increase the offer—was picked as the best by 29 percent of those surveyed. It's an easy choice to understand but harder to justify. It would allow you to please your manager without reneging on your agreement with the seller. If your boss is hotheaded and doesn't listen to other viewpoints, expressing disagreement could be dangerous.

This approach is troubling, however. It leaves the boss believing that you'll do what he told you, when in fact you won't. Maybe the boss will never know. But you will. To rationalize the deception in your own mind, you have to believe that he doesn't deserve to know the whole truth. And if he is deceitful and overbearing with you, perhaps he doesn't. That's a

gloomy conclusion to reach, however. It would certainly affect your dealings going forward. You'll have to keep your head down and your mouth
shut. That's not a great way to live.

As an alternative, consider Mark Twain's advice. "Always do right," he
said. Here that could mean having a forthright conversation with your
boss, rather than circumventing his wishes. You could try to persuade
him that it's not in the company's interest for it (or you) to get a reputation for being devious. Twain also said that doing right "will gratify some
of the people and astonish the rest."

In any case, there's a moral to this story if you look at it from the boss's
perspective. It's hard to judge another negotiator's performance if you're
not sitting next to him or her. At best, you'll know only half of the story.
Maybe the negotiator isn't pushing hard enough to advance your firm's
interest. Or perhaps he or she isn't as scrupulous as you hope. That's all
the more reason for having clear and verifiable rules for what behavior is
permissible and what is not.

Finally, there's a lesson for dealing with negotiators who represent
others, which is often the case in business dealings. Knowing the extent
of your counterpart's authority is essential. It's dangerous to make commitments to people who can't reciprocate with binding promises of their
own. If they can't give you a yes or a no, the most you should give them
is a maybe.

DRAWING A LINE

Acting responsibly doesn't require a doctorate in moral philosophy, but it
does mean knowing your core values before negotiation begins. There are
tried-and-true tests that can help you not cross the line separating right
and wrong.

- Universality check. Could you recommend that everyone in your
  situation act this way?
- Reciprocity check. Would you want others to treat you this way?

- Publicity check. Would you be comfortable if your actions were fully and fairly described in a newspaper or online?
- Trusted-friend check. Would you be comfortable telling your best friend, spouse, or children what you are doing?
- Legacy check. Is this how you want to be known and remembered?

If a flag goes up on one of these checks, it's a warning that you may be compromising your principles. If more than one test makes you squirm, change your plans or risk shame and regret.

Good intentions aren't enough. Research shows that powerful people who are convinced about their own rectitude may be *more* likely to transgress. Time and time again, we see self-righteous politicians from both sides of the aisle sermonize about other people's behavior, only to end up in the tabloids themselves. People with more humility about their capacity to resist temptation take care to avoid situations where their willpower might be tested.

Being mindful of the company that you keep is also important. Back in the scenario about buying the cabin from its elderly owner, I noted how the image of a kindly grandmother could elicit generosity. But don't assume that applies to everyone. In fast-paced, high-pressure organizations, it's easy for people to adopt an us-against-the-world attitude that justifies crushing outsiders without compunction.

Remember the energy traders at Enron who were audiotaped gloating about profiting from the 2000–01 California power crisis? One of them asked about the state's efforts to recover Enron's excess charges, or as he termed it, "All the money you guys stole from those poor grandmothers." They went on to describe "Grandma Millie" with profanity-laced contempt. For them, grandmothers had come to personify easy prey, ripe for exploiting. Maybe if these same people worked for a company with a different ethos, they would have had a more compassionate outlook.

Our moral sensitivity may slacken over time as well. I have a colleague who served on Los Angeles County's Regional Planning Commission. We'll call him Norman. His agency has powerful influence over what gets developed in an area that spans hundreds of square miles.

A few months after his appointment, Norman received a fancy smoked ham from Forest Lawn, a company that operates cemeteries throughout the region. He asked his assistant, "What's this about?" She told him that Forest Lawn had a tradition of sending hams to commissioners every Christmas season. "They like to stay on good terms with us, as they're always looking for new sites to develop." Norman told the assistant to send back the gift immediately.

Nevertheless, the following year, another ham appeared. Norman meant to return this one as well, but he was busy, and so was everyone else. When his assistant reminded him, Norman said, "Oh, just use it for our office party tomorrow night." Norman sampled some of the ham himself. It was delicious.

Another year passed. It was early December, and Norman caught himself thinking, "I wonder when my ham is going to arrive." Good for Norman to recognize that he was starting down a slippery slope. What at first seemed to him like a clumsy bribe had become an entitlement. It's a trap any of us can fall into.

Learning also involves gauging what rules your counterparts play by. Studies show that most people rate themselves well above average when it comes to ethical behavior. In fact, a newsmagazine poll asked people whom they thought would get to heaven. Bill Clinton was a toss-up, getting 52 percent backing from respondents. Former basketball star Michael Jordan did better, at 62 percent. Mother Teresa topped the two American men with 79 percent. But she was not the highest. That honor went to "yourself," with 87 percent.

If feeling morally superior were just self-flattery, it would be harmless. But if we tend to see people we negotiate with as having lower standards than we do, at best we become distrustful. At worst, we may feel that we have to be as ruthless as we suspect them to be. Impugning bad motives to others can also be a way of justifying shady practices on our part. But there are some people who treat negotiation as a winner-take-all battle. We don't want to be naïve. After all, there is nothing fair about splitting the difference between our reasonable offer and someone else's ridiculous demand. As Sean Connery's Irish cop character in *The Untouchables* says, it's folly to bring a knife to a gunfight.

Don Schnabel and the team that fashioned the Citibank land assembly strove to be fair with owners but played tough when they had to. They were gracious to the elderly tenants who were reluctant to move. Likewise, after purchasing a restaurant, they kept it open so that the employees would continue to have paychecks. They honored their word to the church from which they bought air rights. But they also went toe-to-toe with professional holdouts who were angling for top dollar.

CHARACTER

When *Getting to Yes* was published three decades ago, it was rightly praised for making the case for collaborative, value-generating negotiation. The authors maintained that rather than being "a sermon on the morality of right and wrong, it is a book on how to do well in negotiation." Nevertheless, some readers felt that it had a sanctimonious tone. A reviewer friendly to its overall thrust admitted to being put off by "a certain take-it-or-leave-it righteousness in the new religion."

In sharp contrast, Herb Cohen's bestselling *You Can Negotiate Anything* (which appeared around the same time) was criticized from the opposite direction. Although Cohen tipped his hat to the win-win philosophy and extolled Jesus Christ and Socrates as "ethical negotiators," his actual advice was, as one reviewer put it, "laced with enough manipulative ploys to make Niccolò Machiavelli nervous." Even some of the stories that Cohen told about himself had a heartless edge.

For instance, Cohen described an unsettling incident in front of a New York hotel. As he arrived in a cab, there was a crowd pressed around a police barricade and gaping upward. According to the doorman, someone on the eleventh floor was threatening to jump. "Gee, that's too bad," Cohen said. As he entered the lobby, he felt "upset at the thought of a fellow human being tumbling to the sidewalk."

Then his story takes an unexpected turn. This isn't a tale of how a gifted negotiator raced to the elevator and talked a desperate man off the ledge. Instead, Cohen strode directly to the front desk. His mood changed when the clerk told him that there weren't any rooms available, even though he had a reservation. In Cohen's own words, here's what happened next:

> *"'Hold it!'" I snapped. "You do have a room! You know the guy on the eleventh floor? The one who's causing all that commotion outside. He's checking out!"*
>
> *The windup? The guy didn't jump. The police corralled him but checked him into a different facility for psychiatric examination. I got his vacant room.*

It is true that Cohen had no role in pushing the stranger into despair, nor was he rooting for a suicide. And it's true that somebody else would have eventually gotten that empty room, so why not him?

What's missing in Cohen's own account is compassion. His self-absorption led him to construe another person's misery as his own good luck. It's not the outcome that seems unseemly. Rather, it's the haste with which he reached it. His behavior required a change of attitude, a narrowing of perspective. Within a few seconds, the "fellow human being" perched on the ledge became in Cohen's eyes "the one who's causing all that commotion." That less sympathetic characterization suited his need for a room.

This incident took place many years ago. Cohen may feel differently about the situation now. And we all have weak moments and blind spots. The best protection against them is stepping back and reminding ourselves of who we aspire to be.

My friend Jim Golden is a personal injury defense lawyer with considerable experience in the trucking industry. One company he represents operates eighteen-wheelers that drive a combined million miles every day. Inevitably, there are collisions with smaller passenger vehicles. Deaths and horrible injuries result, sometimes followed by long and costly lawsuits. The conventional defense strategy in these kinds of cases is to stonewall and drag out the process. Victims' families and injured survivors are often in a financial squeeze. Under pressure, they frequently settle cheaply.

This was long Jim's approach, though the thought of compounding other people's suffering made him increasingly uncomfortable. He got to a point where he decided he couldn't do it any longer. Right after the next fatal accident, Jim got his client's permission to try a different tack. He telephoned the funeral home handling arrangements for the driver of the other car—a man with two young children—and asked if the family would like a representative of the trucking company to attend the service. He had no idea what the response would be, but a few hours later, he was told that the answer was yes.

Jim flew halfway across the country and stood in back of a packed church. When the service was over, he waited and then introduced himself to the victim's widow. "We are very, very sorry," he said, "for your loss." Those were his only words, but his voice cracked as he spoke.

Two weeks later, he called the funeral home again to see if the family had a lawyer or some other representative he could talk to about the accident. He got the name of a local attorney, arranged a meeting, and flew out again, this time for a longer conversation. Jim explained that the company's technical team had completed an investigation of the accident. It appeared that the truck driver was at least partially at fault. "We can negotiate a final settlement later," he said, "or if that doesn't work out, the case can go through the courts." In the meantime, however, he worried about how the family was doing. He knew nothing could alleviate their emotional distress, but he didn't want them to be struggling with financial problems on top of that.

As he spoke, Jim reached into his pocket, pulled out an envelope, and slid it across the desk. "Here's a check that may help—no strings attached," he said. "I'm sure they're going through a horrible time. We just don't want to make it any worse."

The other lawyer looked at Jim, stunned. "No strings?" he asked. "No obligations on our part? No releases or waivers?"

"None at all," Jim answered. "I'll be glad to sign whatever document you'd like to draft in order to confirm that."

The lawyer opened the envelope. His eyebrows rose. The check was for $25,000. "If you think the family needs more to get by," Jim said, "let's talk about it." He also volunteered to share all the information that the company had already gathered about the accident. Less than two months later, the two lawyers reached a full settlement.

Now Jim begins all his negotiations this way. To his surprise, his offer to attend victims' funerals is almost always accepted. It's a heavy duty for him, but the gesture is appreciated. He's not surprised that his approach often leads to early settlement. Jim thinks his own openness unfreezes other people, at least much of the time, and allows them to dispense with their emotional agendas. Experience has taught him that the "person who is the most aggressive, the most brazen, the most angry, is often, if you dig down underneath, the most fearful."

Dread of negotiation may be fear of being disrespected, exploited, or proven incompetent. Jim believes that when people mask their fear, they try to protect themselves by hitting first before getting bashed themselves. When both parties have that attitude, conflict escalates, whether it's in the schoolyard or in negotiation. "I think if you can get past the fear," he says, "the animosity, then maybe you don't have to prove things to other people—or yourself."

Jim is a look-you-straight-in-the-eye kind of guy and an intense listener. When he walks into a settlement conference, he exhibits both compassion and confidence. By slashing litigation costs, he has reduced his company's insurance premiums and put more money into victims' pockets. Jim's approach to negotiation isn't a trick or gambit. Instead, it's how Jim encourages the best in his negotiation counterparts by summoning the best in himself.

My colleague Andy Wasynczuk has written a case study that examines Jim's work. I use it in my own course, as it sparks spirited discussion for a full eighty-minute session. The buzz continues long afterward. Early one afternoon, as I gathered my notes and started back to my office, I overheard one student who'd boiled down Jim's message to its essence. "To know the right thing to do," she said, "you need to know who you want to be."

KEY POINTS

- Decide what you owe others in regard to fairness, candor, and the negotiation tactics you employ.
- Recognize that your counterparts may have different expectations and principles than your own.
- Do what you can to encourage ethical behavior from others.
- Be realistic, but take care not to rationalize questionable conduct just because you suspect your counterparts may not behave ethically.
- Remember that in the end, your actions define your character.

Appendix

Twenty-five Reasons to Embrace Chaos in Negotiation—A Strategic Road Map

PRECEPTS

1. **Negotiation is a dynamic, interactive process.** Goals, interests, non-agreement alternatives, and, hence, potential solutions evolve as we negotiate. The changes are driven by our own actions, those of our counterparts, and external events. They can also be due to new ways that we (and others) construe the environment in which we operate.

   Changes in circumstances and perceptions may be significant or relatively small. They may be beneficial or to our detriment. Rarely are circumstances at the end of negotiation exactly as we anticipated at the beginning.

2. **The better we manage and cope with the inherent uncertainty and unpredictability of negotiation, the more effective we will be.** Even in seemingly simple situations, it's hard to see the current landscape with perfect clarity. It's harder still to predict exactly how things will unfold. Learning, adapting, and influencing are thus key elements of negotiation strategy and the tactics that implement it.

   The actions we take and the statements we make to learn more about the negotiation environment, however, are also signals that are read (or misread) by our counterparts. Their perceptions will influence their actions and, hence, alter the world in which we must function. Thus, we must balance the strategic costs of how we endeavor to learn as well as the benefits.

3. **Omniscience about the present, let alone the future, isn't possible.** We must therefore act, often in real time, on incomplete and ambiguous information, even when the stakes are high. A bias for action is important, but we must prepare for surprises, pleasant and otherwise.

4. **The foregoing precepts all demand formulating robust strategy and executing nimble tactics.**

ASSERTIONS

5. **Conventional negotiation theory implicitly assumes a static environment by focusing on the individual decision maker instead of the interaction of the parties. It largely ignores problems (and opportunities) inherent in the dynamic nature of negotiation.** Familiar concepts and techniques (such as working from interests and improving one's BATNA) are important but do not in themselves prepare practitioners for the complexity of real-world negotiation.

6. **In negotiation, we don't have complete control over our destiny. Exactly where we end up and how we get there are determined also by the needs, perceptions, and nature of our counterparts.**

7. **Striving for a degree of control that is beyond our reach is not in our interest.**

8. **A fresh look at negotiation is required, one that focuses on the interaction between the parties (their dance, so to speak) rather than just the steps of a single party.**

9. **Our success in negotiation turns on both luck and skill: luck, in terms of our circumstances and whom we deal with; skill, in regard to our ability to analyze our situation and influence it positively.** Our counterparts are often as smart, determined, and fallible as we are. With potential partnerships and collaboration, encouraging counterparts to expand their vision and flexibility is usually to our advantage. By contrast, in some disputes, being at least a step ahead of others in respect to discernment and agility is beneficial.

10. **We can learn to manage strategic complexity and interpersonal dynamics in two complementary ways.** Illuminating the implicit practices of master negotiators is one avenue. Another is adapting principles and techniques from other domains in which people collaborate, create, or compete with one another (such as jazz, improv theater, psychotherapy, sports, and even warfare).

STRATEGIC PRINCIPLES

11. **Deliberate, ongoing learning is a critical element of effective negotiation strategy.** It's essential to recognize what we do—and *don't*—know about what may develop. Rigid plans and untested assumptions hamper effective learning.

12. **Having clear objectives provides discipline and focus in negotiation, but that advantage must be weighed against openness to unexpected opportunities or obstacles that may warrant revising our strategy.**

13. **Well-crafted strategies thus should contemplate not just likely outcomes but also best-case and worst-case scenarios.** In some cases, that may require devising a plan B. In others, undertaking parallel negotiations with different potential partners may be wise. In all cases, it's useful to set benchmarks and trip wires to activate alternative plans, including possible exits.

14. **A strategic direction should be chosen that will seek vantage points and generate opportunities to test assumptions.** Reconnaissance is especially important in the early stages of negotiation, when direction may be set. It is also important to optimize (as opposed to maximize) the number and nature of different paths to our ultimate goal. We must balance the option value of alternatives against the possible strategic advantage of commitment to a particular course of action.

15. **Ongoing learning informs us how best to influence the actions and perceptions of our counterparts, where possible, and how best to adapt to their behavior where necessary.**

16. **As negotiation unfolds, some options will close, while others emerge.** Achievement of initial goals may still be possible, though perhaps through different means. New or unexpected conditions may call for a fundamental shift in strategy, including the execution of a plan B or ending the negotiation.

TACTICAL POINTS

17. **Many of the dynamic factors that inform broad strategy have micro-equivalents in moment-to-moment interactions.** How parties generally engage each other and define the task is enacted by the specific things that they do and say.

18. **Tactics and interactions must serve and be consistent with general strategy. Aggressive gambits seldom promote constructive relationships.**

19. **Negotiators must on the fly learn, adapt, and influence in both collaborative and competitive interactions.**

20. **Learning is an ongoing process of observing, orienting, deciding, and acting.** We must begin negotiation with a clear set of expectations but be prepared to discard them when they do not match the situation at hand.

21. **Learning goes well beyond simply uncovering other parties' substantive interests and perceived options (and the corresponding value of possible carrots and sticks).** Specifically, it includes recognizing how best to engage others in regard to our demeanor, voice, and tempo. It also entails gauging if and how others can be influenced to act in a way that advances our interests.

22. **Maintaining situational awareness requires emotional balance and presence of mind.** Paying heed involves more than merely processing the literal words that others speak. It also includes sensing their unspoken emotional nature and needs. Our own internal doubts and distractions can distort our perceptions.

    Emotional balance requires comfort with uncertainty and lack of total control. It also involves mastering paradoxes, such as being simultaneously calm and alert, patient and proactive, and creative and grounded.

NEGOTIATION SUCCESS

23. **Measuring negotiation success is hard.** We seldom know what our counterparts might have been willing to agree to, so we can't access precisely how much value might be created and captured. Initial aspirations are an imperfect benchmark, as they may be unrealistically high or low.

    Impasse may occur for a variety of reasons: strategic behavior, interpersonal issues, or a failure of imagination. In some cases, there simply may be no room for agreement. Correspondingly, if we achieve an excellent outcome, it could be due to our skill and creativity, but maybe we were just lucky. Perhaps our counterpart was desperate for a deal or negotiated poorly.

24. **As a result, negotiation is a "wicked environment" for learning.** Because negotiation is a complex process, isolating specific causes and effects is difficult. It is important to avoid mislearning from an outcome, good or bad, of a particular case. To learn from experience, we should focus on how we negotiated. Were we agile strategically and tactically?

25. **Negotiation is an important, recurring process in our professional and personal lives.** Even modest improvement in our skills can significantly improve our well-being. It can help us reach agreements that might otherwise slip through our fingers. It can enable us to create value through mutually beneficial trades. It can empower us to resolve small quarrels before they become major disputes. By negotiating well, we also benefit others—in our organizations, our homes, and our communities.

Acknowledgments

As a graduate student, I took a negotiation seminar from Jim White, who happened to be visiting from the University of Michigan. In the first session, we did a simulation in which half of us played salespeople for a furniture manufacturer. The others were assigned to be buyers for a retail store. Each side received confidential instructions, and then we were paired up to negotiate a price for a mattress order. Even though each duo had been dealt the same cards, some buyers managed to get a bargain, while others paid much more than necessary. In the debriefing, we analyzed what tactics drove success and what explained failure. In simulations that followed, we tested our skill at settling lawsuits, handling family disputes, and resolving labor deadlocks. The fact that I remember these details decades later tells you that I was hooked from the start. I had found my calling.

Just as important—and just as fortuitous—that same year marked the launch of an interdisciplinary course on law and public policy taught by an all-star team of faculty. From the Harvard Law School, there was Phil Heymann, later deputy attorney general; Larry Tribe, the eminent constitutional scholar; and Stephen Breyer, who now sits on the United States Supreme Court. From Harvard's Kennedy School of Government, we had economists Richard Zeckhauser and Edith Stokey; Howard Raiffa, a towering figure in decision science; and Tom Schelling, who later became a Nobel laureate. For a full year, we students sat back and enjoyed the ride as our teachers debated how to divide scarce resources, allocate risk, and promote efficiency. It was in this class that I first learned about game theory, decision trees, and linear programming. One didn't have to be a genius to connect the conceptual dots, as many of those analytic tools mapped well to negotiation. (Just think of a personal injury claimant weighing the bird in the hand of a settlement offer against taking the chance of going to court and either winning more or losing everything.)

And so my professional career began. Using the basics that I had just learned, I first taught negotiation at New England Law School in Boston. At the time, it was one of only a handful of schools to offer such a course. Now negotiation is a standard part of the curriculum in professional programs throughout the United States and, increasingly, in universities throughout the world.

Later I moved to MIT, where I joined a research team studying contentious environmental disputes that involved dozens of parties, huge costs, and complex technical issues. These real-world cases didn't really fit the analytic boxes I had been taught. Other perspectives were needed to understand how such controversies arose and how, on occasion, they were constructively resolved.

Once again I was doubly lucky, for this was also when the Program on Negotiation was created. PON is an interuniversity consortium of Harvard, MIT, and Tufts faculty who share an interest in negotiation but who work in a wide variety of disciplines and fields. In those early years, we hosted regular "devising seminars" at which practitioners would dump real-world challenges in our laps. One month our guest might be an FBI hostage negotiator. The next month, it could be a federal official trying to site a repository for radioactive waste from nuclear power plants. After a guest would describe his or her particular case, our band of psychologists, anthropologists, urban planners, organizational theorists, and legal types would jump in with ideas from our various perspectives.

All of which is to say that I've had the good fortune to have great negotiation teachers and colleagues right from the start. I am deeply grateful to each one of them. I only wish that I had the wit to compose a rhyming tribute in the spirit of the *New Yorker*'s annual Christmas poem, "Greetings, Friends!," into which I could drop each of their names. And there are so many of them, I can thank only a relative few in the space here.

Certain colleagues contributed significantly to the ideas in this book. Most of what I know about improvisation I learned from Frank Barrett, an organizational theorist and gifted jazz pianist. Kim Leary has taught me about psychodynamics and emotion. Debbie Kolb opened my eyes to how power is transacted in the shadow of explicit negotiation. Larry Susskind and Jim Sebenius have continually challenged my thinking in enormously helpful ways.

Many other colleagues and friends have generously shared their knowledge, support, and good company. These include Larry Bacow, Susan Carpenter, Amy Cuddy, Clark Freshman, Ran Kuttner, Carrie Menkel-Meadow, Richard Paisner, Barbara Pizer, Frank Sander, Sandra Sucher, Noah Susskind, Gerry Williams, and Gerry Zaltman. Bob Mnookin is on the list as well, though he warrants a special bow, as he introduced me to my agent, Jim Levine, who understood the core of my book even when it was in rough form. Jim helped shape the proposal, sharpened the writing, and found the right home for the book.

Thanks to the support of the Harvard Business School, where I've been these past twenty years, I've had a succession of smart and creative research associates. They have really been more like collaborators. Those whose research is reflected in this book include Lakshmi Balachandra, Captain David Dixon, Jill Morris Green, Jane Juliano, Jenny Illes, Georgia Levenson Keohane, Ellen Knebel, Dana Nelson, and Julianna Pillemer. It was a privilege to work with them, and it is a continuing delight to watch them make their way in the world.

I'm grateful as well to my MBA and executive students—thousands of them, at this point—who were patient with me as I tested ideas in the classroom and searched for ways to express them effectively. Jazz teacher and horn player Ed Sarath taught me that in order to be creative, improvisers need to be 80 percent in their comfort zone but 20 percent beyond it. I live by that principle in the classroom, though that has meant that some of my pedagogical experiments failed. I'm sorry for any collateral damage and hope that my stumbling didn't discourage students from taking risks themselves.

Students provided many of the examples I describe in this book, sometimes long after having been in my course. Other friends have told me great negotiation stories as well. I'm especially grateful to Jeff Ansell, Courtney Cowart, Tim Crouse, Charlie Davidson, Erin Egan, Jim Golden, David Hoffman, Lt. Colonel Leonard Lira, Jack Parker, Sandy Ritchie, Derek Sanderson, and Colin Smith.

A half dozen people I've named to this point also read earlier drafts of the book. I am deeply grateful for their encouragement and their candid criticism. Thanks to them, I was able to clarify and provide support for some of my conclusions. They also helped me see what had to be scrapped. Rather than implicate those readers, I'll simply bow to them deeply, grant them deniability, and take sole responsibility for the finished product.

Turning ideas in one's head into words on a page is a physical act. So is turning those pages into a book. For many years, my assistant MaryAlice Wood was my partner in that enterprise, as drafts were revised and chapters were shuffled around. I am deeply grateful for MaryAlice's patience, dedication, and friendship. Three years ago, Christina Lau took over the daunting task of managing me. The care, insight, and good humor that she brought to this work will serve her well as she embarks on her legal career.

I also thank Kim Ducharme, working in collaboration with Chris Pullman, for creating the illustrations in this book. Using words alone to describe the dynamic, nonlinear nature of negotiation is a challenge. Kim's freehand drawings have helped bring improvisation to life. And in conjunction with the book, thanks also go to Jesse McDougall and Cally Wheeler for designing and developing my website (www.michaelwheeler .com). Readers can find research updates, analysis of current negotiations in the news, and instructive videos on the site.

Hearty thanks to the talented crew at Simon & Schuster. Emily Loose, who was my editor initially, pushed me to reorganize the book and add important new material—specifically, the chapters on critical moments, closing, and negotiation ethics. Ben Loehnen, who saw the book home, pared my prose so as to make it more compelling. He reminded me that good writing, like jazz, is about the notes that you don't play. Brit Hvide masterfully managed the production process and Jonathan Evans is the best production editor I've ever had the good fortune to work with. (And I apologize for ending that sentence with a preposition.) I'm most grateful, as well, to Akasha Archer for her work on the interior design.

Finally, profound thanks to Candace, Kate, and Cally for their love and support. Their patience, optimism, and humor have seen me through.

Notes

Chapter I: Embracing Chaos

1 *As manager of a private investment firm*: Jay Sheldon is a former colleague of mine. He has asked me to use a pseudonym. That will be my practice throughout this book. I'll provide sources for examples that have been written about elsewhere.

2 *colleagues at the Program on Negotiation*: The program was founded in 1983 and is based at the Harvard Law School. PON hosts academic conferences, offers executive training programs, and publishes the *Negotiation Journal*. Its website is www.pon.harvard.edu.

3 *The late ambassador Richard Holbrooke*: PON awarded Ambassador Holbrooke its Great Negotiator Award in 2004. In his acceptance remarks, he said, "This award honors the art of negotiation. I say 'art' intentionally because it is not a science and never will be." For a summary of his comments, see www.pon.harvard.edu/events/richard-holbrooke-receives-the-2004-great-negotiator-award.

3 *UN special envoy Lakhdar Brahimi*: His comment was made during a seminar that was held when he received PON's Great Negotiator Award in 2002. Video of the event is available from the program's clearinghouse: www.pon.harvard.edu/shop/great-negotiator-2002-lakhdar-brahimi-2.

3 *Dell has also done very well*: See Donald Dell, *Never Make the First Offer (Except When You Should): Wisdom from a Master Dealmaker* (Portfolio, 2009), p. 27. His advice about assuming there is something that you don't know appears on page 59. (Emphasis added.)

4 *Tom Green is a remarkable negotiator*: Tom joined the Massachusetts Attorney General's Office after seven years on Wall Street. His knowledge of law and finance made him an important member of the team that coordinated the multistate settlement with the major tobacco companies. See *Tobacco Negotiations*, a case study by Michael Wheeler and Georgia Levenson (product number 899049), July 30, 1998, Harvard Business Publishing.

7 *The story of how*: The Citibank land assembly negotiations are described in greater detail in chapter 4, "Plan B." See also Peter Hellman's article "How They Assembled the Most Expensive Block in New York's History," *New York*, February 25, 1974, pp. 30–37.

7 *The board of a co-op*: See Wade Lambert, "Ever Hear the One About the Lawyers and the Window Bars," *Wall Street Journal*, March 23, 1994, p. 1.

8 *The groundbreaking negotiating text*: Bruce Patton joined Roger Fisher and William Ury for the second—as well as subsequent—editions of *Getting to Yes* (Penguin Books, 1991).

9 *Books such as Jim Camp's*: See Jim Camp, *Start with No: America's Number One Negotiating Coach Explains Why Win-Win Is a Disastrous Strategy, and How You Can Beat It* (Crown Business, 2002).

10 *A lot of good work*: These books include *Beyond Reason: Using Emotions as You Negotiate* by Roger Fisher and Daniel Shapiro (Penguin Books, 2006); *Getting Past No: Negotiating in Difficult Situations* by William Ury (Bantam Books, 1993); and *Difficult Conversations: How to Discuss What Matters Most* by Douglas Stone, Bruce Patton, and Sheila Heen (Penguin Books, 2010). Other contributions to negotiation literature have been made by David Lax and James Sebenius, most recently in *3-D Negotiation: Powerful Tools to Change the Game in Your Most Important Deals* (Harvard Business School Press, 2006); Robert Mnookin, Scott Peppett, and Andrew Tulumello, *Beyond Winning: Negotiating to Create Value in Deals and Disputes* (Harvard University Press, 2004); Lawrence Susskind and Patrick Field, *Dealing with an Angry Public: The Mutual Gains Approach to Resolving Disputes* (Free Press, 2010); and Deborah Kolb, Judith Williams, and Carol Frohlinger, *Her Place at the Table: A Woman's Guide to Negotiating Five Key Challenges to Leadership Success* (Jossey-Bass, 2010).

10 *The standard model doesn't capture*: None of my colleagues denies the dynamic nature of negotiation. See, for example, Lax and Sebenius, *3-D Negotiation*, p. 253, who state that "negotiating effectively isn't like following a recipe that is written out before you start." They note that key factors "tend to stay in play and to evolve, often dramatically," hence you must "continually update and adjust your approach."

12 *Savvy real estate brokers*: See Timothy Wilson, *Strangers to Ourselves: Discovering the Adaptive Unconscious* (Cambridge, Mass: Harvard University Press, 2002), pp. 164–65.

Part I: A Sense of Direction

17 *You'd be surprised*: Charlene Barshefsky served as US trade representative, the country's top trade negotiator, from 1997 to 2001. In 2004 she received the Great Negotiator Award from the Program on Negotiation. For the quotation,

see *Charlene Barshefsky (B)*, a case study by James Sebenius and Rebecca Hulse (product number 801422), March 29, 2001, Harvard Business Publishing.

Chapter 2: A Map of the Pyrenees

19 *Many years ago*: Well-known organizational theorist Karl Weick recounted this story in an interview by Diana Coutu, "Sense and Reliability: A Conversation with Celebrated Psychologist Karl E. Weick," *Harvard Business Review*, April 2003, p. 86. Weick commented, "In crises especially, leaders have to act in order to think, not the other way around."

21 *Herb Cohen recounts stories*: His story about buying a $489.50 refrigerator for $450 can be found in the paperback edition of *You Can Negotiate Anything* (Bantam Books, 1982), pp. 31–37.

21 *But asking can be risky*: Arvind Gupta is a pseudonym of a justifiably well-regarded negotiation teacher.

22 *Compare Arvind's blunder*: Liz and Tony Weiler are pseudonyms of old friends of mine who told me this story as it was unfolding.

24 *it's a matter of comparing two paths*: The best, most practical introduction to decision analysis is *Smart Choices: A Practical Guide to Making Better Decisions* by John Hammond, Ralph Keeney, and Howard Raiffa (Harvard Business, 1999).

26 *When Harvard economist Richard Zeckhauser*: The experiment is described in Howard Raiffa, *The Art and Science of Negotiation: How to Resolve Conflicts and Get the Best out of Bargaining* (Cambridge, Mass.: Harvard University Press, 1982), p. 52.

27 *this was a lose-lose negotiation*: Stubbornness may have been part of the reason for the 2012–13 stalemate. Each side may have been convinced that the other would blink in the face of mounting losses. But there's another explanation, as well: internal dynamics. Tough bargaining took place inside each group. Every NHL team wanted to cap its payroll expenses, but teams turning a profit had different incentives than those running losses. (It's rumored that some of the latter were actually losing less money by being shut down.) Likewise, some members of the players' union had been earning thirty times as much as their less talented teammates. Those stars had more at stake, but most also had the resources to ride out the impasse. Marginal players had less to fall back upon. It likely was hard for each side to build internal consensus over what would ultimately be acceptable. The story of the 2004–05 lockout is told in a case study by my colleague Deepak Malhotra and his research associate Maly Hout, *Negotiating on Thin Ice: The 2004–2005 NHL Dispute (A/B)* (product numbers 906038/906039), February 14, 2006 (Harvard Business Publishing).

28 *A few years ago*: The following story was told in detail by *Wall Street Journal* reporter Daniel Michaels, who had confidential access to all the parties as the negotiation progressed. "Airbus and Boeing Duke It Out to Win Lucrative

Iberia Deal," *Wall Street Journal*, March 10, 2003, p. 1., http://faculty.wash-ington.edu/sundar/MM-BBUS320/Fun-READINGS/Airbus-Boeing%20 for%20Iberia%20Deal.pdf.

29 *Nobel laureate Tom Schelling*: The capacity to commit oneself, Schelling ex-plains in his "Essay on Bargaining," even if it is to a dangerous course of ac-tion, is a form of bargaining power. The essay is the second chapter in his *The Strategy of Conflict* (Harvard University Press, 1981).

29 *Fox Television's prominence*: See Richard Sandomir, "Fox Network Outbids CBS for Rights to Pro Football," *New York Times*, December 18, 1993, p. 1.

29 *Putting a toe in the water*: I'm grateful to Sandy for letting me tell this story.

30 *It's a strategic planning technique*: For a fuller description of this technique, see Gary Klein, *Intuition at Work: Why Developing Your Gut Instincts Will Make You Better at What You Do* (Doubleday-Currency, 2003).

32 *Studies show that negotiators*: Deborah Zetik and Alice Stulmacher, "Goal Set-ting and Negotiation Performance: A Meta-Analysis," *Group Processes & In-tergroup Relations* 5, no. 1 (January 2002): pp. 35–52. This meta-analysis of almost two dozen studies showed that negotiators who held specific and chal-lenging goals outperformed others whose aims were lower.

32 *In a recent experiment*: See Adam Galinsky, Geoffrey Leonardelli, Gerardo Okhuysen, and Thomas Mussweiler, "Regulatory Focus at the Bargaining Table: Promoting Distributive and Integrative Success," *Personality and Social Psychology Bulletin* 31, no. 8 (August 2005): pp. 1087–98.

33 *Fortunately, they didn't fall*: Hikers use the phrase "bending the map" to de-scribe how people convince themselves that they aren't really lost. (For ex-ample, "The map says that there's supposed to be a lake here, but it must have dried up.")

Chapter 3: Prospecting

36 *To illustrate the importance of preparation*: The results of this exercise are de-scribed and analyzed in "First Let's Kill All the Agents," a chapter I wrote in a collection edited by Robert Mnookin and Lawrence Susskind, *Negotiating on Behalf of Others: Advice to Lawyers, Business Executives, Sports Agents, Diplo-mats, Politicians, and Everybody Else* (Sage Publications, 1999), pp. 235–62.

37 *Because it considers only price*: See Max Bazerman, "Negotiator Judgment: A Critical Look at the Rationality Assumption," *American Behavioral Scientist* 27, no. 2 (November 1983): pp. 211–28, at 215–18.

39 *We'll start with the deal triangle*: At first glance, the triangle here may look the same as those depicting Pareto superior deals, but this is constructed dif-ferently. In this construction, your baseline is an indifference curve located

by different outcomes that you *value the same*. In the Pareto diagram, the horizontal and vertical axes are scales on which ascending value of different deals is measured.

41 *Research suggests*: See Arvind Rangaswamy and G. Richard Shell, "Using Computers to Realize Joint Gains in Negotiations," *Management Science* 43, no. 8 (August 1997): pp. 1147–63. This study suggests that preparing for negotiation by thinking more rigorously about one's own trade-offs stimulates negotiators to find more value creating solutions.

48 *Jack Binion, a celebrated Las Vegas casino operator*: See symposium transcript, "How to Play Your Hand: Lessons for Negotiators from Poker," *UNLV Gaming Law Journal* 2, no. 2 (December 2011): 231–53, http://scholars.law.unlv.edu/glj/vol2/iss2/5.

54 *Swarthmore College psychologist Barry Schwartz*: See Barry Schwartz, *The Paradox of Choice: Why More Is Less* (Harper Perennial, 2005). For the research on happiness, see Sheena Iyengar, Rachael Wells, and Barry Schwartz, "Doing Better but Feeling Worse: Looking for the 'Best' Job Undermines Satisfaction," *Psychological Science* 17, no. 2 (2006): pp. 143–50.

55 *Consider Hollywood producer*: See Jerry Weintraub, *When I Stop Talking, You'll Know I'm Dead: Useful Stories from a Persuasive Man* (Twelve, 2010), pp. 199–201 (the John Denver story) and 268–69 (*Ocean's Eleven, Twelve*, and *Thirteen*).

Chapter 4: Plan B

57 *The Citibank Center*: The Citibank land assembly negotiations mentioned briefly in the first chapter are described in Peter Hellman's article "How They Assembled the Most Expensive Block in New York's History," *New York*, February 25, 1974, pp. 30–37. *Holdouts!* by Andrew Alpern and Seymour Durst (McGraw-Hill, 1984) describes this case and other contentious real estate negotiations.

67 *Just as that new tower*: See Calvin Trillin, "U.S. Journal: Atlantic City, N.J.—Land Assemblage," *New Yorker*, January 8, 1979, p. 44.

69 *The Walt Disney Company should have*: For a fuller description of this case, see Michael Wheeler and Georgia Levenson, *Disney: The Third Battle of Bull Run* (product number 909030), December 9, 2008, Harvard Business Publishing; and Marcia Synnott, "Disney's America: Whose Patrimony, Whose Profits, Whose Past?," *Public Historian* 17, no. 4 (Fall 1995): pp. 43–59.

Part 2: Improvising

73 *Some situations are like*: Ambassador Richard Holbrooke, who mediated the Dayton Accords ending the bloodshed in the former Yugoslavia, received the Program on Negotiation's Great Negotiator Award on November 12, 2004.

Chapter 5: Presence of Mind

75 *First, there's Donald Dell*: See Dell, *Never Make the First Offer*, pp. 1–5.

75 *Then there's Chris Robbins*: I'm grateful to my colleague Kim Leary for telling me about Chris Robbins. (The latter name is a pseudonym.)

77 *Tom Wolfe's novel*: See Tom Wolfe, *A Man in Full* (Dial Press Trade Paperback, 2001), pp. 31–53.

77 *The classic* Getting to Yes: See Fisher, Ury, and Patton, *Getting to Yes*, 2nd ed. (Penguin Books, 1991), pp. 17–39.

77 *Later in his career*: See Fisher and Shapiro, *Beyond Reason*.

79 *Averell Harriman, a diplomat*: See obituary by Steve Neal, *Chicago Tribune*, July 27, 1986. "Mr. Harriman liked the nickname so much that he used it as his code name in confidential diplomatic cables, and he collected stuffed crocodiles and silver crocodile pins."

79 *Bruce Wasserstein, the late New York investment banker*: See Laurence Grafstein, "M&A . . . and Bruce," *New Republic*, October 15, 2009; www.newrepublic .com/article/economy/ma-%E2%80%A6-and-bruce.

79 *Arnaud Karsenti, a young real estate developer*: See Margie Kelley, "Arnaud Karsenti: Irrepressible Entrepreneur, Optimist, Global Dealmaker," *HBS Alumni Bulletin*, June 2006, p. 23.

81 *Mihaly Csikszentmihalyi, author*: See Mihaly Csikszentmihalyi, *Flow: The Psychology of Optimal Experience* (Harper & Row, 1990), p. 203.

81 *Several years ago*: See Julianna Pillemer, Kimberlyn Leary, and Michael Wheeler, "Negotiating with Emotion," *Harvard Business Review*, January–February 2013, pp. 96–103.

82 *To get a deeper understanding*: For more information about the ZMET method, see *Marketing Metaphoria: What Deep Metaphors Reveal About the Minds of Consumers* by Gerald and Lindsay Zaltman (Harvard Business Press, 2008) and the Olson Zaltman Associates website, www.olsonzalt-man.com.

82 *The subjects in our study*: To see how a sample of our subjects describes its emotions about negotiation, visit the site for this project: www.people.hbs.edu/mwheeler.

88 *Sports psychologists such as Robert Nideffer*: See Robert Nideffer, "Getting Into the Optimal Performance State," www.taisdata.com/articles/optimal.pdf.

88 *Mihaly Csikszentmihalyi describes*: See Csikszentmihalyi, *Flow*, p. 4.

88 *Studies suggest that stress*: See Sian Beilock and Thomas Carr, "When High-Powered People Fail: Working Memory and 'Choking Under Pressure' in Math," *Psychological Science* 16, no. 2 (February 2005): pp. 101–5.

88 W. *Timothy Gallwey, author:* See W. Timothy Gallwey, *The Inner Game of Tennis: The Classic Guide to the Mental Side of Peak Performance,* rev. ed. (Random House, 1997), pp. 75–78.

89 *Legendary UCLA basketball coach:* See Andrew Hill with John Wooden, *Be Quick—But Don't Hurry! Finding Success in the Teachings of a Lifetime* (Simon & Schuster, 2001), p. 69.

89 *Champion race car driver:* Stewart describes this experience in *George Harrison: Living in the Material World,* a Martin Scorsese documentary about George Harrison. It also can be found at http://davetrott.campaignlive .co.uk/2010/01/06/god-is-in-the-detail. Elsewhere Stewart is quoted as saying, "when I am driving really well, I always have plenty of time." See http://jalopnik.com/5616728/what-i-learned-from-jackie-stewart-in-a-flurry-of-feathers-and-blood.

90 *The best negotiators are:* See Ury, chap. 1, "Go to the Balcony," in *Getting Past No,* pp. 31–51.

91 *The General Mills company offers:* See Daniel Gelles, "The Mind Business: Yoga, Meditation, 'Mindfulness'—Why Some of the West's Biggest Companies Are Embracing Eastern Spirituality," *Financial Times,* August 24, 2012, p. 1, for the quotations by Janice Marturano and Bill George.

91 *David Hoffman, a Boston-based mediator:* See Daniel Bowling and David Hoffman, eds., *Bringing Peace into the Room: How the Personal Qualities of the Mediator Impact the Process of Conflict Resolution* (Jossey-Bass, 2003).

91 *Mindfulness has deep roots:* See Shunryu Suzuki, *Zen Mind, Beginner's Mind* (Shambhala Publications, 2011), p. 2.

91 *Psychologist Ellen Langer:* See Ellen Langer, *The Power of Mindful Learning,* (Boston: Addison-Wesley, 1997), p. 10.

92 *As Csikszentmilhalyi says:* See Csikszentmilhalyi, *Flow,* p. 21 (emphasis in the original).

96 *Also remember the promotion-priming:* See Galinsky, Leonardelli, Okhuysen, and Mussweiler, "Regulatory Focus," pp. 1087–98.

Chapter 6: The Swing of Things

97 *Jazz trumpeter Wynton Marsalis says:* This quotation is from the prologue to the Ken Burns Public Broadcasting Service documentary *Jazz,* which Marsalis hosted.

97 *The late Richard Holbrooke:* PON awarded Ambassador Holbrooke its Great Negotiator Award in 2004. For a summary of his comments, see www.pon .harvard.edu/events/richard-holbrooke-receives-the-2004-great-negotiator-award.

97 *The Roots have remained*: Tariq "Black Thought" Trotter's remark is from an interview on National Public Radio's *Weekend Edition* on December 18, 2011.

101 *Jazz great Herbie Hancock has described*: My colleague Frank Barrett heard Hancock interviewed.

102 *As Flow author*: See Csikszentmilhalyi, *Flow*, p. 204.

103 *Sigmund Freud stressed*: See Jeremy Safran and Christopher Muran, *Negotiating the Therapeutic Alliance: A Relational Treatment Guide* (Guilford Press, 2000), p. 36.

103 *Trumpeter Miles Davis*: The quotation can be found in Adam Shatz's review of John Szwed's *So What: The Life of Miles Davis* (Simon & Schuster, 2002). The review appeared in the Sunday Book Review of the *New York Times*, December 29, 2002, p. 11.

103 *George Shultz, in his memoir*: See George Shultz, *Turmoil and Triumph: My Years as Secretary of State* (Charles Scribner's Sons, 1995), p. 763.

104 "*It is not enough to be*": See Frank Barrett, "Creativity and Improvisation in Jazz and Organizations: Implications for Organizational Learning," *Organization Science* 9, no. 5 (September–October 1998): pp. 605–22, at 617. Most of what I have learned about improvising, I've learned from Frank.

105 *According to Barrett*: See Frank Barrett, *Yes to the Mess: Surprising Leadership Lessons from Jazz* (Harvard Business Review Press, 2012), p. 175.

107 "*He's yakking and talking*": See Sally Abrahms, "Richard Holbrooke Receives the Great Negotiator Award," *Harvard Law Today*, January 2005, p. 1. A summary of that article appears at http://www.law.harvard.edu/news/bulletin/2005/fall/feature-intro.php.

108 "*provocative competence*": For more on this theme, see Barrett, chap. 7, "Leadership as Provocative Competence," in *Yes to the Mess*, pp. 135–60.

108 *Saxophonist John Coltrane*: See Barrett, "Creativity and Improvisation," pp. 605–22, at 609.

108 *Benny Goodman's famed Carnegie Hall*: This performance and Phil Schaap's commentary can be seen at the beginning of episode six, "Swing: The Velocity of Celebration—1937–1939," in the Ken Burns 2001 documentary series *Jazz*.

108 *Fear of mistakes is a great inhibitor*: The quotations in these two paragraphs from Stephen Nachmanovitch's *Free Play: Improvisation in Life and Art* (Jeremy P. Tarcher/Putnam, 1990) are from p. 52 and p. 64, respectively.

109 *Ed Sarath, former head*: Ed Sarath examines the essential interplay between, and value of, working within and beyond one's comfort zone in *Improvisation, Creativity, and Consciousness: Jazz as an Integral Template for Music, Education, and Society* (SUNY Press, 2013). Using concepts from music theory, he shows how probing unfamiliar territory breaks down normative cognitive structures, and, in so doing, gives rise to new conceptual and creative possibilities.

109 *"I don't like a comfortable person"*: The quotation is from the 2002 documentary *The Miles Davis Story,* available at http://www.amazon.com/Miles-Davis-Story-George-Avakian/dp/B00007CVRL/ref=sr_1_1?s=movies-tv&ie=UTF8&qid=1363360526&sr=1-1&keywords=miles+davis+story.

109 *"You better have something to play"*: See Paul Berliner, *Thinking in Jazz: The Infinite Art of Improvisation* (University of Chicago Press, 1994), p. 102.

110 *Donald Dell tells about*: See Donald Dell with John Boswell, *Never Make the First Offer*, p. 38.

112 *Long before Dick Costolo became*: See Nick Bilton, "A Master of Improv, Writing Twitter's Script," *New York Times*, Business Section, October 7, 2012, p. 1.

112 *Bill Ury's 2007 book*: See William Ury, *The Power of a Positive No: Save the Deal, Save the Relationship—And Still Say No* (Bantam Books, 2007).

114 *And the power of having that attitude*: See Alison Wood Brooks, "Get Excited: Reappraising Pre-Performance Anxiety as Excitement" (unpublished doctoral thesis, the Wharton School, University of Pennsylvania, 2013).

115 *Gerry Williams, a pioneer in the negotiation field*: Gerry was a pioneer in negotiation research and teaching. He is now an emeritus professor at Brigham Young University.

117 *An Appreciative Mind-Set*: For more on this theme, see Barrett, chap. 8, "Getting to 'Yes to the Mess,'" in *Yes to the Mess*, pp. 161–84.

117 *The late investment banker*: See Laurence Grafstein, "M&A . . . and Bruce," *New Republic*, October 15, 2009; www.newrepublic.com/article/economy/ma-%E2%80%A6-and-bruce.

118 *Several years ago*: See David Hajdu, "Wynton's Blues," *Atlantic Monthly*, March 2003, pp. 43–55.

Chapter 7: Situational Awareness

120 *It took the maverick intelligence*: Material on Colonel Boyd in this chapter is drawn from several sources, including Robert Coram, *Boyd: The Fighter Pilot Who Changed the Art of War* (Little, Brown and Company, 2002); Grant Hammond, *The Mind of War: John Boyd and American Security* (Smithsonian Institution, 2001); and Frans Osinga, *Science, Strategy, and War: The Strategic Theory of John Boyd* (Routledge, 2006). For further examination of the links between military doctrine and negotiation strategy, see Michael Wheeler, "The Fog of Negotiation: What Negotiators Can Learn from Military Doctrine," *Negotiation Journal* 29, no. 1 (January 2013): pp. 23–38.

120 *Former Israeli prime minister Shimon Peres*: See Michael Benoliel with Linda Cashdan, *Done Deal: Insights from Interviews with the World's Best Negotiators* (Platinum Press, 2005), p. 127.

120 *US Marine Corps doctrine defines: Warfighting*, Marine Corps Doctrinal Publication 1, U.S. Marine Corps, rev. ed. (June 1997), p. 95. Hereafter cited as *Warfighting*. The manual can be found online on various sites, including, as of this writing, www.fs.fed.us/fire/doctrine/genesis_and_evolution/source_materials/MCDP-1_warfighting.pdf. The fact that it is publicly accessible suggests that the success of strategy depends on how well it is executed.

121 "Machines don't fight wars": Boyd is quoted in Raymond Curts and Douglas Campbell, "Avoiding Information Overload Through the Understanding of OODA Loops, A Cognitive Hierarchy and Object-Oriented Analysis and Design," *Proceedings of the 2001 Command and Control Research and Technology Symposium*, U.S. Naval Academy (June 2001). Boyd gave many presentations. He apparently expressed this idea in a variety of ways. One website (www.oocities.org/heratyk/milquote1.html#b) cites him as saying both "People, ideas, and hardware—in that order!" and "Machines don't fight wars. People do, and they use their minds."

121 *In the seeming chaos*: See Hammond, *Mind of War*, p. 32.

123 *Erin Egan was merely*: Erin is a former student of mine. I appreciate her generosity in allowing me to describe her negotiation experiences.

123 *Researchers call what*: See Karl Weick, *Sensemaking in Organizations* (Sage Publications, 1995); Weick and Kathleen Sutcliffe, chap. 6, "How to Manage Mindfully," in *Managing the Unexpected: Resilient Performance in an Age of Uncertainty* (Jossey-Bass, 2007), pp. 149–73; and Coutu, ""Sense and Reliability," p. 86.

123 *In basketball, it's called*: See Jackie MacMullan, "Cousy Getting to Point: New Award Honors Best College Guard," *Boston Globe*, June 26, 2003, p. C-8.

124 *A clever experiment*: This study is cited in Sheena Iyengar, *The Art of Choosing* (Twelve, 2010), p. 193.

124 *Chess writer and chess master Graham Burgess*: See Graham Burgess, *The Quickest Chess Victories of All Time* (Cadogan, 1998), p. 4.

124 *As Graham reflects*: See Burgess, *Quickest Chess Victories*, p. 5.

124 *Newly hatched chicks*: See David Myers, *Intuition: Its Powers and Perils* (Yale University Press, 2002), p. 54.

125 *They speak of identifying*: See *Warfighting*, pp. 92–93.

127 *In* Streetlights and Shadows: See Gary Klein, *Streetlights and Shadows: Searching for the Keys to Adaptive Decision Making* (MIT Press, 2009), p. 153.

127 *Consider, for example, this exchange*: For an analysis of this case, see www.airdisaster.com/special/special-af90.shtml. Although more than thirty years old, the transcript is still used in training flight crews and other teams where clear communication is essential.

128 *Contrast the Potomac case*: For excerpts of the radio communication between Captain Sullenberger and flight control, see Sharon Otterman and Matthew

Wald, "F.A.A. Releases Flight 1549 Tapes," *New York Times, City Room,* February 5, 2009, http://cityroom.blogs.nytimes.com/2009/02/05/faa-releases-flight-1549-tapes-2.

129 *He wasted no time*: In the year after Sullenberger's water landing, analysts tested different flight simulator models to see if he actually could have piloted his crippled plane back to LaGuardia. See Andy Pasztor, "'Hudson Miracle' Gets Closer Look," *Wall Street Journal,* May 4, 2010. Studying all the data, a few researchers now believe that he might have made it back safely. That's a big "might," however, as even some of them concede that it's uncertain whether he could have cleared high-rises in Midtown Manhattan. In any event, the pilot had only a couple of minutes, not months, to weigh his options. He simply had the instrument readings right in front of him.

130 *In their book* Make Your Own Luck: See Eileen Shapiro and Howard Stevenson, *Make Your Own Luck: 12 Practical Steps to Taking Smarter Risks in Business* (Portfolio, 2005), p. 10.

130 *Psychological research*: See Amos Tversky and Daniel Kahneman, "Loss Aversion in Riskless Choice: A Reference-Dependent Model," *Quarterly Journal of Economics* 106, no. 4 (November 1991), pp. 1039–61.

130 *Vacillation is a cardinal sin*: See David Freedman, *Corps Business: The 30 Management Principles of the U.S. Marines* (HarperBusiness, 2001), p. 7.

130 *A player looking forward*: See Gary Kasparov's review of *Chess Metaphors: Artificial Language and the Human Mind* in the *New York Review of Books,* February 11, 2010.

130 *Having a bump plan*: Freedman, *Corps Business*, p. 182.

131 *Academy Award winner*: Russell Crowe's comment is from an interview on *Inside the Actors Studio,* which aired January 4, 2004.

131 *Stirring the pot*: Colonel Boyd never wrote a book—or even an article, apparently—on his theories, but he did amass an ever-growing set of overheads that he used in his presentations. It was entitled "Patterns of Conflict" and is available (in different versions) on the web, including in the bibliography for the Wikipedia entry for "Patterns of Conflict." Boyd's characterization of the early military theories of Napoléon I appears on page 37 of that version of the material.

131 *Jenny Rudolph conducts research*: Dr. Rudolph's work is summarized and extended in J. Rudolph, J. B. Morrison, and J. Carroll, "The Dynamics of Action-Oriented Problem Solving: Linking Interpretation and Choice," *Academy of Management Review* 34, no. 4 (October 2009): 733–56. It was based on Dr. Rudolph's doctoral dissertation conducted at the Center for Medical Simulation (CMS).

133 *French philosopher*: I came upon Émile Chartier's aphorism in David Ullman's article, "'OO-OO-OO!' The Sound of a Broken OODA Loop," *CrossTalk: The Journal of Defense Software Engineering* 20, no. 4 (April 2007): pp. 22–25, at 23.

134   *A leader who ruled*: The Gadafi quotation is from Max Rodenbeck, "Libya: The Losers," *New York Review of Books*, October 13, 2011. There are conflicting stories of how Gadafi died, though video suggests strongly that he was killed by rebel forces.

134   *"Plans are worthless"*: The quotation is from an Eisenhower speech to the National Defense Executive Reserve Conference in Washington, DC (November 14, 1957), in *Public Papers of the Presidents of the United States, Dwight D. Eisenhower, 1957*, National Archives and Records Service, Government Printing Office (1958), p. 818.

135   *The further ahead we think*: See *Warfighting*, pp. 83–84.

135   *"The task denotes"*: See *Warfighting*, p. 89.

136   *Karl Weick*: See Klein, *Intuition at Work*, pp. 200–7. Klein notes a dilemma in crafting instructions. "The art in describing your intent," he says, "is to give as little information as you can. The more details you pack in, the more you obscure your main points. But if you leave out an important consideration, you run the risk that the person will be confused at a critical decision point."

136   *On June 5, 1944, the eve of the Normandy landings*: To view General Eisenhower's full message and to hear an audio recording, see www.army.mil/d-day/message.html.

136   *Tucked into his wallet*: To view General Eisenhower's handwritten note, see www.archives.gov/education/lessons/d-day-message.

137   *In 1997, Marine Corps*: See *Counterinsurgency*, FM 3-24 (Washington, DC), Department of the Army, December 2006), p. 8–3.

137   *In 2007, Major Leonard Lira*: See Leonard Lira, chap. 27, "Design: The US Army's Approach to Negotiating Wicked Problems," in *Venturing Beyond the Classroom*, Vol. 2 in the *Rethinking Negotiation Teaching* series, eds. Christopher Honeyman, James Coben, and Giuseppe De Palo (DRI Press, 2011), pp. 511–28, at 519.

138   *Lira had initially organized forums*: From recent correspondence with Leonard Lira.

138   *Lira turned to other*: See, for example, Jack Kem, *Design: Tools of the Trade*, Fort Leavenworth, KS: US Army Command and Staff College (May 2009), http://usacac.army.mil/cac2/repository/Materials/Design.pdf; see also Peter Checkland and John Poulter, *Learning for Action: A Short Definitive Account of Soft Systems Methodology, and its Use for Practitioners, Teachers, and Students* (Wiley, 2006).

138   *This change in negotiation strategy*: See Chris Argyris and Donald Schon, *Organization Learning: A Theory of Action Perspective* (Addison-Wesley, 1978); Donald Schon, *The Reflective Practitioner* (Basic Books, 1983); and Chris Argyris, "Teaching Smart People How to Learn," *Harvard Business Review*, May–June, 1991, pp. 99–109.

138 *In 2003, in the early days*: For more on the incident that follows, see Dan Baum, "Annals of War: Battle Lessons—What the General Don't Know," *New Yorker*, January 17, 2005, pp. 42–48. See also chap. 3, "The Mosque of Ali," in Christopher Hughes, *War on Two Fronts: An Infantry Commander's War in Iraq and the Pentagon* (Casemate, 2007).

Part 3: Managing the Process

141 *Consider Northern Ireland*: Senator Mitchell has frequently mentioned the two years of "failure" and one day of negotiation success in Northern Ireland. This specific comment was made at an INSS Conference in Tel-Aviv, Israel, December 18, 2008, "Security Challenges of the 21st Century: The US and Israeli Roles in the Middle East Under Changing Political Circumstances." It appears on page 8 of the transcript.

Chapter 8: Openings

146 *We videotaped real estate professionals*: The tapes (titled "Negotiation of a Commercial Lease") and a related negotiation exercise are available from the Program on Negotiation's case clearinghouse: www.pon.harvard.edu/shop/category/audio-cd/?sort=custom

158 *Amy, a social psychologist*: For an introduction to her work, see Amy Cuddy, Peter Glick, and Anna Beninger, "The Dynamics of Warmth and Competence Judgments, and Their Outcomes in Organizations," *Research in Organizational Behavior* 31 (2011): pp. 73–98; and Cuddy, Glick, and Susan T. Fiske, "Universal Dimensions of Social Cognition: Warmth and Competence," *Trends in Cognitive Science* 11, no. 2 (February 2007): pp. 77–83.

159 *Amy and her colleagues*: See Dana Carney, Amy Cuddy, and Andy Yap, "Power Posing: Brief Nonverbal Displays Affect Neuroendocrine Levels and Risk Tolerance," *Psychological Science* 21, no. 10 (October 2010): pp. 1363–68.

161 *Opening up your physical stance*: See Amy's 2012 TED talk "Your Body Language Shapes Who You Are," www.ted.com/talks/amy_cuddy_your_body_language_shapes_who_you_are.html.

161 *On September 16, 2001*: Courtney Cowart spoke at a Kennedy School of Government forum on rebuilding the World Trade Center. The event was held on October 7, 2002.

Chapter 9: Critical Moments

163 *Daniel Yin was back*: A set of cases that I have developed tell the following story in greater detail. They are available from Harvard Business School Publishing and are entitled *Kidnapping Negotiation*, A through D, product numbers 899026 through 899029, August 16, 2000.

170 *He triages*: His comment was made during a seminar that was held when he

received PON's Great Negotiator Award in 2002. Video of the event is available from the Program's Clearinghouse: www.pon.harvard.edu/shop/great-negotiator-2002-lakhdar-brahimi-2.

172 *Bill describes this technique*: See Ury, *The Power of a Positive No.*

173 *For years, the Humane Society*: From an NPR *Morning Edition* interview and story by Steve Inskeep, "How Two Bitter Adversaries Hatched a Plan to Change the Egg Business," February 10, 2012, www.npr.org/templates/run-downs/rundown.php?prgId=3&prgDate=2-10-2012.

174 *According to the* New York Times: See *New York Times*, January 22, 2009.

174 *Lisa Tschorn was meeting*: Lisa Tschorn is a pseudonym.

175 *What's the best way*: Deborah Kolb and Judith Williams, chap. 3, "Resisting Challenges," in *Everyday Negotiation: Navigating the Hidden Agendas in Bargaining* (Jossey-Bass, 2003).

179 *Kolb and Williams call dances*: See Deborah Kolb and Judith Williams, *The Shadow Negotiation: How Women Can Master the Hidden Agendas That Determine Bargaining Success* (Simon & Schuster, 2000).

180 *Bill Gates and Steve Jobs*: See Walter Isaacson, *Steve Jobs* (Simon & Schuster, 2011), pp. 177–79.

181 *Years ago, a young comic*: This story is from an *On the Record with Bob Costas* interview with Larry David that aired on HBO in 2003.

Chapter 10: Closing

190 *That kind of lore*: For solid advice, see G. Richard Shell and Mario Moussa, *The Art of Woo: Using Strategic Persuasion to Sell Your Ideas* (Penguin Books, 2008); Robert Cialdini, *Influence: The Psychology of Persuasion* (HarperBusiness, 2006), and his more recent *Yes! 50 Scientifically Proven Ways to Be Persuasive* (with Noah J. Goldstein and Steve J. Martin, Free Press, 2008); and Deepak Malhotra and Max Bazerman, chap. 7, "Strategies of Influence," in *Negotiation Genius: How to Overcome Obstacles and Achieve Brilliant Results at the Bargaining Table and Beyond* (Bantam Books, 2007).

190 *Sheena Iyengar*: For a provocative analysis about how freedom of choice is valued differently in various cultures, see Iyengar, *Art of Choosing.*

192 *Former New York City detective*: See Diane Coutu, "Negotiating Without a Net: A Conversation with the NYPD's Dominick J. Misino," *Harvard Business Review*, October 2002, pp. 49–54.

193 *The sale of a $3 million*: For these examples of difficult real estate closings, see Patrick O'Gilfoil Healy, "Closing Day Disasters," *New York Times*, April 24, 2012, p. 1.

196 *A young couple*: See Elaine McCardle, "The Personal Touch: More Homebuyers Are Writing Letters to Sellers to Personalize, Help Seal the Sale," *Boston Globe*, April 25, 2004, pp. G-1 and G-4.

196 *Relationships matter*: See Weintraub, *When I Stop Talking*, pp. 89–90.

197 *We'll close with another*: Derek Sanderson generously shared this story with me. He describes his salary negotiations—and other aspects of his remarkable life—in *Crossing the Line: The Outrageous Story of a Hockey Original*, coauthored with Kevin Shea (Triumph Books, 2012).

Part 4: Mastery

201 *You need, I think*: Brahimi made this comment during a seminar when he received the Program on Negotiation's Great Negotiator Award in 2002. Video of the event is available from the Program's Clearinghouse: www.pon.harvard.edu/shop/great-negotiator-2002-lakhdar-brahimi-2.

Chapter II: Silk Purses

203 *A major publishing house*: George Brockway, the former president of W. W. Norton, told me this story.

204 *In the 1990s*: See George Gendron, "Real Men Don't Litigate," *Inc.*, May 1, 1992, www.inc.com/magazine/19920501¼059.html. Southwest posted a video of the contest on YouTube: www.youtube.com/watch?v=EwU9m4oCtRE.

205 *Recent studies by Evan Polman*: See Evan Polman and Kyle J. Emich, "Decisions for Others Are More Creative Than Decisions for the Self," *Personality and Social Psychology Bulletin* 37, no. 4 (April 2011): pp. 492–501.

205 *In the movie* Heist: *See* www.imdb.com/title/tt0252503/quotes.

209 *The second puzzle*: See Rob Walker, "Take It or Leave It: The *Only* Guide to Negotiating You Will Ever Need," *Inc.*, August 1, 2003, p. 75.

211 *People who believe*: See Max Bazerman, "Negotiator Judgment: A Critical Look at the Rationality Assumption," *American Behavioral Scientist* 27, no. 2 (November–December 1983): pp. 211–28, at 215–218.

211 *Stephen Nachmanovitch*: See Nachmanovitch, *Free Play*, p. 133.

212 *The late actress Ruth Gordon*: See www.enjoy-your-style.com/ruth-gordon-quotes.html. "To get it right, be born with luck or else make it. Never give up. Get the knack of getting people to help you and also pitch in yourself. A little money helps, but what really gets it right is to never—I repeat—never, under any conditions, face the facts."

212 *Claude Lévi-Strauss called it*: See Ted Gioia, *The Imperfect Art: Reflections on Jazz and Modern Culture* (Oxford University Press, 1988), p. 615. Gioia writes:

"Like the *bricoleur* who assumes that there must be a tractor somewhere in that pile of junk, the improviser assumes that there is a melody to be worked out from the morass of rhythms and chord changes."

212 *Unburdened by their bloody history*: Holbrooke recounted this story in a panel discussion when he received the Great Negotiator Award in 2004. See *Harvard Law Today*, January 2005, p. 1. (This is also the source of the Holbrooke reference in the next paragraph.)

212 *According to Nachmanovitch*: See Nachmanovitch, *Free Play*, p. 43.

213 *And* spark *is the right word*: See Andy Clark, *Being There: Putting Brain, Body, and World Together Again* (MIT Press, 1997), p. 66.

213 *Albert Einstein said that many*: See John Kao, *Jamming: The Art and Discipline of Business Creativity* (HarperCollins, 1996), p. 48.

213 *German scientist Friedrich Kekule*: See Myers, *Intuition*, p. 61.

213 *When asked how he thought*: The Bill Clinton quotation is from the 2006 documentary *Wordplay*.

214 *Studies by Leigh Thompson*: See Dedre Gentner, Jeffrey Loewenstein, Leigh Thompson, and Kenneth Forbus, "Reviving Inert Knowledge: Analogical Abstraction Supports Relational Retrieval of Past Events," *Cognitive Science* 33, no. 8 (November–December 2009): pp. 1343–82, which cites the prior studies and related work.

216 *Many years ago*: See Kim Phillips-Fein, *Invisible Hands: The Businessmen's Crusade Against the New Deal* (W. W. Norton & Company, 2010), for a political assessment of Boulware's tactics.

216 *Screenwriter-producer Robert Kosberg*: The quotation is from an interview ("The Art of the Pitch") conducted by Noah Adams on *All Things Considered*, which aired on NPR on February 19, 1997.

217 *Babson College professor Lakshmi Balachandra*: "Pitching Trustworthiness: Cues for Trust in Early-Sage Investment Decision-Making," unpublished PhD dissertation at Boston College, 2011.

218 *Skilled psychotherapists have a keen*: Laura Abraham, "Can This Marriage Be Saved?," *New York Times Magazine*, August 12, 2007, p. 28.

219 *When other efforts at peacemaking*: My mediator friend who shared this story asked that his name not be used.

Chapter 12: Wicked Learning

226 *You can find*: To take the test and understand your score, see Schwartz, chap. 4, "When Only the Best Will Do," in *The Paradox of Choice*, pp. 77–98, at 80–81.

228 *Robin Hogarth, author*: See Robin Hogarth, *Educating Intuition* (University of Chicago Press, 2001), pp. 89–90.

230 *In the movie*: The movie is based on a novel by Barry Reed, *The Verdict* (Simon & Schuster, 1980).

230 *She accepted an $165,000 settlement*: See "Blind Student: No Regrets About Taking Lower Malpractice Settlement," *Daytona Beach Morning Journal*, March 27, 1975, p. 3A.

231 *We know that positive things*: See Daniel Gilbert, *Stumbling on Happiness* (Vintage Books, 2005).

234 Built to Win: See Lawrence Susskind and Hallam Movius, *Built to Win: Creating a World-Class Negotiating Organization* (Harvard Business Press, 2009).

235 *UN diplomat Lakhdar Brahimi*: The comment that follows was made during a seminar that was held when he received PON's Great Negotiator Award in 2002. Video of the event is available from the Program's Clearinghouse: www .pon.harvard.edu/shop/great-negotiator-2002-lakhdar-brahimi-2.

Chapter 13: Fair Enough

236 *Every time we sit down*: For an extensive examination of ethical issues in negotiation, see the articles and essays collected in Carrie Menkel-Meadow and Michael Wheeler, eds., *What's Fair?: Ethics for Negotiators* (Jossey-Bass, 2004). See also Robert Mnookin, *Bargaining with the Devil: When to Negotiate, When to Fight* (Simon & Schuster, 2011); G. Richard Schell, chap. 11, "Bargaining with the Devil Without Losing Your Soul: Ethics in Negotiation," in *Bargaining for Advantage: Negotiation Strategies for Reasonable People* (Penguin Books, 2006); and Malhotra and Bazerman, *Negotiation Genius* (Bantam Books, 2007), in particular, chapter 9, "Confronting Lies and Deceptions," and chapter 10, "Recognizing and Resolving Ethical Dilemmas."

245 *Recent scientific findings*: See Jonathan Haidt, "The New Synthesis in Moral Psychology," *Science* 316, no. 5827 (May 18, 2007): pp. 998–1002. See also Jonathan Haidt, *The Righteous Mind: Why Good People Are Divided by Politics and Religion* (Pantheon Books, 2012).

249 *Good intentions aren't enough*: See Joris Lammers, Diederik Stapel, and Adam Galinsky, "Power Increases Hypocrisy: Moralizing in Reasoning, Immorality in Behavior," *Psychological Science* 21, no. 5 (May 2010): pp. 737–44.

249 *Remember the energy traders*: To hear the X-rated conversation, go to www .youtube.com/watch?v=DOLNWF5QMxY.

249 *Our moral sensitivity may slacken*: Norman is a pseudonym. I'm grateful to him for sharing this story.

250 *In fact, a newsmagazine*: See Douglas Stanglin et al., "Oprah: A Heavenly Body?" *U.S. News & World Report*, March 31, 1997, p. 18.

251 *The authors maintained*: See Fisher, Ury, and Patton, p. 154.

251 *A reviewer friendly*: See Carrie Menkel-Meadow, "Legal Negotiation: A Study

of Strategies in Search of a Theory," *American Bar Foundation Research Journal* 8, no. 4 (Autumn 1983), pp. 905–37, at 919.

251 *In sharp contrast*: See Cohen, *You Can Negotiate Anything*. Cohen's reference to Jesus Christ and Socrates is at p. 20. Cohen describes the episode that follows on p. 227.

251 *his actual advice was*: A. Press, C. Glass, and D. Foote, "Winning by Negotiation," *Newsweek*, October 26, 1981, p. 86.

252 *My friend Jim Golden*: For more on Jim's openhearted and practical approach to negotiation, see Jim Golden, "The Negotiation Counsel Model," *Negotiation Journal* 24, no. 3 (July 2008): pp. 371–78.

254 *My colleague Andy Wasynczuk*: See Andrew Wasynczuk, Katherine Dowd, and Sara del Nido, *Golden Rule* (product number 909017), October 27, 2010, Harvard Business Publishing.

Index